May your cinch never pinch
Josie

Gone Ridin'

© Copyright 2003

First Edition

By Josie Rusho

Josie Rusho

CREDITS

Published by:	Outpost Books
Printed:	The Craftsman
Cover graphics:	Cecilia McGuire
Editing:	Terri Sandoval & friends
Photography:	Co-riders and Family
Maps & Illustrations:	Josie Rusho
Front cover photo (Lion Rock):	Madeleine Bratt
Back cover (Alpine Lakes Wilderness) photo:	Karla E. Smith
Back cover wildlife photos:	Josie Rusho & Cliff Holsclaw
Formatted:	Will Wanner

BE ADVISED

It is a continuing learning experience to be with our mounts. Be as safe as you can and when in doubt, don't do it! Prepare as well as you can and use caution and common sense. The reward is a lasting memory of a trip well planned and time successfully spent in the regions we love. There is no place like the United States of America, the land of the free. Take good care of it and use it. This land is truly your land!

The contents of this book are meant to be a general guideline to trails and trail riding and cannot replace your own judgement for your mount and situations. The responsibility is solely up to each individual for safety and actions taken. This book's coverage is not intended to make your decisions for you. Check ahead with Forest Services for trail conditions as they change from year to year. A horse has its own mind and there are gambles involved when the choice is made to ride them. There are potential risks and hazards being involved with livestock, this book does not allow for the disclosure of all of them.

ACKOWLEDGEMENTS

I'd like to express thanks to my other half, Cliff and son Nick for being patient while I was investigating the trails for <u>Gone Ridin'</u>. I am also grateful to Cliff Holsclaw, Madeleine Bratt, and Karla E. Smith for their superb cover photographs. Nick, thanks for helping me with computer questions. To my friends and riding partners: Your presence is invaluable as we explore new lands in the Pacific Northwest, thanks for all your great snaps as well! A special thanks goes to Donna Evans and Madeleine Bratt for sharing their words on several trails. To Cecilia McGuire, thanks for your talented graphic design on the cover. The crew at the Craftsman and Will Wanner, thanks for getting the book formatted and printed out. I wish to say thanks to Don Hampton, for shoeing my horses and Terri Sandoval & friends for editing this book for me. A hart-felt thanks goes to Mary Seth for rescuing my manuscript at a critical point. I would like to acknowledge the Ranger Districts in Oregon State for going over the manuscript for accuracy before it went to press: Middle Fork and the McKenzie River Ranger Districts, and in Washington State: Naches and Cle Elum Ranger Districts.

TABLE OF CONTENTS

OVERVIEW

Hi fellow horse lovers, welcome to the exciting world of trail riding in the Pacific Northwest's Cascade Mountains and deserts. With the experience under my belt of writing two previous trail-guide books; <u>Grab Your Tails and Ride the Trails</u> and <u>Trail Blazing the Northwest</u> with the help of an old riding buddy, Rene Ogan, I'm delighted to go solo and present my newest adventure, <u>Gone Ridin'</u>. I have personally ridden all of the trails in this book with the exception of a handful, which are identified as you read them. <u>Gone Ridin'</u> features over 200 miles of the Pacific Crest National Scenic Trail. One hundred plus miles are in Oregon and over one hundred in Washington as well. The difficulty of trail ranges from rugged terrain near the Canadian Border to the High Desert areas in Central Oregon. Also included in the book are some areas that have no assigned trails, sometimes overlooked because they are not on maps or in the Wilderness or National Forests, but certainly worth riding. <u>Gone Ridin'</u> has something for every level of riding. There are placid lake basins, cascading waterfalls, huge volcanoes, dense forest, arid barren ridges, cool wide rivers and quiet running streams with sweeping meadows beside them. The majority of trails in this book are rated in the "Moderate" range, with few "Challenging" trails, as this is what I find most enjoyable. Horse camps are described as well as directions to trailheads, connection trails, and stories to amuse you. The trails range from beginner level to hard-core. There are tons of pictures, and a few sketches. Hints and camp lists are included as well, information and Forest Service addresses are listed to help make your trip safe and worry-free. Camp grub recipes for the hungry trail rider are included also. In the back of <u>Gone Ridin'</u> is a table with over 150 more trails that I have ridden in the Pacific Northwest, with brief a description, and a list of the maps you'll need to explore them.

Josie

AUTHOR'S STORY

I was born and raised in the beautiful state of Colorado, growing up outside the town of Boulder. During our childhood, my sister and I, for years, shared a single, family owned mare. Later, my sister and I raised and trained several horses entering and riding in play-days, in parades and rode many trails. For recreation we held our own half-mile races, jumped our steeds over fallen trees and cooled off by swimming our horses in the local ponds.

As an adult, when I lived in the states of Nevada and California I experienced riding fifty-mile endurance races. After logging one thousand miles in equine endurance races, I found myself riding endurance rides for other horse owners in the states of Nevada and Utah. Additional wonderful equine experiences I have had include riding a pony express race, grand entries in rodeos and competing in calf penning contests.

I currently reside in Ellensburg, Washington with my husband and son where I have lived since 1986. We have a place in the country northwest of Ellensburg, where I have just room enough to enjoy my horses, laying hens, cats and ever-faithful dog Tess. While living here, I have had the chance to experience working on a cattle ranch helping with the spring calving, roundups, and the branding and castration of calves. These events added to my earlier experience of milking dairy cows, working the counter in a local butcher shop, and raising calves.

My passion currently, and for the past few years, is about riding the Pacific Northwest's trails and writing books for trail riders to enjoy and explore for themselves. Recently, I have been branching out working on several other books, about campfire stories and a children's book about, you guessed it; "Horses".

I am glad to be in the saddle riding and writing once again, about the equine trails that I have found in the Pacific Northwest, while riding my favorite horse that I raised Ali and relying on my backup horse, Inky. Going. Going, Gone Ridin'!

Enjoy the book Josie

DEGREE OF DIFFICULTY

Moderate:

Most any seasoned rider-horse team should be able to ride trails with the "Moderate" rating. It can include rolling terrain with short steep sections or long steady climbs and may have some narrow sections of trail, or be on an open ridge on wide trail and may also have vague tread, but on easy terrain. A moderate rating of a trail can include drop-off spots, rocks, bridges, ruts, loose footing, mud, water crossings, logs and or gates; or simply be a flat wide path. I will describe in detail what the trail includes in the description. After all this is why I wrote the book, so you can get and idea of what you're getting into before you ride it.

Challenging:

The trails with the "Challenging" rating are only for hard-core riders with seasoned trail horses. Even then proceed with caution and use common sense. These ratings are assigned to trails that have one or more of the following: severe pitch, deep mud or ruts, sheer drop-offs, slick wet ground or hard-packed dirt with little traction that has extremely narrow or crumbly-soft footing and dangerous water crossings not recommended for livestock. The "Challenging" rated trails may have snowfields or low maintenance trails ending in a lot of debris or fallen logs. These trails may be in high altitudes, or maybe they are extremely long or have a vague tread in difficult terrain.

If a trail is a combination of the ratings listed above you'll find it reads like this example: "Moderate-Challenging" (extremely narrow at top). The rating that best describes the majority of the trail will be the first word listed and the exception will be in parentheses. Ride where you are sure you can, better to be safe than sorry! Plan in advance and do your homework, make those calls to the Ranger Stations and if at all possible talk to a Wilderness Ranger for the latest trail reports. Here are a few questions to ask them. Have the trails been cleared? Where is the snow level, and is there any lingering snow on the trail? Are these trails open to livestock? Be sure to ask about the trailhead access and road conditions and any camping questions as well.

MAPS

(Green Trails Maps are referred to the most and GTM is the abbreviation used)

1.	Green Trails Maps
	P.O. Box 77734
	Seattle WA 98177
	206-546-6277

2.	Nature of the Northwest
	800 NE Oregon St. Room 177
	Portland OR 97232
	503-872-2750

Ranger Stations can be contacted for Forest Service and Wilderness maps; every chapter has a listing for the closest district to the region. Always use updated maps. You may want to get several different maps, as there is a wide variety in detail, as some show more than others do. If a trail crosses a National Forest Boundary or Ranger District the mileage may be recorded in several districts on the back of the Green Trails Map.

TREAD LIGHTLY IN THE WOODS

Treading lightly means more trails staying open to equestrians. A few simple rules followed will benefit us all and can make a big difference as to how others view us as a whole. The Forest Service is working with horse clubs all the time to help ensure that the forests stay available for us to ride in. Compiling a list of each other's needs, they start with basic skills and people-power available to do the work needed, a working relationship is formed. Sometimes the work the clubs do is traded for parking passes issued by the Forest Service. Projects can be building horse camps and trailheads, putting in many hours on the trails and preparing for work to be done. The lumber is bought, volunteers are gathered, schedules are made to fit the time and location for the job to take place. Next, the mules and horses are loaded down with building supplies. Depending on where in the woods the work is to be done, sometimes helicopters are brought in to drop-off the fixens needed for new bridges and whatever repairs the trail needs to be made safe for us to use. Let's help them by doing our part and our share in assuring that horsemen and women are welcome visitors in the woods. It is all about taking charge of our destiny and demonstrating some responsibility. The list below is a start on how you and I can take part in putting out our own "welcome" mat on the forest doorway.

➢ **Watering your animals-** Pick a rocky shoreline at a lake to water to help avoid bank erosion. Since livestock is not allowed along lakeshores except for watering, be sure and picket or high-line your horses at least 200' from the shoreline.

➢ **Feed for packing in-**Use feed that is seed-free to keep unwanted plant species from being introduced.

➢ **On the trail-** Going single file keeps the soil erosion to a minimum, especially in wet conditions. Trail switchbacks are engineered to avoid erosion and prolong the life and accessibility of the trail. Use them and avoid short cutting switchbacks. Short cutting speeds up erosion, increases the difficulty of the trail and is expensive to repair.

➢ **Containing animals-**Avoid tying to small trees and keep animals that are prone to pawing in hobbles or high-line them between trees, this helps protect the vegetation and erosion problems. Use tree-savers (a barrier around the tree to reduce scaring on the trunk) when high-lining animals. Some places have a time regulation for tying livestock. Call ahead to the Forest Service to find out more information for where you're going to visit. When you picket your horses, move them around from time to time to prevent overgrazing.

➢ **Breaking camp-**After breaking camp, be sure to fill all holes with dirt and sprinkle the top with pinecones and needles, and be sure to spread the manure thinly so it will dissipate quickly.

➢ **Trash-**The motto for taking care of your trash is "You pack it in, you pack it out"! This applies to trash, garbage and food scraps.

➢ **Human waste-**Both fish entrails and human waste need to be buried. Dig a hole at least 6-8 inches deep and at least 200' from any water source, trail or camp. These "cat holes" need to be widely dispersed.

➢ **Soap-**Use low phosphorous soaps to wash body, hair and dishes. Make sure you are at least 200' from any water source when doing these activities. This will help prevent any unwanted nutrients from entering the lakes and streams.

➢ **Water-**Open water sources in the woods may be contaminated by human or animal waste, so be sure to purify water before drinking it.

➢ **Fire-**A campfire may be prohibited within 100' of a permanent trail system and water source in some areas, check with the Forest Service before building one. The Forest Service encourages a non-smoking policy, if you do please pack out the butts! In the Alpine Lakes Wilderness-Washington, campfires are permitted at most locations below 5,000' on the *east side* of the Cascade Mountains and below 4,000' on the *west side* of the Cascades. Exceptions include various lakes below those elevations where campfires are specifically prohibited within ¼ to ½ mile of lakes. Contact the Forest Service for specific information and observe posted signs along the trail. Also, never leave a campfire unattended. Instead, extinguish the fire completely and make sure it is out. It's often best not to have a campfire going if you don't need one for cooking or heat. This saves firewood and cuts down on air pollution.

➢ **Leave it-**It is illegal to take archaeological artifacts from any National Forest.

➢ **Party size-**In Oregon Wilderness areas, the limit for a group is 12 people and 12 pack and saddle stock. Some areas in Oregon have adopted the same rules as Washington State, if the number of heartbeats is a concern to your group size, **call the Forest Service to check the area you are visiting.** In Washington the group size in the Wilderness is limited to 12 beating hearts this includes livestock.

➢ **A simple message-**If you see something on the trail that you feel the Forest Service needs to be aware of leave a message on the Wilderness sign-in board or call them. They are glad to have extra ears and eyes on the trails. Help them help us. They also like it when you tell them what an awesome job they do!

➢ **Find your way-**A rock cairn is used to guide you through an area that may be vague or hard to negotiate, look for a series of piled rocks, line them up and presto you have found the trail. A blaze in a tree is also used to help guide you, this time it will help you through the forest. Look for an elongated scrape in the tree-bark, it is usually about eye level when you are on horseback. Trail numbers and letters; sometimes you'll see a regular trail number followed by either a decimal number or a letter behind it. This usually means the trail is a spur trail to the main trail. Let's use an example; the main trail number may be #1399, the spur trail number would either be #1399.1 or #1399A, which both mean the same trail, this goes on and on using .2 and B behind the main trail number.

➤ **Motors in the Wilderness-**Anything with a motor, including chain saws and motor bikes are not allowed in the Wilderness. Only the Forest Service or Sheriffs Department can use motorized equipment in an emergency. Mechanized devices such as mountain bikes are also prohibited.

➤ **Camps-**Be sure when making camp that it is placed in a spot previously made, or a designated camp to reduce impact on the forest. Check ahead, caching of camp supplies to reserve a camp spot is prohibited in certain areas, call ahead to the Forest Service for more information. Caching of supplies and leaving unattended camps is limited to 48 hours in the Alpine Lakes Wilderness in Washington.

➤ **Wild animals-**Refrain from approaching wild animals, they may attack you. Some wild animals may be startled by our presence and some are protecting their young hidden in the timber or meadows. Others are just plain unpredictable, stay safe and keep your distance!

➤ **Blending in-**Dressing and camping with earth tone colors while visiting the Wilderness is one way to meld with the mountains, and some believe that it is easier on the eyes.

CAMP LISTS

What to bring on your trip for the human:

❑ **MONEY-**Cash, check or even credit cards are a must on any excursion.

❑ **CAMP SUPPLIES-**Wash cloth, sleeping bag or bedding with pillow, fire wood, newspaper for fire starter, lawn chair, hammock, mosquito repellent, solar shower, flash light with extra batteries, hot dog fork, lantern, camp fuel, camp stove, matches, grill and a small table.

❑ **FIRST AID-**Lotion for insect bites, Ibuprofen, antacid, Band-Aids, antiseptic ointments, gauze, tape, anti-inflammatory, cleansing agent, antihistamine, scissors, tweezers, dental floss, vitamin B complex (taken daily I think, keeps the bugs from biting as bad) and medicine for allergies.

- **CLOTHES**-Bring cold and hot weather clothes, and a swimsuit. A warm cap to wear at bedtime, sure beats trying to stay "under cover" to keep those ears warm. Be sure to include shoes, boots, and some flip-flops (for bathing or swimming in a lake or stream). I love to have my favorite slippers on hand as well.

- **FOOD AND DRINK**-Bring more food than you think you can eat, guaranteed someone in your party will forget something, plus you may eat more than you do at home due to increased activity.

- **KITCHEN**-For cleaning the dishes, bring dish soap, hand soap, dish towels, scrubber, and at least 2 dishpans one for washing and one for rinsing. For storing food and cooking on the BBQ, load up on plastic bags for garbage, sandwich size and gallon size, foil, foil bags made for filling with foods, plastic wrap, stirring and flipping utensils, hot mitt and a thermos. For general use at camp, you'll need a can opener, bottle opener with cork screw, coffee pot, hot and cold cups, bowls, matches, pots, pans, silverware, paper plates, paper towels, and a shot glass. Add anything else you can think of, it is better to have too much than to have left something out.

- **TOILETRIES**-A mild bath soap, shampoo, toothbrush, toothpaste, floss, lotion, shaver, bath towels, cotton swabs, comb and brush are what you'll need to bathe. A few more personal hygiene items include; tissues, eyewash, lip balm, toilet paper, nail clippers (toe and finger), a small sewing kit, and if you are doing things outside, remember to bring that solar shower and curtain. Add to your list as you see fit.

- **WATER**-When camping I'll bring along a minimum of 30 gallons and refill as needed.

- **COOLER**- Even if you have a refrigerator in your camper, bringing a cooler makes sense, store extra food or drinks in here. When using it for cold storage, on top of your ice and food, be sure to put a thick layer of newspapers, so when you open the lid all of the cold doesn't escape, you'll find the ice lasts much longer. Check out the new propane fueled coolers that even have wheels to roll around on.

- **TOOLS**-Here are a few essentials for camping, they include; a shovel, rake, broom, tarp, wire cutters, scissors, flares, super glue, hammer, pliers, jumper cables, an assortment of wrenches, bailing wire, extra batteries, flash light, and duct tape. It is also nice to have a tire inflating machine that hooks up to your cigarette lighter, a cellular phone, blocks for your wheels or to level your camper with, and a "drive up on jack" for the horse trailer. A regular jack will be needed for the truck and remember to put in a star wrench to loosen the bolts with. A few more important things to have are, some motor oil, ax, saw, CB radio, gun with extra ammunition and a "Leatherman" type of tool, and spare tires (truck and trailer).

❑ **GETTING THERE**-A state map is a basic need to go anywhere. Also make sure to have a Wilderness or National Forest map and if a GTM is available, include that as well. Take the maps to a local store that does lamination and have all maps that are accompanying you on the trail laminated. Roll them tight and slide them in between your saddle and the saddle pad, beneath the horn area. Remember to bring the best Pacific Northwest trail-guide book available with you. (You know which one I mean!)

What to bring on your trip for the horse:

❑ **ON THE ROAD**-The driver of the truck hauling the horse trailer may want to have a brand inspection and health paper for each horse being hauled issued from their home state, in case a state trooper stops them. Check with your veterinarian, to clarify what the rules and penalties are pertaining to the state you are visiting.

❑ **HAY**-I always use the same type of hay at home as I do when camping. If your horse is on pasture at home, you may want to pen them up for a couple days prior to your camp trip, feeding only hay. It's wise to keep your horses diet constant to avoid upsetting their digestive systems. I "free feed" up to ½ bale (2-wire) a day for a hard working horse.

❑ **GRAIN**-If you are going to grain your animal, make sure that they are used to eating grain ahead of your trip. Again keep the same routine. I only grain ½ coffee can per day, and only when the horse is being used every day.

❑ **SALT**-Bring salt for your animal when camping. Either loose or solid works well, I use plain white salt to avoid doubling up on some minerals that may be in their other feeds. Small blocks of salt are available and are easy to handle.

❑ **TREATS**-A few apples or carrots in his dish are a special surprise for your mount, and well deserved at the end of a hard day on the trails.

❑ **BLANKETS**-Use heavy, light or none if it is hot outside. When animals are contained in a small area, they are not moving around like they be would at home. It is beneficial for the horse to wear a blanket that keeps the body heat in, especially after being ridden day after day. A lot of energy is expelled to stay warm without a blanket on; use a sheet if the bugs are bad and the weather is hot.

- **HOUSING-**There are many choices to house your horse in camp, portable corral, hobbles, electric fence or a high-line with a tree saver (protective barrier between the line and the trunk of the tree, grain sacks work well). These are the most popular ways to contain livestock, although some people even put their horses in the trailer at night.

- **CLEAN UP-**Wheelbarrows come in fold-up models now-a-days to scoop and transfer the poops to the manure bins in horse camps, some camps provide wheelbarrows and sometimes manure forks too. Bring big heavy trash bags, some horse camps require you to move the "road apples" away from camp to a dump site area.

- **WATER-**There are several ways to haul water for your horses. I use a "dry camp" system, it is a large heavy plastic container shaped like a saddle rack and holds 30 gallons of water. It can be carried either on top of the horse trailer in the hayrack or can be used as an extra saddle rack in the tack room. You could also get yourself 5-gallon containers and strap them on to the fenders of the trailer or stash them wherever they will fit. I have found that using one bucket for my horse to drink from and another to fill it with works well. I like to fasten the stationary bucket with a Velcro strap to my portable corral so if an accidental tip-over happens, it will release in case of emergency.

- **TACK-**Saddle, saddle pads (Wool pads are the best as they are breathable. I buy the reversible ones, when they get dirty on one side, just flip it over for double the wear.), pommel bag, saddlebags, halter, lead rope, bridle, reins, crupper, breast collar, brushes and a hoof pick. An important item to include is a water bottle (I get the ones that can filter water so if I run short on water I can fill up in a stream or lake.) I consider this part of my tack, don't leave your trailer without water!

- **ON YOUR SADDLE-**Clip on snaps, extra leather pieces, a hoof pick on a string can easily be added to any saddle. Pommel bag and saddlebags with water bottles and coats area must. Keep cruppers, breast collars, and back cinches snug against the horse for safety, we don't need any loose straps where a branch may get tangled in and spook or gouge our steeds! Always pack your bags as if you are going overnight.

- **FIRST AID PACK FOR IN THE SADDLE BAGS-**Antiseptic ointments, gauze, tape, tissue, electrolytes, sponge, fishing line and hook are some good ideas to pack. Here are a few more, anti-inflammatory medicine, suture needle and thread, lighter or waterproof matches. A space blanket, water purifying tablets, cleansing agent, Phenybutazone (Bute.), which is used for the horse to reduce pain, and a tranquilizer to calm, are all things I have in my bag. Also a signal mirror, plastic bag (use if rain gear is forgotten), Band-Aids, smelling salts, anti-histamine, antacids, and throat lozenges are helpful items to include. The first aid pack can be wrapped into an amazingly small wad, put in a locking plastic bag, then secure with a tourniquet.

❑ **IN YOUR TRAILER-**Use what makes sense. I keep boots, hats, gloves, tack, horse treats, buckets, hand warmers, glow sticks, gun, ammunition, belt, holster, grooming equipment, maps, and a sleeping bag in my trailer. I also have enough extra tack to outfit a horse completely. Keep food, tools, buckets, hay hooks, tree savers, flashlight that attaches on a strap around the head, grain pans and a spare tire along with anything else that makes you feel prepared. A hanging shoe bag makes for easy access to the little things that tend to get buried, maps rolled up store nicely in the shoe bag. A large rubber tub with a lid is helpful to store bulky items in. Coats, raingear, a small bag containing a dry set of emergency clothes, horse blankets and ropes can be stored on the wall-hooks. Trail food, full or half-chaps (for warmth and protection on your legs), baby wipes used for clean ups and small kitchen towels, as well as a roll of toilet paper and some paper towels are all handy items to carry. A trailer ball-lock in case you need to leave your trailer to go to town, hoof dressings and horse medicines, bran with mineral oil (soaked together for ½ hour with warm water for a sick horse) are included in my list. Water is essential as well as a manure fork, a small broom, and tire blocks. Always leave a note where you are going, especially if there is no sign-in box at the trailhead or if riding alone.

❑ **IN THE POMEL & SADDLEBAGS-**Food, extra food, water, binoculars, camera with spare film, vet wrap; duct tape and bright colored surveyor ribbon (used to mark trail or signal with). Lip balm, sunscreen, sunglasses, whistle, small container with fly repellant on a rag (for the horse) are items to include in the saddlebags. Tee Tree Oil (antiseptic as well as a fly repellant for horse's face and for human use too) and a candle, are all essentials to have with you. I put a glow stick (glows for up to 12 hours), old drivers license, paper and pencil (pens break, pencils can be re-sharpened), cowboy scarf (soaked in water can cool you all day) in my packs. If you are carrying a firearm concealed, be sure to have your permit on you. Always pack an "Easy Boot" to use in case of a thrown shoe, candle (or a small Sterno can) and extra food fit nicely inside of the boot for traveling. Some people pack their phone in the saddlebags.

PREVENTION-Look over everything at least once a year for needed repairs. Check floorboards in the trailer for signs of wear, make sure you have the proper amount of air in all your tires and tighten lug nuts if needed. Tune up that truck and G0!

CAMP GRUB

CASCADE CREST WILD EGGS – SERVES 4

1 Cup sliced mushrooms
¾ Cup chopped onion
½ Cup diced green or red pepper

2 Cans (small) sliced black olives

¾ Cup shredded cheddar cheese
8 Eggs
¾ Cup shredded Parmesan or
Romono cheese
½ Cup herb butter (see recipe below)

In a large skillet, sauté onions and mushrooms in herb butter over low heat until tender. Over medium heat crack-open the eggs and add them to the mushroom and onions. Mix in the remainder of ingredients except the cheese. Top with cheese when the eggs are cooked the way you like. Serve with a side of bacon or sausage; add pan-fried bread and grapefruit juice for a rib sticking meal.

TEANAWAY PAN FRIED TOAST – SERVES 2

4 Slices of bread   ½ Cube of butter

In a large skillet, melt half the butter and bring to medium heat. Lay the bread down in the butter until golden brown, flip the bread and add the other half of the butter. Cook until brown and good!

THREE SISTERS IMITATION CRAB SALAD- SERVES 4

1 Cup celery, finely chopped
1 Cup mayonnaise
cheese
2 Pounds of imitation crab

3 Cans (small) sliced black olives
1 Pound shredded medium cheddar

2 Medium size onions

In a large bowl, flake imitation crab and then add the remaining ingredients. This makes a good salad on a bed of lettuce or use as a dip for crackers or chips. Quick and easy and can be made a day ahead.

INDIAN HEAVENLY 'SMOORES – SERVES 4

1 Large bar of "Caramello"
(chocolate-caramel)
1 Bag of big marshmallows

1 Box of cinnamon graham crackers

Lots of napkins or damp wash cloths

Toast your marshmallows skewered on a campfire stick over hot coals until lightly brown and gooey. Slide onto a graham cracker, insert a square of chocolate, wait a minute and smoosh down with one more cracker or eat open-face. UMMM!

11

THREE FINGER JACK HAM SPREAD – SERVES 4

1 Small jar of sweet pickle relish   1 Cup mayonnaise
2 Pounds of ground ham (your local butcher shop will do this for you)

Mix all ingredients together. Uses for either sandwich spread or on crackers, sit back to a leisurely lunch.

MOUNT HOOD SNOWBALLS – SERVES 4

3 Cups of just picked huckleberries (frozen ones work too)
1 Cup whipped cream

Mix together and enjoy a cool dessert after a hot day on the trail.

RAINIER HERB BUTTER-GOOD ON LOTS OF THINGS

2 Garlic cloves (raw or roasted)   2 Tablespoons of parsley
1 Cube of butter   2 Tablespoons of oregano

Whip all ingredients together and refrigerate for a couple hours. Use it on chicken, eggs or crackers. This can be made a head of your trip and keeps well.

MT. BACHELOR DUTCH OVEN MONTEREY CHICKEN – SERVES 4

4 Boneless chicken breasts   1 Cup herb butter (recipe above)
3 Cups breadcrumbs mixed with finely grated Parmesan cheese   1 Pound
Monterey Jack cheese
Peanut oil   8 Tooth picks
1 Cup melted butter

"Squirrel again?"

Pound chicken breasts to ¼ inch thickness (wrap loosely in plastic wrap before pounding for easy clean up). Place the skin side of the chicken breast down and generously smear herb butter on top of chicken. Place several slices of Monterey Jack cheese on top of butter mixture. Roll and secure with 2 toothpicks per breast. Dredge chicken in melted butter and then roll in breadcrumb mixture. Place in a Dutch Oven pan with a small amount of peanut oil in bottom. Cook over charcoals until juice runs clear and chicken is done, 25 minutes at 400 degrees is a good time and heat guide.

PACIFIC CREST TRAIL #2000

The Pacific Crest National Scenic Trail will be referred to as either Pacific Crest Trail or PCT #2000. This chapter is a conglomeration of sections of the PCT #2000 that I have ridden in the Pacific Northwest region. The terrain I've crossed varies from the rocky lava fields with dry and desert air to muddy, foggy, fern laden jungle type of mountains. My friends, Donna Evans and Madeleine Bratt have also contributed to the writing of this chapter. This trail will be described from the southern most area in Oregon, going to the northern portion in Washington as it cuts a swath across the Cascade Mountains. The total trail extends 2,600 miles connecting Canada and Mexico. Portions were built as early as the 1920's. The Pacific Crest Trail that I am going to write about is perched atop the Pacific Crest of the Cascade Mountain Range. The Ranger Districts to contact for trail information is listed by each trail description. Remember to keep livestock at least 200' from water sources when staying longer than it takes to water them. Camp 100' back from the PCT #2000.

Northwest Forest Parking Passes are available at Forest Service offices, they are required at designated trailheads.

Head 'em up and move them out!

Josie at Charlton Lake (Waldo Wilderness)

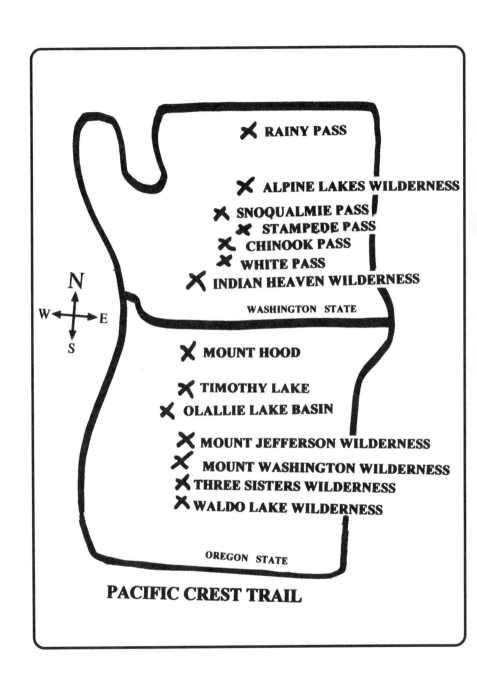

RAINY PASS

ALPINE LAKES WILDERNESS

SNOQUALMIE PASS

STAMPEDE PASS

CHINOOK PASS

WHITE PASS

INDIAN HEAVEN WILDERNESS

WASHINGTON STATE

MOUNT HOOD

TIMOTHY LAKE

OLALLIE LAKE BASIN

MOUNT JEFFERSON WILDERNESS

MOUNT WASHINGTON WILDERNESS

THREE SISTERS WILDERNESS

WALDO LAKE WILDERNESS

OREGON STATE

PACIFIC CREST TRAIL

Trail #2000	Page

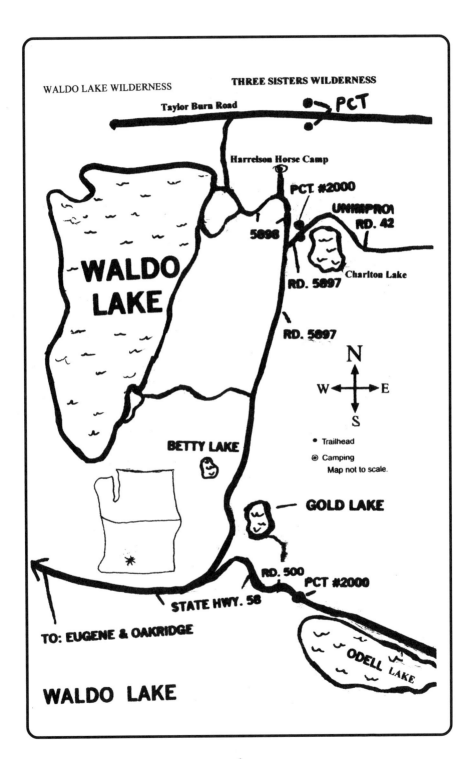

WALDO LAKE WILDERNESS   THREE SISTERS WILDERNESS

Taylor Burn Road

PCT

Harrelson Horse Camp

PCT. #2000

UNIMPRO

RD. 42

5898

WALDO LAKE

Charlton Lake

RD. 5897

RD. 5897

N

W   E

S

BETTY LAKE

- Trailhead
- Camping
  Map not to scale.

GOLD LAKE

RD. 500

PCT #2000

STATE HWY. 58

TO: EUGENE & OAKRIDGE

ODELL LAKE

WALDO LAKE

16

PCT #2000 WALDO LAKE AREA

(Maiden Peak Trail north to Brahma Lake) in Oregon

Distance:	15.4 Miles
Altitude:	5500'-6500'
Map:	Waldo Lake Wilderness
Difficulty:	Moderate

Directions: This portion of the PCT #2000 is located in South Central Oregon. Drive State Highway 58 and turn north on Forest Service Road 5897. You can access this section of the PCT #2000 from a variety of trails that connect to Forest Service Road 5897. Or access it from Harrelson Horse Camp off of Forest Service Road 5898 to Road 511, which is attained by continuing north on Forest Service Road 5898 when Forest Service Road 5897 turns toward Charlton Lake.

Connecting Trails: 3681, 3663, 40, 3595, 19, 3593, 19.3, 4364 (4363)

Horse Camping: Harrelson Horse Camp offers several campfire rings, garbage service, tables and an outhouse. There is room for lots of rigs, big or small at the large turnaround. No potable water here, there are people camps nearby that have potable water. Water for the animals is accessed by riding down Harrelson Horse Trail #4363, about ½ mile to Waldo Lake. No fee was required when I visited in 2000.

McKenzie River Ranger Station
State Highway 126
McKenzie Bridge, OR 97413
503-822-3381

Middle Fork Ranger District
46375 Highway 58
Westfir, OR 97492
541-782-2283

Williamette National Forest
211 E. 7th Ave. (P.O. Box 10607)
Eugene, OR 97440
541-465-6521

Trail Description: This 15.4 mile fragment of the PCT #2000 will be described from Maiden Peak Trail #3681 going north to Brahma Lake in the Three Sisters Wilderness. Leaving Maiden Peak Trail #3681 the first couple of miles of trail appear less traveled and has low maintenance, I found logs down here and there. Riding among the evergreen trees, the path alternates rising and declining for 15.4 miles with no huge elevation changes. My friend Sandy and I scanned the horizon and picked out big treed peaks to the west, Mount Fuji and Mount Ray. The PCT #2000 teams up with 2 other trails to make a 4-way intersection, Bobby Lakes Trail #3663 leaves to the west and Moore Creek Trail #40 goes toward Bobby Lakes. In about 1.5 miles more, Twin Peak Trail #3595 exits to the right (east). Ride upward for 500' to the high-point of the trail at 6,500', you may find late lingering snow from the previous winter in this area. The path is fun and along this stretch you can make some time. Views of white Diamond Peak are behind you to the southwest and the Three Sisters Mountains are ahead of you. Boulders are lined alongside the trail in places. Gliding down gently you'll reach a network of trails by Charlton Lake, they are an Unnamed Trail #19 and Charlton Lake Trail #3593. (Unnamed Trail #19 leaves again after skimming the west shore of Charlton Lake). Ride across Forest Service Road 5897-4290 and head uphill again traveling through a semi-burnt area on the west slope of Charlton Butte. You'll be in the "Taylor Burn" area for about 3-4 miles, stay on the trail to avoid hidden holes and exposed roots from the inferno that raced across the area in 1996. There are several ponds laced with lily pads floating lazily. Notice that the green around the wetlands looks odd and out of place among the charred remains of the fire. Lily Lake Trail #19.3 sign is crisply toasted, a grim reminder of the forest fire. Harrelson Horse Trail #4364 (4363) leaves to the west (left) and is unsigned. Spotty burnt areas of standing dead timber look like sticks of black licorice, which somehow are being held up in the soft sandy soil. You'll ride, winding in and out of green forest and burn moonscape all the way down to the glistening Taylor Lake. Ride across Forest Service Road 4636-600 (which by the way, is NOT a road you want to drive with a horse trailer!). Enter the Three Sisters Wilderness, passing Irish Lake and continue the trek to Brahma Lake in moist green forest. You'll find lakes, ponds and brackish puddles everywhere and blankets of green velvet moss beds. The PCT #2000 zigzags as it comes to rest for a moment at the east shoreline of Brahma Lake. This is a clean, clear lake with nice flat rocks to sit on and bask in the sun. Have a well-deserved break and maybe a refreshing swim too. The footing for the horses in this area is ideal. This morsel of the PCT #2000 runs parallel to Oregon's 2nd largest lake, Waldo Lake, although the trees hide the lake from view. For more trails and details about this area look in the Waldo Lake Wilderness and the Box Canyon Horse Camp chapters of this book, you may want to look up information on the web at www.fs.us./.r6/wilamette. Have fun!

*NOTE: The sign at Harrelson Horse Camp reads Trail #4363, and the Waldo Lake Wilderness Map reads Trail #4364. The PCT #2000 is on the Waldo Wilderness Map, however is not in the Wilderness. The Waldo Wilderness Map shows the name of Twin Peak Trail #3595 incorrectly as Twins Trail #3595.

HINT-At a Back Country Horseman meeting in Yakima, Washington the president of the chapter, informed us how a cardboard egg carton filled with wood chips and topped off with left over melted down candle wax, makes a great fire starter for a campfire. He is right!

One of the lakes in the Three Sisters Wilderness

PCT #2000 THREE SISTERS WILDERNESS AREA

(Southern section)

(From Trail 16 north to Trails 3517 & 3515, near Elk Lake) in Oregon

Distance:	9.3 Miles
Altitude:	5200'-5600'
Map:	Three Sisters Wilderness
Difficulty:	Moderate

Directions: This portion of the PCT #2000 is located in Central Oregon approximately 40 miles west of
Bend. From Bend, drive west on Cascade Lakes Highway 46 use Elk Lake, Six Lakes, or Winopee Lake
Trailheads to access the PCT #2000 in this area see your map for details.

Connecting Trails: 16, 3510, 33, 3526, 3326.1, 14, 3517, and 3515

Horse Camping: Nearby camping at Todd Lake Horse Camp, Quinn Meadows (reservation only), or Cultus Corral. Todd Lake Horse Camp is near Todd Lake Trailhead on Road 46. It is small; holding 4-5 sites and has a camp host. There is no fee yet! Quinn Meadows Horse Camp is a busy place. It is also on Highway 46, located near Elk Lake. With 22 sites and 4 stalls to each site, a fee is required. My favorite camp is Cultus Corral; it is south of both Todd and Quinn camps. Drive Highway 46 to gravel road 4630, go 1 mile on Road 4630. It has room for 200 people, 12 sites 4 corrals for each site, a fee is required.

Sisters Ranger Station
P.O. Box 249
Sisters, OR 97759
541-549-7700

Bend Ranger District
1230 NE 3rd Suite A262
Bend, OR 97701
541-388-5664

Trail Description: This 9.3-mile section of the PCT #2000 will be described going north from a 4-way intersection with Trails #16 and #3510 to another link of trails, they are, Trails #3517 and #3515. Ride in the forest, it is a short way around the east side of Packsaddle Mountain to reach the edge of the Mink Lake Basin. There are too many lakes to name! Snowshoe Trail #33 leads to the east. A series of trails depart as you make your way along this beautiful area on great trail, the trails are marked with destination signs rather than with trail numbers (refer

Josie and Ali ride the PCT in the Three Sisters Wilderness

We rode across this snowfield

to your map for the numbers). You'll pass Mink Lake Trail #3526 exiting to the west (left). There is one narrow spot on a blind corner, with a rock slide area to negotiate across. Meet with Porky Lake Trail #3326.1 going west (left). Several wonderful wooded miles glide under you and your mount. Travel by sparkling lakes and again you'll meet Mink Lake Trail #3526, which this time will cross the PCT #2000, and Trail #14 departs to the right (east). There are several shelters in the area; one is at Mink Lake. Ride by Reserve Meadows, you can water your animals here, where you'll find lush feed. The area is covered in lakes and meadows. Go past Dumbell Lake to reach Trail #3517 going to the west (left) toward Fisher Lakes and Trail #3515, which goes north toward Horse Lake. If you enjoy easy trails with nice footing and tons of lakes this is the place for you. For more information on this area, see the brief description table in the back of the book, look under Three Sisters Wilderness. The Waldo Lake Wilderness and Box Canyon Horse Camp chapters have trails in this area as well.

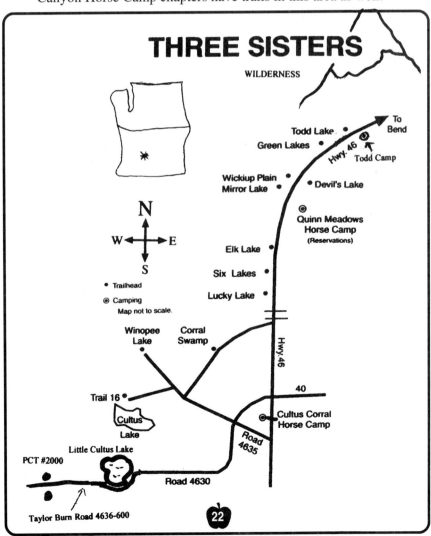

THREE SISTERS

WILDERNESS

To Bend

Todd Lake
Green Lakes

Hwy. 46

Todd Camp

Wickiup Plain
Mirror Lake

Devil's Lake

Quinn Meadows
Horse Camp
(Reservations)

Elk Lake

N

W ← → E

S

Six Lakes

Lucky Lake

• Trailhead
◉ Camping
Map not to scale.

Winopee
Lake

Corral
Swamp

Hwy. 46

40

Trail 16

Cultus Corral
Horse Camp

Cultus
Lake

Road
4635

Little Cultus Lake

PCT #2000

Road 4630

Taylor Burn Road 4636-600

22

PCT #2000 THREE SISTERS WILDERNESS AREA

(Middle section)

(From Trails 2 & 3516 near Elk Lake, north to Racetrack Meadows) in Oregon

Distance:	13.3 Miles
Altitude:	5200'-6520'
Map:	Three Sisters Wilderness
Difficulty:	Moderate

Directions: This portion of the PCT #2000 is located in Central Oregon approximately 40 miles west of Bend. From Bend, drive west on Cascade Lakes Highway 46, Elk and Devils Lake Trailheads can be used to access the PCT #2000 in this area, see your map for details.

Connecting Trails: 3516, 2, 3515, 20, 3527, 12.1, Unnamed Trail, 3547, 3511

Horse Camping: Nearby camping at Todd Lake Horse Camp, Quinn Meadows (reservation only), or Cultus Corral. Todd Lake Horse Camp is near Todd Lake Trailhead on Road 46. It is small; holding 4-5 sites and has a camp host. There is no fee yet! Quinn Meadows Horse Camp is a busy place. It is also on Highway 46, located near Elk Lake. With 22 sites and 4 stalls to each site, a fee is required. My favorite camp is Cultus Corral; it is south of both Todd and Quinn camps. Drive Highway 46 to gravel road 4630, go 1 mile on Road 4630. It has room for 200 people, 12 sites 4 corrals for each site, a fee is required.

Sisters Ranger Station
P.O. Box 249
Sisters, OR 97759
541-549-7700

Bend Ranger District
1230 NE 3rd Suite A262
Bend, OR 97701
541-388-5664

Trail Description: This 13.3 mile section of the PCT #2000 will be described from a 4-way intersection with Trails #3516 and #2 near Elk Lake north to Racetrack Meadow Trail #3511. In a nice cool forest, begin a 4.3-mile ascent up and over Koosah Mountain at 6,520' and down to Sister Mirror Lake, where Trail #3515 joins. The trail narrows a bit on the north face of the mountain. As the path flattens, Sister Mirror Lake unfolds before your eyes in a post card setting with South Sister's image reflected on her waters. Just beyond the lake, Mirror Trail #20 leaves going east (right), then Nash Lake Trail #3527 hooks in from the west (left). Ride around the east side of the House Rock and into the fragile and vast openness of Whickiup Plain, to the edge of massive Rock Mesa Obsidian Flow. "Charity", the pet name for the South Sister Mountain, is the big sister standing before you, topping out at a whopping 10,358 feet. You'll pass Wickiup Plain Trail #12.1 and then in 1.2 miles an unnamed trail both going to the east (right). Coming in to view is The Wife Mountain; she is pretty tall too, standing at 7,054'. Long slopes guide you back into the forest again, down in, then back up and out of a gully, with a spring in the bottom, pass Trail #3547 (James Creek Shelter is 1 mile up this trail. Refer to the note at the bottom of the page). Ride along the side of the South Sister Mountain for 4.2 miles more to reach Racetrack Meadow Trail #3511 (the ground in this area is growing, the Forest Service told me it has grown 3-4 inches in just a matter of a year or two, this was in 2002). Views are of buttes and of The Husband Mountain, he is slightly taller than his wife measuring up at 7,524 feet. For more information on this area, see the brief description table in the back of the book, look under Three Sisters Wilderness.

*NOTE: The Three Sisters Wilderness Map shows different numbers assigned to the same trail. On the back of the map it reads #3546 and the front it shows #3547.

HINT-Need to make an emergency call on your cell and can't get reception? Go to the top of a hill and try again.

Terri and Champ ride by a lava cinder

Terri stops to reflect on the wondrous Wilderness

Theresa and Roy make their way down Opie Dildock Pass

(Northern section)

(Obsidian Falls north to Scott Pass) in Oregon

Distance:	7.8 Miles
Altitude:	6400'-6890'
Map:	Three Sisters Wilderness
Difficulty:	Moderate

Directions: This section of the PCT #2000 is located in the heart of Oregon, west of the town of Sisters about 15 Miles. It can be accessed from a number of spots, McKenzie Pass on Road 242 (this road has a 35'length restriction for your rig), or jump in at any of these trails: Obsidian #3528, Scott #3531 or Scott Pass #4068, see map for details.

Connecting Trails: 3528, 3528.2, 3531, 4068

Horse Camping: Camps in the area include Sisters Cow Camp and Whispering Pines Horse Camp. To drive to Sisters Cow Camp, take paved Road 242 west out of Sisters about 1 mile, and turn left on Road 15 (Pole Creek Road) which starts paved, then becomes gravel, follow the sign to the camp at about the 2 mile-point. There are 3 large spots for your horses, two are corrals and one is wire. They share a water trough, outhouses, fire pits and tables are available. No fee is charged. The settings for both these camps are under ponderosa pines. Whispering Pines Horse Camp is reached from the same directions, except stay on Road 242 for about 5 miles, then turn left onto gravel

Camp neighbors, Roy and Theresa ride the PCT

Road 1018 camp is on the left side of the road. Whispering Pines includes 9 sites, a group area, outhouse, corrals, campfire pit, table, and trash service. Water for horses is in the creek. There is no potable water, so bring your own. A fee is charged.

Sisters Ranger Station	Bend Ranger District
P.O. Box 249	1230 NE 3rd Suite A262
Sisters, OR 97759	Bend, OR 97701
541-549-7700	541-388-5664

Trail Description: This 7.8 mile segment of the PCT #2000 stretches from Obsidian Falls and goes north through the magnificent Three Sisters Wilderness to Scott Pass. If you experience no other portion of the PCT #2000, I suggest you do this one! It is a "Heavy Use" area and if you use the Obsidian Trailhead you must obtain a permit from the Forest Service to ride here. Beginning from the long fall of the Obsidian Falls and the intersection of Obsidian Trail #3528, the PCT #2000 will carry you up the mountain's side. With mist on your face and roaring in your ears from the cascading glacier waters, you'll find yourself on the laps of "Hope" and "Faith", they are the North and Middle Sisters Mountains, both are over 10,000 feet high. Their big sister "Charity" is an arm's length away to the south. The PCT #2000 runs on the west side of these gals. You'll ride around the bottom of numerous glaciers. Glacier Way Trail #3528.2 departs going west (left) here. Skirt Little Brother Mountain and Collier Cone and climb up the most awesome set of switchbacks on open terrain. You can see the whole path to the tip-top of the mountain, where Opie Dilldock Pass greets you, this is the high-point of the trail at 6,890'. Passing Minnie Scott Spring, where the only grove of trees grows, for miles. The views from here on a clear day are breathtaking, white snow against coal-black obsidian rock and dark blue sky; it is a cornucopia for your senses. There may be a snowfield across the trail on the north slopes of the mountains where it stays cold and shady longer, be sure to call ahead for trail information. Ride down to a large meadow to merge with Scott Trail #3531 the "Old Scott Party route". The trail goes around the west and north side of Yapoah Crater. There are awesome cinder cones that the path goes up and over (Wonders never cease how these trails get built, hats off to the builders!). Ride on a more level trail as you make your approach to Scott Pass and Scott Pass Trail #4068. You may want to continue a few extra feet to the north to water the animals at South Mattieu Lake. If you can take time on your trip to visit the Dee Wright Observatory at McKenzie Pass, I'm sure you'll find it worth the effort. We'll pick the trail up on the other side of McKenzie Pass a ways. For more information on this area, see the brief description table in the back of the book, look under Three Sisters Wilderness.

PCT #2000 MOUNT WASHINGTON WILDERNESS AREA

(Big lava flow near McKenzie Pass north to Santiam Pass) in Oregon

Distance:	13.3 Miles
Altitude:	4650'-5800'
Map:	Mount Washington Wilderness
Difficulty:	Moderate

Directions: This part of the PCT #2000 is located in Central Oregon, west of Sisters and northwest of Bend. You can access the area described from Santiam Pass off of Highway 20-126. From Highway 20, turn south on paved Forest Service Road 2690; follow the signs almost to the end of the paved road and Big Lake. Turn left on Road 811, toward the PCT Trailhead.

Connecting Trails: Unnamed Spur Trail

Horse Camping: There is primitive camping at the trailhead in a small meadow, you'll find a trail behind the meadow that leads to a small lake for your stock to get a drink, bring potable water. There are also primitive camp spots all along the dirt Santiam Wagon Road 811 and Road 810. Stay on the main roads, as the terrain is sandy, deep in spots and you may get stuck if you detour from the packed roads.

Josie and her mare at the "Black Wilderness" the lava stopped here!"

28

Sisters Ranger Station	Detroit Ranger District
P.O. Box 249	HC Box 320
Sisters, OR 97759	Mill City, OR 97360
541-549-7700	541-854-3366

Bend Ranger District
1230 NE 3rd Suite A262
Bend, OR 97701
541-388-5664

Trail Description: The 13.3 mile-portion of the PCT #2000 will be described in 2 parts. From Big Lake 3.6 miles north to Santiam Pass and from Big Lake south 9.7 miles to the base of Belknap Crater at the big lava flow near McKenzie Pass.

Going North: Leaving the PCT #2000 Trailhead near Big Lake going north to Santiam Pass, is a sandy and pine lined path. You can make good time through this area as the ground is mostly level. Views of Mount

Madeleine rides past the snarled snags that line the PCT

Washington are over your shoulder; Hayrick and Hoodoo Buttes, as well as Sand Mountain are to the west (left). At the halfway-point, you'll find a lake on the west (left) side of the trail. Cross several dirt roads and reach Santiain Pass and Highway 20-126.

Going South: From the PCT #2000 Trailhead near Big Lake the path sets out to the south for 9.7 miles towards McKenzie Pass. A grand trail waits for you, with excellent footing for the animals. At the 1-mile point, a spur trail exits down to a youth camp along Big Lake's east shore. The sound of splashing water, echoes of children's voices and the roar from motor boats float up to you as you catch the sun gleaming off gigantic Big Lake below. This trail climbs modestly around the west side of Mount Washington and passes many seasonal washes stemming from Mount Washington. As you stroll along, sometimes under a thick canopy of trees and other times the forest turns strikingly bony, bear grass and ferns adorn the forest floor. This section of the trail has a surprisingly minimal amount of rocks for its length. Leave civilization behind and travel past alpine meadows to discover the views ahead of Mount Washington and Belknap Crater. Notice a rock cairn beside the trail to the east (left) at about the 3 mile-point. After consulting the map, it looks as if this would be where a spring is, but it is not the spring, the spring is just a stone's throw away in a meadow, too bad it is down in a hole and not accessible for livestock to drink. Continue riding, passing more seasonal creeks and come upon some good size meadows with lots of feed. Ride past some boulders in rich forest with more wash areas. Mount Washington juts out of the ground as if begging to have his picture taken. Reach a level plateau on open

Josie and Bandit at the trailhead to the Pacific Crest Trail at Mount Washington Wilderness

terrain, the high-point of the trail at 6,000'. The trail goes around an open hill to overview a small rock slide made up of huge boulders. The only water spots my friend Madeleine and I found on a hot August day were at Lower and Upper Washington Ponds. The way is marked with a rock cairn, as it is off-trail. The water is on the south (right) side of a vague side path on a shelf. The upper pond is to the northeast of the lower pond about 120' up the hill. There was tender grass by the lower pond and nice shade for a cool break when we visited. Ride in more old growth forest, reaching an area where the snow and wind has sheered off some trees at their waistline; this looks like an avalanche chute. Two of the Tree Sisters Mountains and Belknap Crater are in full view. This ride has deep forest with hemlock trees (Washington State's state tree) as well as weathered bony skeleton snags, meadows, ponds and lots of views, you can see Mount Jefferson to the north as well. The sandy trail gently slopes down to "The Black Wilderness", which is a forsaken area around the impressive Belknap Crater (standing at 6,872' high) and is entirely lava-covered earth. Ride down to the edge of the lava field, it is a wall of gray razor sharp crags that are unforgiving to anyone or anything! Unfortunately after weighing the pros and cons of continuing, we ran our hands over the lava rocks to test its sharpness, then we turned back. The abrasive bubbly rock (frozen in time) is extremely sharp. We didn't want our horse's feet to be chewed up by this wonder of nature. We got lots of great snap shots and called it a victory! This is a "MUST SEE" area and is well worth the trip. Besides Mount Washington you'll see Mount Jefferson, Three Fingered Jack, Sand Mountain, Hoodoo Butte, and Hayrick Butte (looks like a crew-cut hair do). It is a wonderful part of the PCT #2000 with slight

One of the two Washington Ponds

Madeleine and Josie at the foot of Mount Washington

grades that most any rider-horse team can handle. We'll skip the north side of Santiam Pass (I hear it is pretty narrow) and jump back on the trail near Jack Lake, see ya there!

HINT-Before leaving on a ride be sure to leave a note in your truck or at home as to where you have gone. Do this especially if there is no sign-in box at the trailhead.

"IT MUST BE THE FULL MOON"

Unbeknownst to my friend Madeleine and me, we picked the busiest weekend of the year to visit the Santiam Pass and Big Lake Area. There was an endurance race with 30, 50, 75 and 100 miler's being ridden, which meant that the road in front of our campsite had horses clip-clopping by till dawn. The 100 miler's have 24 hours to complete their route. A children's summer camp was having a grand finale with parents weekend, complete with loud speakers and lots of singing and clapping echoing off of Big Lake. The motorcycles and 4-wheelers were the hardest to endure, we were sure that their regular riding paths were being blocked by the hundreds of horse racers, and their customary parking taken up as well. You need to understand this is a huge area, and it's unusual for this many activities to be crowded in this tight vicinity. Anyway, the motorcycles zipped up and down the dusty 2-track by our meadow non-stop all day, coating our camp with a layer of grime with each breeze they whipped up. They made a turnaround about 100 yards past our camp, so the powder from when they cruised by the first time hadn't settled when they would plow by again on their way back. Last, but not least, there were the punk rockers next door that loved their loud music. None of these activities alone were enough to bother us, but together, WOW! The straw that broke the camel's back was when the rockers started to light off fireworks at about midnight, we were thinking the whole forest would go up into flames any second. I followed Madeleine's cue, at first I thought she had gone around the bend as she was banging a pan with a wooden spoon. Soon we were in the swing of things, pans and big sticks pounding to our hearts content. Energetically we tipped our faces to the sky and started to howl at the full moon, and we danced like naked elves. Things quieted down, but never came to a complete stand still. We knew our only refuge would be the Wilderness, so the next morning at 6 a.m. (only a couple hours after our moon-party) we saddled up and were on the Pacific Crest Trail headed to see Mount Washington and we were none to quiet about it either! The next night wasn't any better, things quieted down about Sunday evening. Sleep deprived, we moved camp on Monday.

Josie

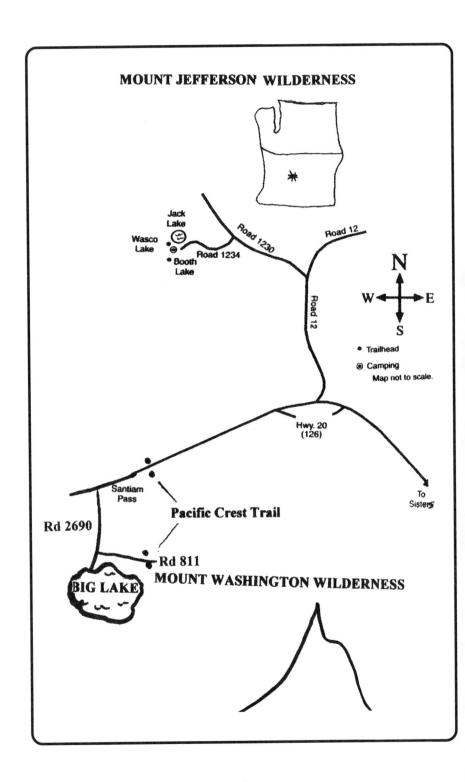

MOUNT JEFFERSON WILDERNESS

Jack Lake
Wasco Lake
Booth Lake
Road 1230
Road 1234
Road 12
Road 12

N
W E
S

• Trailhead
⊚ Camping
Map not to scale.

Hwy. 20
(126)

Santiam Pass
Pacific Crest Trail
Rd 2690
Rd 811
BIG LAKE
MOUNT WASHINGTON WILDERNESS
To Sisters

PCT #2000 MOUNT JEFFERSON WILDERNESS AREA

(Minto Pass north to Rockpile Lake) in Oregon

Distance:	3.6 Miles
Altitude:	5300'-6400'
Maps:	GTM 557 Mount Jefferson
	Mount Jefferson Wilderness
Difficulty:	Moderate

Directions: This short sector of the PCT #2000 is located in Central Oregon. You can access it using trails coming from the Jack Lake area. Drive from Sisters, on Highway 20-126 going west for 13 miles and turn right onto Forest Service Road 12. Then, you need to turn left on Forest Service Road 1234, where you'll find Jack Lake at the top-end of this dusty, rough, winding and steep road. The reward for the trudge up this road is a nice size turnaround; it can get busy here. We like to visit during the week when it's less crowded.

Connecting Trails: 4015 (GTM 65A), 3437,4014

Horse Camping: Jack Lake Horse Camp has 4 corrals, 3 campsites, tables, and an outhouse. Bring potable water, livestock water is at Jack Lake, which is hidden to the north of the trailhead. No fee was charge when we visited. Big Meadows Horse Camp is close by, near Santiam Pass, offering 8 sites. There is a fee charged here, amenities include outhouse, fire pits, corrals and water.

Sisters Ranger Station
P.O. Box 249
Sisters, OR 97759
541-549-7700

Bend Ranger District
1230 NE 3rd Suite A262
Bend, OR 97701
541-388-5664

Detroit Ranger District
HC Box 320
Mill City, OR 97360
541-854-3366

Trail Description: This 4 mile segment of the PCT #2000 is described from Minto Pass going north to Rockpile Lake. Starting at Minto Pass in a succulent green forest at a 4-way intersection with Minto Pass Trail #3437 and Pacific Crest Tie Trail #4015 (GTM 65A), the trail gains 1,000'. This path has some narrow parts as it ducks under a stone wall, all you see is the next corner and some blue sky. Widening out, the trail meets with Rockpile Lake and Wasco Lake Trail #4014. For more information on this area, see the brief description table in the back of the book, look under Mount Jefferson Wilderness.

HINT-Hauling your rig up or down a hill on a washboard road, drive at an angle rather than going straight across the bumps, you'll find it is easier on your rig.

Madeleine and her Arabian mare at Minto Pass

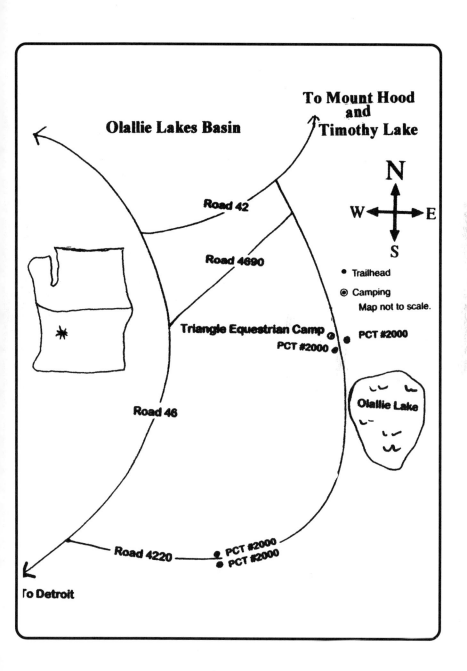

Olallie Lakes Basin

To Mount Hood and Timothy Lake

N
W — E
S

• Trailhead
◉ Camping
Map not to scale.

Road 42

Road 4690

Triangle Equestrian Camp ◉ • PCT #2000
PCT #2000 •

Olallie Lake

Road 46

Road 4220 — • PCT #2000
◉ PCT #2000

To Detroit

PCT #2000 OLALLIE LAKE BASIN

(From Horseshoe Saddle Trail north to OlaIlie Meadow) in Oregon

Distance:	8 Miles
Altitude:	4600'-5700'
Maps:	Mount Jefferson Wilderness
	GTM 525 Brittenbush
Difficulty:	Moderate

Directions: This slice of the PCT #2000 is located in the North Central part of Oregon. There is a chain of trails that crisscross the PCT in this area. Take Highway 26 south from Mount Hood to paved Skyline Road 42 for 18 miles going southwest, the next 4.3 miles of road is one lane paved. At this point you can consult your map for a rough-road shortcut. Or continue 4 miles more to reach milepost 26. Turn south (left) on Forest Service Road 46, which is 2 lane for 6.9 miles, turn left again onto a single lane Forest Service Road 4690, go 8.1 miles more to Forest Service Road 4220. Drive to the right, passing Olallie Meadow and you'll find Triangle Equestrian Camp in 2 miles on the right hand side of the road. It is approximately 49 miles from Estacada to Forest Service Road 4690 and about 23.5 miles from Detroit to Forest Service Road 4690.

Connecting Trails: 712, 714, 735, 719, 720, 706, 716

Horse Camping: There are 8 camp spots at Triangle Equestrian Camp. Tables, fire rings, outhouse and 4 corrals per site are awaiting you, when my friend Madeleine and I visited there was no fee being charged. Water is in a cistern for livestock, bring potable water for yourselves.

Clackamas Ranger District
595 NW Industrial Way
Estacada, OR 97023
503-630-6861

Trail Description: The 8 mile portion of the PCT #2000 that threads through the Olallie Lakes Basin will be described from Horseshoe Saddle Trail #712 north to Olallie Meadow area. Leaving Horseshoe Saddle Trail the PCT begins at the 5,600' level. You'll climb with a view of Mount Jefferson in your rear view mirror, enter a rocky section, Rudy Hill Trail #714 (hiker) exits to the west. Ride around and downhill to see Upper Lake. Double Peaks Trail #735 joins from the west. Descending through a region laced with boulders and lakes pooled everywhere. Pass an unmarked trail to the right. Go down a hillside with some rocky spots, then Red Lake Trail #719 crosses the PCT #2000. Ride along the path as more boulders and rock slides greet you, wander down a slope (Madeleine and I saw a huge black bear here!) to a set of green lakes and Road 4220. Cross the road (there is a small store at Olallie Lake area to the right) and pick the trail up again, ride in forest, passing a pond, the path has great footing for the horses here. Olallie Butte Trail #720 leaves to the west; there are a few rocks in the next mile or so. Pass Lodgepole Trail #706, then come to Russ Lake Trail #716, crossing it the PCT #2000 continues. This is where we turned and followed Russ Lake Trail down to Olallie Meadow. The next section described will be near Timothy Lake and Joe Graham Horse Camp, see you up the road. For more information on this area, consult the brief description table in the back of the book, look under Olallie Lake Basin. Mmost of the trails around here are very rocky, the PCT is the best trail for horses in the area, Olallie Butte Trail #720 is my 2nd choice to ride here. The word Olallie means "Berry".

HINT-When you are hauling your rig something to keep in mind is that a horse does not have any arms to hang on with around tight corners. Also for quick starts and stops, do "Flica" a favor and go slow, ignore the impatient tailgaters, they will always be there, because nobody likes to drive behind a horse trailer.

We stopped for a water break in the Olallie Lakes Basin

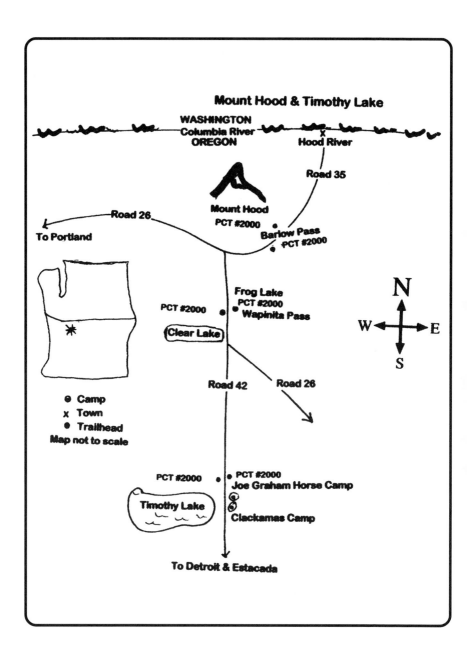

Mount Hood & Timothy Lake

WASHINGTON
Columbia River
OREGON
Hood River

Road 35

Mount Hood
PCT #2000
Barlow Pass
PCT #2000

To Portland
Road 26

Frog Lake
PCT #2000
Wapinita Pass
PCT #2000
Clear Lake

Road 42   Road 26

● Camp
x Town
● Trailhead
Map not to scale

N
W ← → E
S

PCT #2000
Timothy Lake

PCT #2000
Joe Graham Horse Camp
Clackamas Camp

To Detroit & Estacada

PCT #2000 MOUNT HOOD AREA

(From Warm Springs River near Timothy Lake, north to Mount Hood) in Oregon

Distance:	25.7 Miles
Altitude:	3300'-6000'
Maps:	GTM 462 Mount Hood
	GTM 493 High Rock
	GTM 494 Mount Wilson
Difficulty:	Moderate

Directions: This 25.7-mile chunk of the PCT #2000 is located in the North Central part of Oregon. You can hook up to this trail in various spots,

Madeleine rides down a cool timberland section of the PCT

on the north end at Barlow Pass on Highway 35, in the middle at Wapinita Pass on Highway 26 or the southern end at Road 42 by Timothy Lake. From Portland, drive east on Highway 26, from Hood River drive south on Highway 35 the roads meet and turn south onto Road 42 to Joe Graham Horse Camp, it is across from Timothy Lake, the sign is small, if you miss it you will see Clackamas Camp. See map for details.

Connecting Trails: 524, 522, 534, 528, 500, 483, 495,482, 674, 600

Horse Camping: Both Clackamas and Joe Graham Horse Camp have horse camping, however Joe Graham has corrals, Clackamas was still in the process of getting better horse facilities when Madeleine and I were visiting. There is a historical building at Joe Graham; it housed workhorses that helped in putting out wildfires. The camp's host gave us a tour inside the old building. This is a large camp and it fills up on the weekends, you may want to reserve a spot. There are 4 corrals to each spot, fire pits; tables, livestock and potable water are available. You are required to move your horse's dropping into garbage bags (provided by the camp host), then to the garbage bin. There is garbage service, and a rake is available for your use, there is a fee for camping here. Clackamas Camp is to the south and has camping also; you can see it across the big meadow.

Inlet to Timothy Lake

Zigzag Ranger District
70220 E Highway 26
Zigzag, OR 97049
503-622-3191

Trail Description: This 25.7 mile component of the PCT #2000 will be described going from Joe Graham Horse Camp to the south and then to the north.

Going South-The 7.6-mile section of the PCT #2000 from Joe Graham Horse Camp embarks south to Warm Springs River begins at the intersection with Joe Graham Trail #524. Ride under tall timber as the wide trail takes you ½ mile to a carved wooden sign at the junction with Headwaters Trail #524 (not on the map) and Miller Trail #534. In another ½ mile you'll reach a sign that signifies the entrance to the Warm Springs Reservation. *A **warning-***stay on the trail while in the reservation (they have certain rules pertaining to being on this land, you may want to attain more information about this from the reservation). It's a slight trek uphill for the next 4 miles. This is a delightful stretch of trail; you can make some time through here. You'll cross several roads before descending to Warm Springs River on a real nice trail through the forest. One switchback takes you down to the water's edge, next to the river is a spring.

Stop for lunch near Mount Hood

Going North-Setting out from camp, ride the Joe Graham Camp Trail #524, it will take you to the PCT #2000. Take the PCT #2000 1 mile more to Road 42, where it crosses the road and continues toward Timothy Lake. In shadowy timber ride over a rock slide area with bridges, catching a glimpse of Timothy Lake ahead is where Timothy Lake Trail #528 hooks in. There are lots of photo opportunities along here of the robin's egg blue waters of Timothy Lake, you

you may be enticed to go for a swim. Rolling trail with good footing takes you to a series of drawn-out bridges over wet lands and the inlet to Timothy Lake. There is a good watering spot in the inlet for your mounts. The Timothy Lake Trail #528 goes around the lake, the PCT heads north. At the next intersection, Little Crater Lake Trail #500 ties in from the right (east) here you'll find tie rails set up under a canopy of cool trees. It's well worth it to go and see Little Crater Lake, tie up and walk in. It is only ½ mile or so and is a level walk, a small effort to see the deepest blue water you may have ever seen, the water is only 34 degrees, there is a lot of information posted to read. In the next 7.7 miles up to Waplnita Pass you'll cross various roads and ride about 3 miles on a slope with views of Mount Hood. Rhododendron plants hold the hillside captive, pass several clear-cut areas where it is a drop-off on the side of the trail, however the trail is wide enough for most any trail horse to negotiate, watch for roots and rocks. The trail was well maintained when we visited. Blue Box Trail #483 departs to the southeast, just before crossing Highway 26 at Wapinita Pass. From the trailhead parking lot at Wapinita Pass, the trail traverses up the forested mountain on broad trail. Twin Lakes Train #495 joins in 1 mile, the path flattens as Palmateer Trail #482 hooks in, then in less than 2 miles, you'll meet the other end of Twin Lakes Loop, as it will join the PCT #2000. It's a short trek to Barlow Pass, leaving the paved trailhead at Barlow Pass, consider taking a few minuets to read the wooden signs about the historical road. Cross Highway 35 and head up the trail, in just under 6 miles you'll reach Mount Hood. Scale upward on good trail engulfed in cool forest. A short part of the trail has been built up with stones stacked and mortared together across a sheer drop-off area, creating a solid base to ride across. Ride around a corner, you can hear the highway underfoot and can see it over the tip of your boot. The adrenaline is short lived, the trail widens again and the quest to Timberline Lodge continues. Catch peeks of Mount Hood through the meadow and trees, every time it appears bigger. Pass a marker high in the limbs, it is Trail #674 (winter sport). Rein-up in a beautiful alpine meadow and take snaps as you hear the rushing water of White River. Open sandy terrain takes you the remainder of the way, pass Timberline Trail #600 (hiker only), which exits to the right. As you near the apex of this section of the PCT #2000 closing in on the 6,000' level by Timberline Lodge there is some deep sand, be sure to keep an eye on those animals that are prone to rolling! Ford a creek and ride the curves of the hillside, now you can see skiers on the slopes even in August! Massive Mount Hood is standing tall with all its glaciers gleaming in the sun, it is so beautiful,our eyes couldn't get enough. This entire 25.7 miles of trail is in timberland, with the exception of the last 2 miles as you approach Mount Hood. The mountain is 11,235' tall, the trail continues and at one time was considered not suitable to stock, however now it has been improved. For more information on this area, see the brief description table in the back of the book, look under Mount Hood. I'll see you in Washington for the next portion of the Pacific Crest Trail #2000.

HINT-Delegate tasks and supplies when there are few riders, one person can bring the gun, one can bring the water purification bottle, and the other rider brings the saw and so on. We do this with a lot of items, even the food supplies.

Beautiful day to ride to Mount Hood

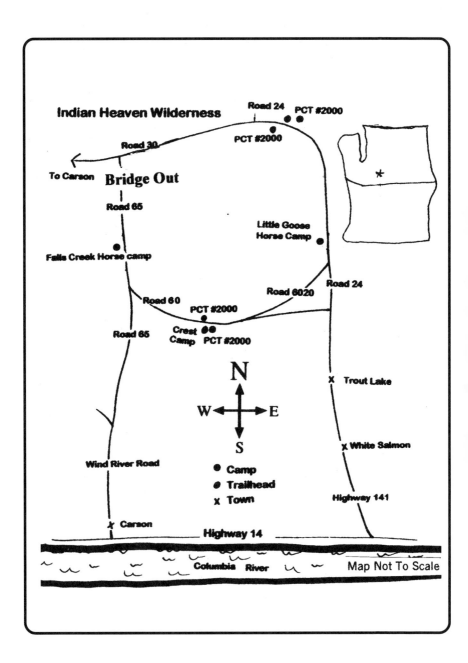

Indian Heaven Wilderness

Road 24   PCT #2000

PCT #2000

Road 30

*

To Carson   **Bridge Out**

Road 65

Little Goose
Horse Camp

Falls Creek Horse camp

Road 24

Road 60   Road 6020

PCT #2000

Road 65   Crest
Camp   PCT #2000

N

x Trout Lake

W   E

S

x White Salmon

Wind River Road

● Camp
● Trailhead
x Town

Highway 141

x Carson

Highway 14

Columbia River   Map Not To Scale

PCT #2000 INDIAN HEAVEN WILDERNESS AREA

(From "Big Lava Bed" north to Surprise Lakes) in Washington

Distance:	17.3 Miles
Altitude:	3000'-5000'
Maps:	Indian Heaven Wilderness
	GTM 365 Lone Butte
	GTM 397 Wind River
Difficulty:	Moderate

Directions: This tidbit of the PCT #2000 is located in Southwest Washington. You may access the trail from an array of places in the Indian Heaven Wilderness Area. There are 2 nice horse camps available, one is on the east and one is on the west side of the Wilderness area. There are primitive camps at the south and north ends of the Wilderness also (see map).

Dark and spooky forest, Josie and Ali

To drive to the Little Goose Horse Camp-This camp is on the east side of the Wilderness, take Highway 14 along the Columbia River to Road 141, go north on Road 141 through the town of Trout Lake to Forest Service Road 24. Drive about 12 miles on Forest Service Road 24, Little Goose Horse Camp is on the west (left) side of the road.

Little Goose Horse Camp's amenities include: 3 sites, table, fire rings, outhouse, ramp, creek water for the livestock, and bring potable water (at one time there was a working spring). When driving in to the camp, the road splits, the upper road is a bit wider than the lower one and they come together again after passing the "people only camp". The horse camp is at the end of the road in a small clearing lined with trees. The area is quite large here, with room to negotiate your rig. No fee was charged to stay here.

To drive to Falls Creek Horse Camp-This camp is on the west side of the Wilderness and is accessed from Highway 14 along the Columbia River also. Turn north on Wind Road 30, toward the town of Carson, next you'll go north (right) on steep, one lane paved Panther Creek Road 65. The road becomes dirt and has some tight turns and narrow spots. Road 65 is washed out about 4 miles past Falls Creek Horse Camp, just beyond Trail #111. Call ahead for updates.

Falls Creek Camp offers: 6 sites, tables, fire rings, outhouse, and water for the livestock is in Falls Creek. Some of the sites are wider than others are and the road is tightly woven in the trees. The sap drips heavily off the trees, when Sandy and I visited we put tarps over our rigs to protect the paint on our trucks. No fee was charged to stay here.

Sandy and Chris by a rock slide at Indian Heaven Wilderness

To drive to the south trailhead and Crest Camp-Follow either of the above directions only this time, turn onto Forest Service Road 60 before reaching either camp and drive to the PCT #2000 Trailhead and Crest Camp. At one time it was a drive through camp, however when Sandy and I were there the road was blocked with a downed tree, in the bushes is a camp spot.

To get to the north primitive camp-drive past Little Goose Camp and reach the trailhead for the PCT #2000, where you'll find roadside parking.

Connecting Trails: 171.1(A), 111, 55, 48, 179, 176, 33, 29, 108, 185, 107, 26

Mount Adams Ranger District
2455 Highway 141
Trout Lake, WA 98650
509-395-3400

Trail Description: The Pacific Crest Trail #2000 will be described in two directions from Crest Camp spot on the south end of the Wilderness at Crest Camp.

Cold weather struck!

Going South: The 4 mile segment of the PCT #2000 gets underway from Forest Service Road 60 at Crest Camp and the "Big Lava Bed", this is an ancient lava flow area. The trees have taken over portions of the tremendous arid bulges of magna-cinders that have been frozen in time. There are tiny flowers and scrawny snags decorating the landscape. The trail split the lava field and the timberland, so you have two types of terrain to experience from one trail, just a matter of feet from each other. Lush and green with soft, spongy forest floor on the one side and hot and dry on the other, both are very interesting but intensely different from one another. In spots the trail sounds hollow when the horse's hooves go across, as it winds around a mountain covered with huckleberry bushes, there is a camp and watering spot along this section. Climb a hillside on some well-placed switchbacks in deep coastal-type forest. We turned around here due to time, so you can explore further yourselves.

Going North: The PCT #2000 embarks north from Crest Camp and begins at a sign, put up by the Delson Family, in memory of their son, they maintain a section of this trail in his honor. This path is chiefly in forest across the Indian Heaven Wilderness for 17-plus miles. Start by climbing mildly from Forest Service Road 60, passing Sheep Lakes, meadows and then Shortcut Trail #171.1(A), which leaves to the west (left). Views are of Mount Adams to the east and Mount Hood to the south, switchback across the sunny side of a huckleberry bush hillside to a hogback. As a bonus you'll see Mount Saint Helens to the west. Ride around Gifford Peak and as the trail levels here, Blue Lake lays in wait for you. Tombstone Lake Trail #55 joins from the east, and Thomas Lake Trail #111 leads to west, this

Chris blends in with the snowy landscape

is about the 8 mile-point. Continue in deep forest and brush laden hillsides, crossing rock washes you'll see East Crater above you and East Crater Trail #48 leaves east. Lemei Trail #179 is the next trail you'll merge with, going to the east as well. Pass several lakes to find Elk Lake Trail #176 headed west and in just over ½ mile, Indian Heaven Trail #33 goes east. As you can tell this area is teaming with trails and is a sublime place to spend a vacation and never ride the same path twice. Placid Lake Trail #29 heads down to the west; this is the high-point of the trail at 5,000'. Bird Mountain hails above to the east of the PCT #2000; you'll pass several more lakes and a rock slide. A succession of trails exit as you make your way to Forest Service Road 24, they are: Cultus Creek #108 going to the east, Wood Lake #185 and Sawtooth Mountain #107 coming in from the east also (this last trail use to be a part of the PCT). Ride down to the tip of Sawtooth Mountain and switchback on broad trail through more flourishing huckleberry fields to meet Forest Service Road 24. This concludes this section of the PCT #2000; it is a great area to visit with many views, and minor elevation changes, lots of lakes and of course big juicy huckleberries to eat in late summer! For more information on this area, see the brief description table in the back of the book, under Indian Heaven Wilderness. Next we will go to the William O' Douglas Wilderness Area at White Pass.

HINT-Flashlight batteries store longer when they are turned around when not in use.

"CAMPER ENVY"

The night was long as the storm raged through the woods, the sound of snags falling near camp had turned a peaceful trip into a wait n' see trip. We had five grand days of riding and it was 80 degrees when we arrived. Suddenly the weather changed. My friend said, she was happy that I bought a camper instead of a canopy to stay in. That night she padded herself with five blankets a wool hat and scrunched down in her shell in her truck. It struck her without warning, when she heard the sound of my heater coming on that night. The dreaded "camper envy" was taking her over. Being the wonderful person she is, she was able to overcome the emotion and join me the entire next day as we hunkered inside the camper to wait out the horrible storm.

Josie

PCT #2000 WILLIAM O' DOUGLAS WILDERNESS AREA

(From White Pass north to American Ridge Trail) in Washington

Distance:	20.1 Miles
Altitude:	4100'-5700'
Maps:	GTM 303 White Pass
	GTM 271 Bumping Lake
Difficulty:	Moderate

Directions: This shred of the PCT #2000 is located in South Central Washington. To access, drive Highway 12 to White Pass, which is between the towns of Morton and Yakima. Day parking is available at the White Pass Horse Camp located on the north side of the highway, look for a small sign that leads to camp, it is on the east side of the ski area.

Connecting Trails: 1107, 60, 57, 1156, 44, 45, 980, 43, 971, 22, Laughingwater Creek, 990, 958

Madeleine at White Pass

Horse Camping: White Pass Horse Camp has a small loop and has an outhouse, tables, and fire pits. Livestock water is in Leech Lake. A camp fee is required to stay here.

Naches Ranger District
10237 Highway 12
Naches, WA 98937
503-653-2205

Trail Description: Begin your 20.1 mile trek starting at White Pass at the 4,400' level and head north toward American Ridge Trail #958. This part of the PCT #2000 is all in forest with many lakes, and is one of my favorite spots to come and play. The footing is pretty smooth and I never tire of the lakes and huge meadows, along with the endless loop possibilities. Start by skirting the immense Leech Lake on its east shoreline. Ride some long switchbacks up a hillside, then the path flattens out a bit as you approach the intersection with Dark Meadows Trail #1107. Continue up to the 5,200' level, where you'll find Deer, then Sand Lakes. Sand Lake Trail #60 exits to the west (left). Gradually

Tons of large meadows at the White Pass Area

ascend for the next 2 miles to attain the high-point of the trail at 5,700'. Cortright Creek Trail #57 hooks up from the west. Climb down 600 feet in the next 1.2 miles passing Buesch Lake, where Dumbell Trail #1156 intersects. A series of small lakes on a flat stretch carry you to yet another fork. This time with Cowlitz Trail #44, which exits to the right, then in .2 mile the same trail departs to the left (see note at bottom of page). The next couple of miles are fun to ride as the tread weaves in and out between knolls and puddles. Twin Sisters Trail #980 goes to the east (right) and Pothole Trail #45 goes south (left). Still slightly downhill in 1 mile more, Jug Lake Trail #43 merges with the PCT #2000. The next 1.4 miles goes downward passing many meadows, one in particular that seems to be a favorite among people who pack in, is at the 4-way intersection with Bumping Lake Trail #971 and Carlton Creek Trail #22. Here you'll find Bumping River, which you'll need to ford. There can be lots of bothersome bugs, but what do you expect it is a lake basin. It can be quite muddy, depending on the year, as this area gets its share of moister to be sure, and takes a long time to dry out because it's cloudy and foggy a lot. The next 6.4 miles of the PCT #2000 has been written by my good friend Donna Evans.

Last camp out of the season-late October

"Head north climbing away from Bumping Lake Trail #971 on fairly easy switchbacks with good footing. Travel through timber, then into sub-alpine meadows and lakes. Mountain goats have been seen in the surrounding rock hillsides. Nice open views to the south and southeast. The trail climbs past lakes onto open hillsides. You can see Mount Adams to the southwest. At about the 3 mile-point from leaving Bumping Lake Trail #971, Laughingwater Trail comes in from the west and .3 mile more Two Lakes Trail #990 exits to the east. (My husband Dean and I went to visit Two Lakes, on a trail, which goes downhill and then climbs back up a rocky slope to meet back up with the PCT #2000.) At the 5,600' level the trail traverses the ridge a ways, then pops out into the open with an amazing view of Mount Rainier to the west. It seems larger than life! From here the path continues along the west side of the ridge, mostly in the open with the view of Mount Rainier all the while. Staying fairly level up on the ridge, you'll intersect with American Ridge Trail #958, there is a great view of the American River Basin from this ridge. For more information on trails in this area see the William O' Douglas Wilderness chapter in this book."

Donna

*NOTE: The Forest Service noted that the PCT is the division for the name of Trail #44. On the east side of the PCT in the Wenatchee National Forest it is known as "Tumac" and on the west side in the Gifford Pinchot National Forest it is "Cowlitz".

HINT-For quick and easy de-worming of your horse or mule, try this: Mix de-worming paste with a couple cups of cracked corn, then sprinkle an extra cup or two of straight cracked corn on top to disguise the taste of the paste mixture.

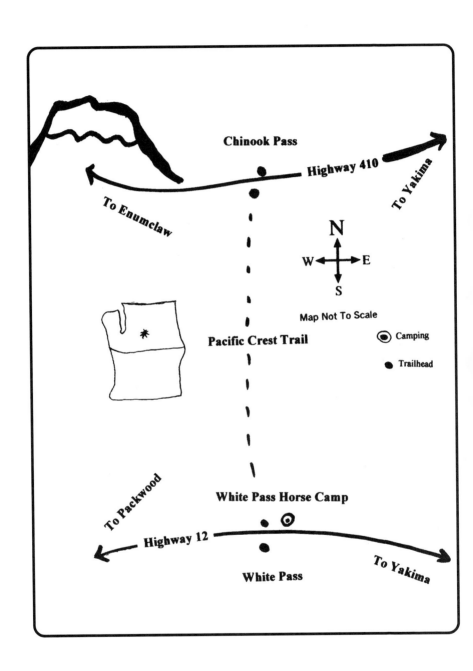

Chinook Pass

Highway 410

To Yakima

To Enumclaw

N
W · E
S

Map Not To Scale

Pacific Crest Trail

◎ Camping

● Trailhead

To Packwood

White Pass Horse Camp

Highway 12

To Yakima

White Pass

PCT #2000 WILLIAM O' DOUGLAS WILDERNESS AREA

(From Chinook Pass going south) in Washington

Distance:	3.5 Miles
Altitude:	5400'-5800'
Maps:	GTM 270 Mount Rainier East
	GTM 271 Bumping Lake
Difficulty:	Moderate

Directions: This section of the PCT #2000 is located in Central Washington. From Yakima, take Highway 12 west and continue straight on Highway 410 to Chinook Pass. Or from the west side of the Cascades, take Highway 410 east out of Greenwater to Chinook Pass. You'll find parking on the north side of the road, with a ramp, hitchin' rail and an outhouse. This can be a busy spot in the peek summer months. "The early bird gets the worm" as the old saying goes, or in this case the parking spot!

Connecting Trails: 968

Naches Ranger District
10237 Highway 12
Naches, WA 98937
503-653-2205

Trail Description: My friend Madeleine rode her mare "Cheyenne" on this section of the Pacific Crest Trail #2000.

Donna and her mare ride between White and Chinook Pass

"You can find the trail west of the parking area on a spur trail. Begin by going southeast from Chinook Pass by way of the overpass above Highway 410. Travel on open slopes around the north and east sides of Naches Peak at 6,452'. Good trail here, but quite steep on your left for a while. You do have some trees on the steep side. Looking over the treetops you'll see Highway 410 in the distance and the wide canyon below. As you ride along, the trail gets rocky in places and you have a rock wall on your right that goes straight up. Further on, it becomes more open and the terrain has more of a gentle slope, where you'll see a small lake on your right. You are in sub-alpine high country and the flowers, plants and trees are absolutely beautiful. The trail is good and well used here. You will reach the top of this section of the PCT #2000 at 5,800'. At this point you'll see the crystal blue Dewey Lake right below at 5,200', and you look out over many mountain ridges to the south, southeast and southwest. Going down you'll see the Forest Service sign and sign-in box. From here the trail is narrow and steep. At the first switchback you can step off the trail to the right to get a view of Mount Rainier. Continue down, still on a narrow trail maneuvering around some rocky areas. Alongside the trail sat some lumber for new bridges, some were completed and we rode across them, nice! Here is a good place to water your horse. Once down you'll see a smaller lake off to your right and Dewey Lake on your left. The trail is wide and soft and the terrain is nice with many beautiful green meadows. Riding at lake-level on the PCT #2000 you will be crossing a rock slide that goes all the way into the lake. At the end of Dewey Lake you'll meet Dewey Lake Trail #968 on your left. From here, the trail starts going up through mud. We came to a rotten bridge, but managed to get around, very muddy! Riding further up, there is a small lake on the right with a mountain peak behind it. There is a creek coming out of the lake, which we crossed. We continued up through more mud and came to a bridge that was impassable, just one board left and deep mud all around. This is the end of this portion of the PCT #2000, as we had to turn around. For more information on trails in this area see the William O' Douglas Wilderness chapter in this book."

Madeleine

*NOTE: A message from the Forest Service-the rotten bridges have been removed, and a fords installed in their place.

"JUST HAPPENED BY"

Madeleine and I just happened to be driving (of course the horses were in the trailer) over the Chinook Pass area and we decided to check out several trailheads. We saw one at Sand Flat that had a lot of rigs parked in it, some were even set up to camp. So we dug around in our maps and low and behold we had one for the area. We picked the Crystal Mountain Trail to ride. We were not disappointed. The trail was gentle at first, going over a bridge and along a power line. It wastes no time in climbing toward the view; several switchbacks took us up to the sky, climbing over brushy hillsides on nice trail with some slouchy and muddy areas, this brings us to the crest of the mountain. This is the closest spot for equestrians to ride up to see Mount Rainier we were almost touching it, it was beautiful. We got lucky and so did the other riders we found at the top, so we took turns taking pictures of one another as the clouds started to roll in. What a nice treat on a late summer day! Watch out for mountain bikers, especially on the weekend, as they love to zip along this trail.

Madeleine and Josie

Madeleine and Josie on Crystal Mountain at Chinook Pass, with Mount Rainier in the background

Chinook Pass

Madeleine talked a hiker into taking a snap of her at Chinook Pass

Sandy and Josie at Government Meadows Shelter

Pacific Crest Trail #2000 Little Naches Area

(From Raven Roost Trail north to Government Meadows) in Washington

Distance:	8.5 Miles
Altitude:	4900'-5800'
Map:	GTM 239 Lester
Difficulty:	Moderate

Directions: The PCT #2000 in this region is located in Central Washington. It can be accessed either from the east, Little Naches or from the west, Greenwater Areas. The nearest practical major road is Highway 410, which is to the south.

Connecting Trails: 951, 945.1(A), 1186

Camping: If packing in you can camp at the shelter alongside the trail, it is huge and has room for lots of people it is like a house!

Naches Ranger District
10061 Highway 12
Naches, WA 98937
503-653-2206

Trail Description: This 8.5 mile part of the PCT #2000 is described from Raven Roost Trail #951 going north to Government Meadows. The PCT #2000 is perched on a forested ridge with Greenwater Valley to the west and the Little Naches vicinity to the east. Heading north, the trail descends passing next to a bare dirt slide area, with a view of Raven Roost across the draw to the east. To the south you'll see the jagged teeth of Fifes Peaks. Manastash Ridge looms in the distance, backed by the Stuart Mountain Range to the northeast. You'll find a small trail leading off the main path that goes to a spring, which may or may not have enough water to bother stopping at. At the 4-mile point, Louisiana Saddle Trail #945.1(A) leaves to the east (right). Ride along a hillside in timber, the path rises and falls periodically. Going past Rods Gap the trail levels as the ridge widens out. Maggie Creek Trail #1186 departs to the southwest. Lush green grassland surrounds Government Meadow. Here the Naches Historical and Wagon Road #1913-684 exits going both east and west just beyond the huge shelter that looks more like somebody's wonderful summer cabin! There is water nearby and plenty of meadow grass here. For more information on this area, see the brief description table in the back of the book, under Little Naches and the William O' Douglas Wilderness.

*HINT-Laminate and roll your map tight. Place it on top of the saddle pad along the horse's spine under the horn area, it rides well stays dry and is handy-dandy.

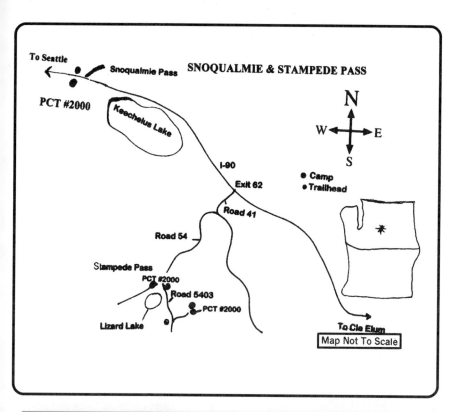

SNOQUALMIE & STAMPEDE PASS

To Seattle

PCT #2000

Snoqualmie Pass

Keechelus Lake

I-90

Exit 62

Road 41

Road 54

Stampede Pass

PCT #2000

Road 5403

PCT #2000

Lizard Lake

To Cle Elum

N
W   E
S

● Camp
● Trailhead

Map Not To Scale

Josie and Lady near Snoqualmie Pass

Pacific Crest Trail #2000 Tacoma, Stampede & Snoqualmie Pass Areas

(Blowout Mountain Trail north to Alaska Lake) in Washington

Distance:	45.3 Miles
Altitude:	3000'-5700'
Maps:	GTM 239 Lester
	GTM 207 Snoqualmie Pass
Difficulty:	Moderate

Directions: This chunk of the PCT #20000 is located in Central Washington. It can be accessed from a wide variety of places. Reach the southern part from either Stampede or Tacoma Passes. From I-90 take exit #62 to the south and follow signs to Stampede Pass using Forest Service Road 41, then Forest Service Road 54 (tune in your CB Radio if the log trucks have their sign out). The trailhead for the PCT #2000 is up above Lizard Lake, turn at Lizard Lake, (just past Stampede Pass) on Forest Service Road 5403, then drive up a small unmarked road on the far side of the lake for about 1.5 miles to a dead end and large loop trailhead. Access the northern part of the PCT #2000 from Snoqualmie Pass (I-90). See the maps for details.

Connecting Trails: 1318, 1338, 1302, 1303, 1033

Horse Camping: There is primitive camping at the trailhead at Stampede Pass, or follow the road downhill ½ mile to Lizard Lake. This is where you are sheltered from the wind better.

Cle Elum Ranger District
803 West 2nd
Cle Elum, WA 98826
509-674-4411

Trail Description: This 45.3 mile link of the PCT #2000 will be described from Blowout Mountain Trail #1318 north to Alaska Lake.

Madeleine rides the PCT near Stampede Pass

64

Donna Evans critiques the first 6 miles of this trail to Tacoma Pass. "The elevation at the junction of Blowout Mountain Trail #1318 and the PCT #2000 is 5,300'. It was raining when my husband Dean and I rode this trail, but we are sure the view south and southeast is probably good of Mount Rainier. The path descends on gentle switchbacks through forest to Tacoma Pass at the 3,500' level."

Donna

From Road 52 at Tacoma Pass ride uphill climbing steadily in forest. Cross a small bridge. Take the opportunity to water your horse near Sheets Pass. The trail clings to the side of a rock slide under the careful watch of Bearpaw Butte. Here on a clear day you'll see Mount Rainer toward the south. The path dips and turns its way to Stampede Pass mostly in forest and clear-cut

Pacific Crest Trail headed down to I-90

areas. When reaching Stampede Pass the elevation is at 3,700' and you have gone 17.5 miles. There is water at Lizard Lake, which is just down the hill on Forest Service Road 54. Crossing Forest Service Road 54, and switchback uphill through evergreen forest to find acres and acres of huckleberry fields. Twist around the hillsides and gullies and cross some log roads. The trail is good as it traverses gently downhill on its way northeast. Views are of Gold Creek Valley, Kendall Peak and Alaska Mountain to the north. Looking to the east and north you'll see the Stuart Mountain Range. Dandy Pass is a great spot to linger and take photos of Mount Rainier. Water can be found near Dandy Pass and again at the intersection with Stirrup Lake Trail #1338, now at the 22.5 mile-point. Contour around a hill on its north slope, it is nice and cool on a hot day in the deep timber. Pass a small lake on the right, the ground is usually muddy through here. Ride uphill for a ways, then down 400' to Twilight Lake. Cross a road and switchback up an old clear-cut area and continue in to the trees. Skirt Mirror Lake on its east shoreline, great swimming hole! Mirror Lake Trail #1302, then Cold Creek Trail #1303 exit at the 26.5 mile-point. Ride up a set of steep rugged switchbacks and around the shoulders of Tinkham Peaks. Pass a rocky section and climb on the east side of Silver Peak. It is narrow and open for about as far as you can throw a stone. You can spot Twin Lakes twinkling like diamonds at the tip of your boot. You'll pass a stair-step part of the trail in either a soggy or green grass area depending on the year. From Olallie Meadow and Creek, you'll ride some road descending toward Snoqualmie Pass Area. Cross a stream and down around a hillside with views to 1-90 below here and there. This is a rugged trail in places with rocks, ruts and roots (the three 'R's of trail riding"). Pass Lodge Lake in dense forest, then Beaver Lake. Civilization is at hand as you see the barren ski slopes at Snoqualmie Pass ahead. Follow under the bones of the lifts down to the gravel trailhead. To reach the next trailhead you need to go under the overpass of I-90 on pavement, with the highway roaring in your ears. It is only 8.3 miles more to Alaska Lake, riding upwards in forest on switchbacks, snaking around the hillside. Commonwealth Trail #1033 exits going north. Continue up, swing around on rugged trail with water cascading down here and there off mossy covered rocks. You'll know Kendall Katwalk when you see it, it's a section of trail blasted across a sheer face of unforgiving gray granite, and it is a one-way trail with a sign telling you so. There is no way to know if anyone is coming, so cross your fingers. Ride a spine between Gravel and Ridge Lakes (no chance to water here). Continue on your trek for 1 mile more to the Bigger Alaska Lake. This concludes this section of the PCT #2000. See you in the Alpine Lakes Wilderness next.

Madeleine near Deception Lakes

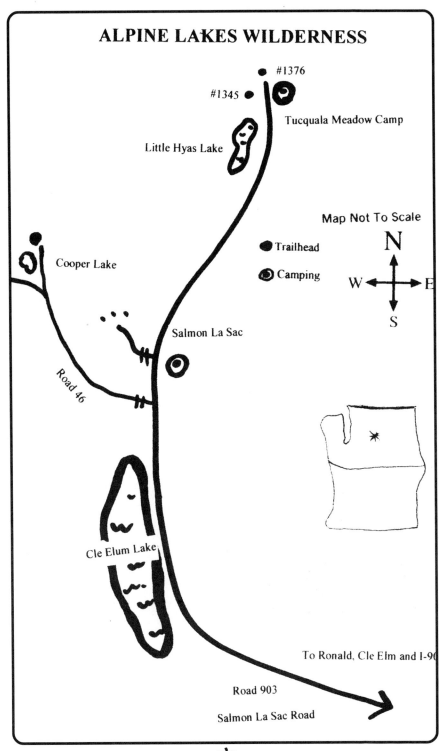

ALPINE LAKES WILDERNESS

#1376

#1345

Tucquala Meadow Camp

Little Hyas Lake

Map Not To Scale

● Trailhead

◎ Camping

N

W ← → E

S

Cooper Lake

Salmon La Sac

Road 46

Cle Elum Lake

To Ronald, Cle Elm and I-90

Road 903

Salmon La Sac Road

68

Pacific Crest Trail #2000 Alpine Lakes Wilderness Area

(From Waptus Burn Trail north to Deception Lakes) in Washington

Distance:	23.9 Miles
Altitude:	3100'-5600'
Maps:	GTM 176 Stevens Pass
	GTM 208 Kachess Lake

Difficulty: Moderate-Challenging

(Coming towards Waptus Lake there are many switchbacks and slouchy spots, near Deception Pass, the tread is soft and narrow with an open drop-off area)

Directions: This slab of the PCT #2000 is located in Central Washington. Access from the Salmon La Sac Area. The nearest Highway is I-90. The nearest towns are Ronald, Roslyn, and Cle Elum.

Josie on her Quarter Horse mare Inky, near Deception Pass

Connecting Trails: 1329.3(C), 1362, 1310, 1337, 1310.1(A), 1365, 1358, 1375, 1345, 1066, 1376, 1059, 1059.1(A)

Horse Camping: Cayuse Horse Camp is located at Salmon La Sac. There are horse corrals, water trough, outhouse, tables, fire pit, potable water and a fee is charged. This is a very busy place in the summer. You'll find primitive camping north of Salmon La Sac along Forest Service Road 4330 and at the Deception Creek, Cathedral Rock Trailheads, which is about 10 miles from Salmon La Sac.

Cle Elum Ranger District
803 West 2nd
CleElum, WA 98826
503-674-4411

Trail Description: This 23.9 mile slice of the PCT #2000 will be described from the intersection of Waptus Burn Trail #1329.3 going north to Deception Lakes. Donna Evans will write the first 8.2-mile stretch of the PCT #2000, she is one of my riding buddies and we see eye to eye on the rating of a trail.

Madeleine on the PCT near Mount Daniel

"Go north on the PCT #2000, and immediately descend on an open, sparsely timbered side of a mountain. From here the views of Mount Daniel, Mount Hinman and Bears Breast are exquisite! Nothing compares. Once you are down the trail a ways, you can clearly see all of Waptus Lake and the mountains to the north, plus the very top of Mount Stuart. The PCT #2000 descends over rocky, open slops with lots of switchbacks. Most of this part is narrow, sloughing off, overgrown and even underslung in places. I hope they fix it soon. There are no steep places on the trail itself because of the amount of switchbacks, however it is a tough path through here. Once down the hill, Dutch Miller Gap Trail #1362 joins in coming from the west. The PCT #2000 now at the 3,000' level continues north; in about 1 mile more the Waptus River Trail #1310 takes off to the southwest. (Waptus River Trail #1310 goes along Waptus Lake, which is a very popular trail with equestrians to reach the PCT #2000, and is 11.2 miles from Salmon La Sac. The views from Waptus Lake's shore toward the south, you can see the ridge you just rode down on.) There are some fairly narrow spots to tend with along Waptus Lake's north end for the next 3 miles or so. You'll pass Spade Lake Trail #1337 (hiker only), and then reach Spinola Creek Trail #1310.1(A) exiting to the right."

Donna

The PCT #2000 follows Spinola Creek up for about 3 miles, gaining 1,000 feet. Travel up a switchback here and there as you make your way across some open rocky spaces, with a narrow spot or two. Level out, Lake Vincente Trail #1365 departs to the left. There is a "User trail" going into a primitive camp area known as Spinola Meadows, where there is feed and a creek nearby to the right. Deep Lake Camps Trail #1358 exits toward the northwest. Ford the outlet creek for Deep Lake and brace for a steady climb out of this basin. The ascent is made easy with the careful placement of well-maintained switchbacks with some rocky spots. It is on an open slope towards the top. Enjoy the rugged views and listen to the far off rush of water spilling off Mount Daniel's Glaciers into the Deep Lake Valley. Memorable pictures have been taken at the top of this hill. Deep Lake seems unreal way down below. Reaching Peggy's Pond Trail #1375 (hiker), then Cathedral Rock Trail #1345, Cathedral Rock's spire stands guard over an alpine meadow. Cathedral Rock to Deception Pass-Do to unpredictable and often hazardous crossing conditions, the Mount Daniel's Ford is no longer recommended for stock. The Forest Service advises riders to use the alternate route, taking Cathedral Pass Trail #1345 down to the junction with Deception Pass Trail #1376 at the end of Forest Service Road 4330. Follow Trail #1376 up past Hyas Lake to Deception Pass, where the Deception Pass Trail #1376 meets with the PCT #2000. (If you for some reason had to use this section this is what you would encounter. Head downhill in timber, where the tread is very narrow in spots, next you'll ride to a wide, swift crossing of Mount Daniel's Creek, with rocks of every size to negotiate around. I have turned around here, as it

Cathedral Rock

was not safe to cross, "better to be safe than sorry". The trail contours around the tip of a beautiful valley where rock-chucks (whistle pigs or marmots) are whistling along the brush and rock slides. Cross several creeks and enter forest again to reach Deception Pass, where a web of trails disperses, they are Lake Clarice #1066, Deception Pass #1376, and Deception Creek #1059.) The next section is also marked with a *warning sign*-trail may not be suitable for stock, the trail has loose, narrow and open tread, however it is short. Next you'll ride on a hillside mostly in deep brush, there were several small bridges in need of repair when I visited. Reaching Deception Lakes Trail #1059.1(A), you know you're only ½ mile from the beautiful Deception Lakes. Mac Peak towers above the lakes. Bring repellent! The final leg of the PCT #2000 will be described at Rainy Pass up north read on.

*NOTE: For more information on this area, refer to the brief description table in the back of the book listed under Salmon La Sac. The alternate route to avoid Mount Daniel's Creek crossing is among the trails listed.

*HINT- Set up a shower in your trailer for privacy. Or get a plastic, ready-made shower stall.

Donna rides in the Alpine Lakes Wilderness

Deep Lake, off the PCT

Dean on the PCT

Waptus Lake

View down Deception gully

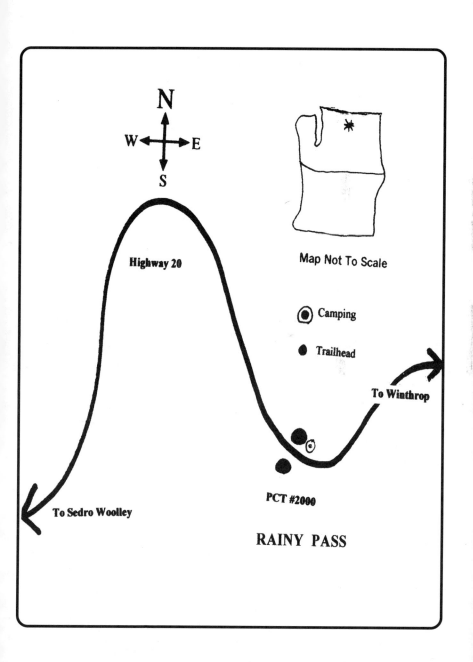

N

W ← → E

S

Highway 20

Map Not To Scale

◉ Camping

● Trailhead

To Winthrop

To Sedro Woolley

PCT #2000

RAINY PASS

Pacific Crest Trail #2000 Rainy Pass Area

(Going both north and south from Rainy Pass) in Washington

Distance:	7 Miles
Altitude:	4800'-6000'
Maps:	GTM 50 Washington Pass
	GTM 82 Stehekin
Difficulty:	Moderate

Directions: This fragment of the PCT #2000 is located in North Central Washington at Rainy Pass on Highway 20.

Connecting Trails: None

Horse Camping: Primitive camping only at the trailhead, bring water or ride south on the trail for 1 mile to a creek.

Trail Description: This 7-mile section of the PCT #2000 will be split into two parts. Going north, 4 miles will be described, and 3 miles will be described going to the south.

North: From Rainy Pass going north 4 miles through forest, the trail heads up from the 4,800' level to the 6,000' level. Starting from the trailhead, the path follows a hillside on long switchbacks, with water coming

Bear

down and across the trail in spots. Sweep around the west side of Cutthroat Peak, the trail is in timber and then brush country. There are several water spots for the animals. The trail was in good shape when I visited. Look up to the northeast to see Cutthroat Pass. This is where time ran out for me and I needed to turn back.

South: From the trailhead going south, cross Highway 20 and go into deep dark forest for 3 miles. Meander along and cross a small swift creek. The trail turns west in deep bushes where you can barely see the trail. I was hoping not to see a bear here as I was riding alone unarmed on my buckskin gelding "Poncho". This looks like a grand place to ride and hopefully you'll have more time than I did to ride this area.

*HINT- For that mess in the horse trailer. Before loading my horse, I put a small pile of loose hay in the spot most likely to have road-apples dropped on. It makes it easier to fork out later.

Moose

WALDO LAKE WILDERNESS

The Waldo Lake Wilderness is a marvelous area for an adventure. There are a total of 84 miles of trails in the Wilderness and gobs more in the adjacent area. The Waldo Lake Wilderness is located 22 miles southeast of Oakridge, Oregon, and about 60 miles southwest of Bend, Oregon. My friend Sandy and I, covered some paths in the Waldo Lake Wilderness and some trails in both Willamette and Deschutes National Forests. A storm caused a dry lightning fire in 1996, which touched Waldo Lake Wilderness. The fire charred 10,400 acres. Harrelson Horse Camp was spared from being burned. Waldo Lake Wilderness area has an array of over 800 lakes and potholes with sandy, pumice beaches. Waldo Lake is one of the largest natural lakes in Oregon. It is 9.8 square miles and 427 feet deep. It is one of the purest lakes in the world, boaters have seen to depths of 120 feet into the cold, blue water. Bring repellent, as the mosquitoes can be thick in June and July. Brook, Rainbow and Kokanee Salmon make their home in Waldo Lake. The terrain is varied and the footing is soft on the majority of the trails. Most of the paths are well used and the views of Waldo Lake, Three Sisters, Taylor Burn, and surrounding mountains are awesome. The Pacific National Scenic Trail #2000 goes through this area and is described in the Pacific Crest Trail chapter of this book. Look for it under "Waldo Lake Area". All of the rides we were on are in the "Moderate" rating category. A few things to be aware of while visiting are; equestrians are not welcome to park and ride trails from the people camps along Waldo & Gold Lakes, and do not attempt to drive your rig on unimproved Taylor Burn Road 514, it is not maintained! Due to the roughness of Taylor Burn Road, a few trails north of there that are in the Waldo Lake Wilderness are described in the Box Canyon Horse Camp (Three Sisters & Waldo Wilderness) chapter. As always, keep stock 200 feet from all water sources when tied.

Directions to Harrelson Horse Camp: Drive State Highway 58 and turn north on Forest Service Road 5897. Continue north on Forest Service Road 5898. At a sharp bend in the road look for Forest Service Road 511. Continue straight (north) on Forest Service Road 511 for ¼ mile to its end and Harrelson Horse Camp, which has a huge turnaround. The horse camp is located northeast of Waldo Lake.

Camp includes: Harrelson Horse Camp amenities include several campfire rings, garbage service, tables and an outhouse. There is room for lots of rigs, big or small at the large turnaround. No potable water here, there are people camps nearby that have potable water. Water for the animals is accessed by riding down Harrelson Horse Trail #4364, about ½ mile to Waldo Lake. No fee was required when Sandy and I visited in 2000.

Northwest Forest Parking Passes are available at Forest Service offices, they are required at designated trailheads.

Get the bridle on and lets ride...

Willamette National Forest
211 E. 7th Ave.
P.O. Box 10607
Eugene, OR 97440
541-465-6521

Middle Fork Ranger District
46375 Highway 58
Westfir, OR 97492
541-782-2283

McKenzie River Ranger Station
State Highway 126
McKenzie Bridge, OR 97413
541-822-3381

Harrelson Horse Camp – Oregon, near the Waldo Lake Wilderness

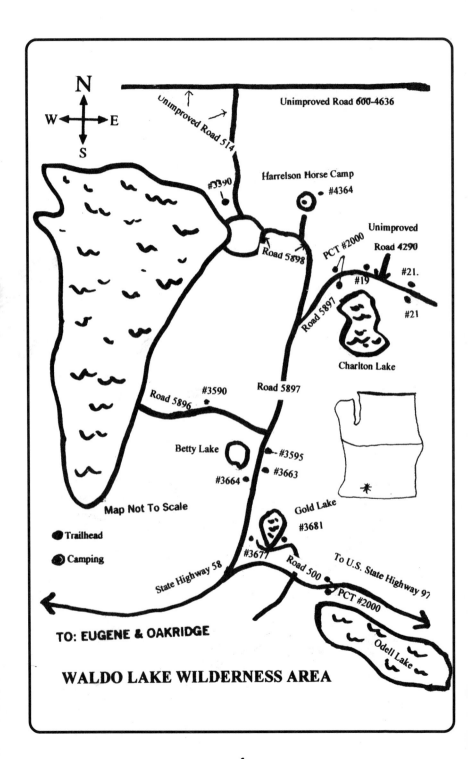

Distance:	1.7 Miles
Altitude:	5500'-5600'
Map:	Waldo Lake Wilderness
Difficulty:	Moderate

Directions: Betty Lake Trailhead is located on Forest Service Road 5897, it is a shared trailhead with Bobby Lakes Trail #3663. Betty Lake Trail #3664 begins on the west side of the road, Bobby Lakes Trail #3663 on the east side. This is the main road leading into the horse camp. For more information read the introduction to this chapter.

Connecting Trails: 3663, 3590

Horse Camping: Harrelson Horse Camp is nearby, read the beginning of this chapter for more information.

Trail Description: Betty Lake Trail #3664 is at the southeast end of Waldo Lake. It heads west from Forest Service Road 5897. The forested path, makes its way over a culvert and rolls slightly downhill, you will see big blue Betty herself and then a pond. Passing several more lakes, the lush, shady trail ends as it meets with Waldo Lake Trail #3590. Loops possible.

*HINT- Hay makes great fire starter.

Wahanna Trail

Bobby Lakes #3663

Distance:	1.5 Miles
Altitude:	5500'-5600'
Map:	Waldo Lake Wilderness
Difficulty:	Moderate

Directions: Drive State Highway 58 and turn north on Forest Service Road 5897. Bobby Lakes Trail #3663 has a shared trailhead with Betty Lake Trail #3664. Bobby Lakes Trail #3663 begins on the east side of the road, Betty Lake Trail #3664 on the west side. Read the beginning of this chapter for more information to reach the Waldo Lake Area.

Connecting Trails: 3664, 2000, 40, 3677

Trail Description: Bobby Lakes Trail #3663 is near the southern end of Waldo Lake. The trail lingers under a canopy of trees, and is mostly level. This trail hooks up with Gold Lake Trail #3677 immediately, continue on Bobby Lakes Trail. You'll catch a glimpse of white capped Diamond Peak. Near Bobby Lake you'll meet with the PCT #2000 and Moore Creek Trail #40. Bobby Lakes Trail #3663 ends at Bobby Lake, which is a beautiful ultramarine color.

Waldo Lake Trail

Charlton Lake #3593

Distance:	1.1 Miles
Altitude:	5430'-5692'
Map:	Waldo Lake Wilderness
Difficulty:	Moderate

Directions: Drive State Highway 58 and turn north on paved Forest Service Road 5897. Turn right (east) on now gravel Forest Service Road 5897-4290, toward Charlton Lake. There is roadside parking by Charlton Lake. Charlton Lake Trail #3593 is easily accessed from Harrelson Horse Camp and the parking is a lot better. Read the beginning of this chapter for more information to find camp.

Connecting Trails: 3590, 2000

Horse Camping: Harrelson Horse Camp is nearby, read the beginning of this chapter for more information.

Trail Description: Charlton Trail #3593 is 1.1 miles long and connects the PCT #2000 and Charlton Lake to Waldo Lake Trail #3590. It is located east of Waldo Lake towards the north end. This trail crosses Forest Service Road 5897 twice: a gravel portion and a paved portion, it also goes over Forest Service Road 5898, which is paved. Charlton Lake Trail #3593 goes downhill from the brilliant Charlton Lake and treks westward to Waldo Lake. Sandy and I saw a swift, jet-black mink run across the trail and disappear into the scrub! The path stays in cool timber. You can ride lots of loops using this trail.

*NOTE: The Waldo Lake Wilderness Map reads 1.6 miles, but the Forest Service told me the mileage is 1.1 for Charlton Lake Trail #3593.

*HINT-Remember to grease the ball on your trailer hitch before connecting. Scrub it often, I have found that WD-40 works well and gasoline removes old grease too. Clean the ball and up under the hitch of the trailer as well. Use the best grease you can, there is some that comes in a foil tube you can buy at automotive stores. It would be better to have no grease than to have old grease that has abrasive sand and dirt collected on it churning with every turn, wearing out your ball.

Clover Meadow #21.1

Distance:	3.2 Miles
Altitude:	5300'-5500'
Map:	Waldo Lake Wilderness
Difficulty:	Moderate

Directions: Drive State Highway 58 and turn north on paved Forest Service Road 5897. Turn right (east) on now gravel Forest Service Road 5897-4290, toward Charlton Lake. Go past Charlton Lake about 4 miles to reach Clover Meadow Trailhead on the north (left) side of the road. Going toward the south (right) is another trailhead, for Round Meadow Trail #21. Forest Service Road 5897-4290 is unimproved so go slow, as it is very bumpy. Limited parking along the roadside only. See the introduction to this chapter for basic information to reach the area; this road leaves before you reach the horse camp.

Josie greets the warm sun at Eddeeleo Lake

Connecting Trails: 21, 18, 19, 19.1, 19.3

Horse Camping: Harrelson Horse Camp is nearby, read the beginning of this chapter for more information and see the map.

Trail Description: Clover Meadow Trail #21.1 is located east of Charlton Butte. Starting from Forest Service Road 5897-4290 Clover Meadow Trail #21.1 goes north. With sandy footing, and rolling hills this path enters a sparse forest and old logging areas. In about ½ mile you'll come upon Unnamed Trail #18 going north (straight). Clover Meadow Trail turns to the left (west). This is a meandering little trail that is lots of fun; it has great footing for your horses too. Negotiate your way up and down maneuvering around small boulders. Clover Meadow Trail #21.1 comes to an end at a 4-way intersection with Lemish Lake Trail #19.1 going right (northeast), Lily Lake Trail #19.3 going straight (northwest) and Unnamed Trail #19 going left (south). Loops possible.

*HINT- Girls are you tired of the weight of your gun pulling down on your belt-line? Does it get in the way when you go to the bathroom? Above your pant waist, not laced in the belt loops is where your gun/holster and Leatherman tool will ride from now on. The belt stays on your waist while you "go". No more droopy pants!

Sandy rides down Twin Peak Trail

Eastern Brook #3552

Distance:	½ Mile
Altitude:	5500'-5600'
Map:	Waldo Lake Wilderness
Difficulty:	Moderate

Directions: No trailhead, access from Wahanna Trail #3583.

Connecting Trails: 3583

Trail Description: Eastern Brook Trail #3552 can be found off the Wahanna Trail #3583 about .3 mile from Taylor Burn Road at Forest Camp. This short n' sweet little trail runs downhill to a beautiful small lake called Eastern Brook, passing a level meadow. The shoreline is difficult to get horse a drink out of because of a rock slide and brush. Consider bringing a collapsible bucket for dipping water out of the lake for your horse to drink. You'll see rhododendron plants on this unused trail.

"DIVINE GUIDANCE"

Have you ever felt like timing is everything? Sandy and I did as we were driving to Waldo Lake Wilderness via the Three Sisters Wilderness Area, following directions we thought would shave at least one hour off our driving time by taking a road listed as "other road " on the map. I did call ahead to the Forest Service to double check that this road was okay for us to tow across. Just as we were about to turn onto the "other road' we were flagged down by an older couple in a small truck. They very politely told us we were **NUTS** and needed to turn around **NOW!** They knew this because this road is a rugged jeep road, and the further you go the worse it gets with no turnaround big enough to accommodate us. They had personal experience on this road that banged up a 4WD truck pretty good. Sandy and I heeded their advice and got out our maps to form plan "B". Later in our trip we road our horses across these roads, yup, they were correct, big boulders, downed trees, uneven ground and steep rocky terrain. We are very grateful for this chance meeting with them, maybe not chance, but divine guidance?

Josie

Fields Lake #3579

(From Taylor Burn Rd. to the S. side of Taylor Butte)

Distance:	1 Mile
Altitude:	5300'-5400'
Map:	Waldo Lake Wilderness
Difficulty:	Moderate

Directions: The trailhead for Fields Lake Trail #3579 is on Taylor Burn Road, which unfortunately is impassable for trucks and trailers, due to its steep pitch and boulders imbedded in the road. See the map for more information.

Connecting Trails: 3580

Trail Description: Begin Fields Lake Trail #3579 by entering the sparse forest on a very wide section of trail that almost looks like it used to be a road. Pass the Waldo Wilderness sign and ride uphill slightly, next to a lush meadow. Ride rolling terrain on this seldom used trail. We saw what looked like a badger hole alongside the trail. Taylor Butte Trail #3580 leaves to the left (east). Enter the Taylor Burn Area and ride down to a large meadow or dry pond. One side of this area is burned, and one is not, you'll see where tiny trees are reclaiming the scorched land. Ride next to Fields Lake. Our smiles turned upside down when we discovered the trail had big logs down, unblocked just enough for hikers, however not enough clearance for my horse and definitely not for Sandy's big 16 ½ hand gelding to get under! The once green trees are left hunched over and they look arthritic. Bent snags they are! The trees are snarled as a bull dogs face. Even though this trail didn't go all the way through, and it was worth the ride. The Forest Service clears hundreds of logs every year out of the burn areas, and all trails were cleared the year we visited, but continue to fall all summer long and will get worse in the next few years.

*NOTE: The Forest Service wants us to know that Taylor Butte Trail #3580 is definitely not good for horse travel. The Forest Service reports that Fields Lake Trail #3570 most likely never will connect to Whig and Torrey Way Trail (the Waldo Wilderness Map shows that it does).

Gold Lake #3677

Distance:	3.8 Miles
Altitude:	4600-5600'
Map:	Waldo Lake Wilderness
Difficulty:	Moderate

Directions: To access this trail, the Forest Service suggests that you use the Fugi Mountain Trail off Road 5897 (main road to Waldo Lake), and that we cannot park and ride from Gold Lake Campground with horses. See the map for details and read the introduction to this chapter to find Waldo Lake Road 5897.

Connecting Trails: 3674, 3682, 3663

Trail Description: Gold Lake Trail #3677 is located south of Waldo Lake, the trail exits Gold Lake Campground headed north. It's an easy rolling trail that runs through dense, dark green forest. However, it had not

There goes Waldo!

been cleared and was a maze of logs for us to negotiate through and was quite arduous. Gold Lake Trail #3677 immediately passes Fuji Mountain Trail #3674 on the left-hand side, going west. After crossing a stream, at the 2.1 mile-point, Mount Ray Trail #3682 leaves, to the left (west). Continue riding north, Gold Lake Trail #3677 flattens out and crosses another stream as it gets ready to end at a "T" intersection with Bobby Lakes Trail #3663. Loops possible.

*HINT- Take Vitamin B complex once a day for at least a week before and during your camping trip and you may find that mosquitoes will avoid you.

"HEY, THE SUN IS GOING DOWN"

My friend, Sandy and I got lazy one day and we fiddled around camp too long. By the time we decided to ride it was 3 p.m. in the afternoon. We still had plenty of time for a 10-mile ride we thought, since in was only late July, the sun will be up for a while yet. The first 6 miles were a piece of cake, then we started getting into a section of the Pacific Crest Trail near Gold Lake that was not maintained very well. By the time we made it to Gold Lake the sunset was brushing strokes of salmon, whisky and plum into the sky. The elongated shadows followed us as we made our way through the timber; the night was encroaching. The trail has to get better here, the terrain is flatter and we were sure that the paths would be traveled more, hence cleared better, right?

NOT! The trail got worse, and there comes a point when you need to ask yourself deep down inside for the answers, then get out of your own way and receive the solutions. We ended up backtracking a couple miles to a road, then riding the road and skipping the area that was so jungle-like. We were able to catch this trail further up the road to reach our camp. Sandy and I were trail riding at daybreak the next day and were relaxing with fluffy sticky marshmallows on long sticks that next night when the sun was saying its good-byes.

Josie

Harrelson Horse Trail #4364

(Map reads #4364 and the sign reads #4363 see note below)

Distance:	3 Miles
Altitude:	5500'-5700'
Map:	Waldo Lake Wilderness
Difficulty:	Moderate

Directions: Read the beginning of this chapter for more information. Harrelson Horse Trail #4364 departs from camp in two different directions.

Connecting Trails: 3590, 2000

Horse Camping: Read the beginning of this chapter for more information.

Trail Description: Harrelson Horse Trail #4364 (#4363) exits two directions from camp; to the northeast for 2 miles, and to the southwest for 1 mile.
  The northeast section: The trail begins in green trees, then enters a charred area climbing gently uphill through the forest to reach the PCT #2000 in just 2 miles.

The southwest section: Harrelson Horse Trail #4364 goes for 1 mile, it starts at camp and heads down toward Waldo Lake through green forest. This section of Harrelson Horse Trail #4364 crosses unimproved Road 514 and ends at the intersection with Waldo Lake Trail #3590. The footing is wonderful for your horses. Lots of loops to ride from here.

*NOTE: The Forest Service informed me that the trail sign at camp is incorrect showing Harrelson Horse Trail #4363, the number for the Harrelson Horse Trail on the Waldo Wilderness Map is correct #4364, the Forest Service will change the sign to the right number.

*HINT: It is a good idea to have your keys on your person in case you and your mount get separated. A key ring that clips to your belt loop is available at hardware stores.

Lily lake #19.3

Distance:	1.8 Miles
Altitude:	5500'-6000'
Map:	Waldo Lake Wilderness
Difficulty:	Moderate

Directions: No trailhead. Access from the trails listed below. Read the beginning of this chapter for more information.

Connecting Trails: 2000, 21.1, 19, 19.1

Trail Description: Lily Lake Trail #19.3 is located north of Charlton Butte and can be accessed from both ends. I will describe the trail starting from the west-end going toward the east-end. From the PCT #2000, Lily Lake Trail #19.3 heads downhill with a view of the distant, pearl white capped Three Sisters Mountains and Bachelor Butte. Switchback downward through a patchy burn area. Lily Lake Trail #19.3 levels

Rigdon Lake Trail

out and drops down again to reach Lily Lake, which has a tip, unharmed by the fire of 1996. After reaching the lovely Lily Lake, you will go slightly uphill to a catwalk ridge between Lily Lake and a pond, then back down into shady pine trees. Riding next to a rock slide and across a hillside, the trail flattens out near a long, tender, green meadow. The trail takes you into a deep muddy, boggy area. Lily Lake Trail #19.3 ends as it comes to a network of trails, which include Clover Meadow Trail #21.1, Lemish Lake Trail #19.1 and Unnamed Trail #19. Loops possible.

"THANKS FOR THE ADVICE"

The Forest Service workers were stationed at Lily Lake and were busy working on trails in the area. They had their mosquito nets over their faces when we came upon them; they looked like beekeepers. We asked them about some of the connecting trails. The crew informed us that the use of Lemish Lake Trail #19.1 at this time was not a good idea for horsemen, as it was not maintained. Call the Forest Service ahead of time to find out the condition of Lemish Lake Trail #19.1 before attempting to ride it. They said several bridges were in nasty shape. Later in our trip we tried to ride Lemish Lake Trail #19.1 from its other end, near Lemish Lake. We just wanted to ride a short distance to the lake. We looked down the path from the trailhead, and saw logs stacked over the trail!

Josie

Maiden Peak #3681

(From the PCT to Road 500)

Distance:	3 Miles
Altitude:	5000'-6000'
Map:	Waldo Lake Wilderness
Difficulty:	Moderate

Directions: Drive State Highway 58 and turn north on gravel Forest Service Road 500. Maiden Peak #3681 Trailhead is near Gold Lake Campground, although there is a spot to park, the Forest Service doesn't want horse people to park near or at the "people only" camps. Read the beginning of this chapter for more information to reach the Waldo Lake Area, where you could ride from other trails to reach this trail.

Connecting Trails: 2000

Horse Camping: Harrelson Horse Camp is nearby. See the map for more information.

Trail Description: This section of Maiden Peak Trail #3681 is located south of Waldo Lake. We rode down from the PCT #2000 to Forest Service Road 500. From the PCT #2000 the path descends quickly, then mellows out a bit as you ford Skyline Creek. There are views of forested Mount Ray and Mount Fuji to the west. The trail drops out onto gravel Forest Service Road 500. This section of Maiden Peak Trail #3681 was used to make a loop in the area.

*HINT- When backing up your trailer if you want to make a tight turn, crank your wheels before you move. If a gentle curve is what you want, wait until you are in motion before turning the steering wheel. Remember your trailer will move backwards, the same direction the bottom of the steering wheel is going.

"THIS COULD HAPPEN TO YOU"

Sandy and I arrived mid-week at Harrelson Horse Camp, no other rigs, cool, we'll have the place to ourselves we thought. It was a hot sultry July afternoon, turns out it was not so deserted. The shadows under the trees were teeming with movement. What a treat to discover big bulls, and cows with an assortment of calves. Elk everywhere! We were obviously scaring them off as we drove in. We set up camp, and as it grew darker we had a marshmallow fire and turned in for the evening. The crunch, crunch followed by munch, munch alerted me out of a deep sleep. I peeked out into the bone white moonlight and was ecstatic to see elk within feet of me crunching on the gravel with their hooves and munching on the tender grass. Their breath smelled like mowed lawn, that's how close they were! They stayed all night and at dawn Sandy and I tried numerous times to capture them on film. They were camera shy and ducked into the security blanket of the woods. We have loads of gray pictures with green-eye spots. Their antics went on each night, except for on the weekend when the camp was too busy even for these brazen beasts. Sunday night they returned again sometimes as many as twelve at a time would stampede between our rigs. Our horses, Ali and Chris, seemed to be used to them, in fact, one dawn I saw two elk rubbing noses with my mare! We decided that they like the left over hay as an additive to their diets, or maybe they just love horses. What do you think?

Josie

Rigdon Lakes #3555

Distance:	2.2 Miles
Altitude:	5500'-5600'
Map:	Waldo Lake Wilderness
Difficulty:	Moderate

Directions: No trailhead. Access from Wahanna Trail #3583, or Waldo Lake Trail #3590. Read the beginning of this chapter for more information on how to reach the Waldo Lake Area.

Connecting Trails: 3583, 3590

Trail Description: Rigdon Lakes Trail #3555 is located on the north end of Waldo Lake. It connects Wahanna Trail #3583 and Waldo Lake Trail #3590. The path follows around the north end of Lower Rigdon Lake, then swings around to the east. Continue on and up to view Upper Rigdon Lake, these two turquoise blue lakes resemble liquid gems. The entire trail is in the 1996 burn, which left the forest defoliated. Rigdon Butte sits above the lakes. I have seen pictures of this area before the fire of 1996, when the trees were tall and green. Now the area is stark, like a moonscape. The contrast is incredible; I found both to be beautiful. Be wary of hidden holes, rocks and exposed burnt roots. They give-way when you least expect it. Lots of loops here!

*HINT- Do you want to use a helmet? I am told the new ones are cooler, the visors are molded on now, so it stays more secure and doesn't rattle. They also keep your head warm and have saved many riders from head injury.

Round Meadow #21

Distance:	3.4 Miles
Altitude:	5300'-5700'
Map:	Waldo Lake Wilderness
Difficulty:	Moderate

Directions: Drive State Highway 58 and turn north on paved Forest Service Road 5897. Turn right (east) on now gravel Forest Service Road 5897-4290, toward Charlton Lake. Go past Charlton Lake about 4 miles, to reach Round Meadow Trailhead. (On the south (right) side of the road.) Going toward the north (left) is another trailhead, for Clover Meadow Trail #21.1. Forest Service Road 5897-4290 is unimproved so go slow, as it is very bumpy. Limited parking available along the roadside only. Read the beginning of this chapter for more information.

Connecting Trails: 21.1, 19

Horse Camping: Harrelson Horse Camp is nearby.

Trail Description: Round Meadow Trail #21 is located east of Charlton Lake. Starting from Forest Service Road 5897-4290, Round Meadow Trail #21 goes southwest. With sandy footing, and rolling terrain this trail enters a scanty forest. Bright green and wet, Round Meadow offers lots of feed. After skirting the meadow the path takes you to a "T" intersection with Trail #19. Here you'll find a small creek to water your horses. Loops possible.

*HINT-For chafing use "Carmex or Bag Balm," they work well, a little bit goes a long way!

Salmon Lakes #3585

(From Waldo Lake Trail to Wahanna Trail)

Distance:	.8 Mile
Altitude:	5500'-5500'
Map:	Waldo Lake Wilderness
Difficulty:	Moderate

Directions: No trailhead. Access from either Waldo Lake Trail #3590 or Wahanna Trail #3583. Read the beginning of this chapter for more information for reaching the Waldo Lake Area.

Connecting Trails: 3590, 3583

Trail Description: This .8 mile section of Salmon Lakes Trail #3585 was used for making a loop on the northwest side of Waldo Lake. The trail is mostly flat and passes a rock slide. You'll see two stunning lakes. This is a path that is less traveled than Waldo Lake Trail #3590. Many places to explore from here.

Six Lakes #3597
(To Lower Eddeeleo Lake)

Distance:	2.5 Miles
Altitude:	5000'-5500'
Map:	Waldo Lake Wilderness
Difficulty:	Moderate

Directions: No trailhead. Access from Wahanna Trail #3583.
Connecting Trail: 3583
Horse Camping: Harrelson Horse Camp is nearby.

Trail Description: Six Lakes Trail #3597 to Lower Eddeeleo Lake is an exciting trail with lots to pay attention to. The total length of the trail is 6.6 miles and has many old growth trees, the Forest Service says it usually gets at lease one huge tree down across the trail each year, and it takes time to clear. Call ahead to the Forest Service for the trail conditions. This trail is located on the northwest side of Waldo Lake. The path starts from Wahanna Trail #3583 in deep, damp forest with loads of shiny rhododendron plants along the route to the two Eddeeleo Lakes. Head downhill over rocky terrain, then the trail stair steps down. Cross between Upper Eddeeleo Lake on the left side of the trail, which is in full view and you'll find Round Lake hiding to the right, which is a bit smaller. Continue on a rougher section of trail with culverts, rocks and bridges. Ride across a wash area to the tip of Lower Eddeeleo Lake. This is where, sadly for us, there were too many huge logs with steep terrain to contend with to continue on safely. After having a nice dip and then a lunch reluctantly we did an "about-face".

"ED, DEE and LEO"

Sandy and I rode deep into the Waldo Lake Wilderness on the Six Lakes Trail. We found two lakes that are named after three Forest Service workers Ed, Dee, and Leo. Hence "Eddeeleo Lakes", there is an upper and a lower lake.

Josie

Twin Peak #3595

Distance:	3 Miles
Altitude:	5500'-7100'
Map:	Waldo Lake Wilderness
Difficulty:	Moderate

Directions: Drive State Highway 58 and turn north on Forest Service Road 5897. Continue north on Forest Service Road 5897. Twin Mountain Trailhead is located on the east (right) side of the road, just past Bobby Lakes and Betty Lake Trailheads. There is a small circle turnaround for parking. Read the beginning of this chapter for more information.

Connecting Trails: 2000, 19

Horse Camping: Harrelson Horse Camp is nearby. See the map for the location in relation to this trail.

Trail Description: Twin Peak Trail #3595 is located southeast of Waldo Lake. The path begins from Forest Service Road 5897 and goes northeast up to the tips of The Twins. The trail passes a marshy area, where the trees are sparse. Climb steadily to meet the PCT #2000, which heads north and south. There are small water collecting areas and depressions in the ground that were filled with stubborn snow patches, even in late July. We took advantage of this and watered our mounts. The map shows Trail #19 around here somewhere; we looked for it, to no avail. Twin Peak Trail #3595 leaves a meadow area to begin a more strenuous ascent to the crest of the lower Twin Peak. Head up steeply on a barren hillside made of red cinder pumas with snarled, wind whipped trees. Reaching the red-earthen ridge on the lower Twin Peak, the views are spectacular of Waldo Lake to the west, Diamond Peak to the southwest, Three Sisters Mountains to the northeast, Mount Hood to the north, and way off Mount Shasta to the south. Not to mention all the lakes and valleys in between. Ride a ridge along the saddle and climb to the top of the upper Twin Peak for more of the same views. If you are coming from a low elevation, it may be wise for you and your mounts to acclimated to the higher elevations gradually for a few days, before stressing to the 7,100' level. I've read that the view from Twin Peak Trail #3595 at its pinnacle, is as spectacular as Maiden Peak Trail #3681, you'll expend about half as much energy getting here, and it is less traveled, this is why we decided to ride to the top of Twin Peak Trail #3595.

*NOTE: The Waldo Wilderness Map reads the name of this trail as Twins Trail, the Forest Service told me the name is Twin Peak Trail.

Twin Mountain Trail

Unnamed #19

(From Lily Lake Trail south to Metolius Windigo Trail)

Distance:	5 Miles
Altitude:	5500'-6000'
Map:	Waldo Lake Wilderness
Difficulty:	Moderate

Directions: Drive State Highway 58 and turn north on paved Forest Service Road 5897. Turn right (east) on now gravel Forest Service Road 5897-4290, toward Charlton Lake. There is roadside parking by Charlton Lake. Unnamed Trail #19 begins two different ways from Charlton Lake's west shoreline, north and south off of the PCT #2000. These directions give you access to the middle of Unnamed Trail #19. Read the beginning of this chapter for more information.

Connecting Trails: 2000, 21, 99, 21.1, 19.3, 19.1

Horse Camping: Harrelson Horse Camp is nearby. See the map for location.

Trail   Description: Unnamed Trail #19 will be described in two portions from Charlton Lake, first going to the north, then to the south.

Going north from Charlton Lake, Unnamed Trail #19 departs from Forest Service Road 5897-4290. This section is 2.3 miles long. Start by strolling downhill gently in old growth timber, the cool shade is always welcome on a hot day. You'll pass several splendid natural rock gardens made up of giant gray boulders and a variety of flowers with a spattering of moss here and there. Not very often do we ask our horses to jump rather than step across a creek. We found this creek to be an exception. This small creek's edges were badly undercut and it was safer to clear the whole mess rather than risk falling into, then out of unstable roots and mud on the banks. The trail comes to its end at a 4-way intersection with Lily Lake Trail #19.3 to the west, Lemish Lake Trail #19.1 to the north, and Clover Meadow Trail #21.1 to the east.

Going south from Charlton Lake, this section of trail is 2.7 miles long. Exit the PCT #2000 and ride Unnamed Trail #19 around the south shoreline of Charlton Lake. Pass a rock outcropping and observe Gerdine Butte above you. Ride the rolling trail, and then head down to ford a stream. Round Meadow Trail #21 meets from the left (east). Ramble along the stream in nice forest and start rising around a knoll to reach Metolius Windigo Trail #99, which comes in from the east. This is the high-point of this segment of Unnamed Trail #19 at 6,000'. Loops possible.

Squirrel

Wahanna #3583

Distance:	5.9 Miles (plus ½ mile of the Waldo Lake Trail to connect)
Altitude:	5300'-5600'
Map:	Waldo Lake Wilderness
Difficulty:	Moderate

Directions: The trailhead is at the end of Taylor Burn Road at Forest Camp. As of 2002 this road was not passable for horse trailer and truck, due to large boulders and steep inclines, 4-WD only!

Connecting Trails: 3585, 3597, 3590, 3555, 3596, 3581, 3552

Horse Camping: Harrelson Horse Camp is nearby.

Trail Description: I have broken Wahanna Trail #3583 in to two sections because ½ mile of Waldo Lake Trail #3590 is used to link the two ends of the trail together. The path is located to the west and to north side of Waldo Lake. The ½ mile section of Waldo Lake Trail #3590 crosses a bridge near Dam Camp and has nice footing.

The north section of trail - Starting from Waldo Lake Trail #3590 turn toward the north on Wahanna Trail #3583. Ride 4.2 miles in the burnt area, which can be very hot on a sunny summer's day. You may want to water your animals at an oasis, found where 2 ponds connect over the trail. After fording the wet spot, proceed on with views of the scorched Rigdon Butte above you on the east side of the trail. Rigdon Lakes Trail #3555 intersects from the east (right). This is a desolate section of trail all the way to its end. You're in the midst of blackened tree-skeletons and sterile baked sandy soil in the aftermath of the 1996 forest fire. The heat tormented, then fried the limbs of the trees, they are hanging in a frozen state of rigidity. Soon you'll see the huge Wahanna Lake in its desert setting, looks like a nice spot to go swimming. Whig & Torrey Way Trail #3581 exit to the east. Continue riding on for 1 mile weaving your way through a few lucky trees that survived the fire. Eastern Brook Trail #3552 hooks in from the west. Head downhill a bit to the trailhead at Forest Camp. The huckleberry bushes are abundant in this area. See Rigdon Lakes Trail #3555, or Whig & Torrey Way Trail #3581 for loop ideas.

The west section of trail - Starting from the northwest side of Waldo Lake on the Waldo Lake Trail #3590 turn toward the west on Wahanna Trail #3583 and ride 1.7 miles. Six Lakes Trail #3597 exits to the right. Ride in the forest under a canopy of evergreens. Traveling through thick forest you'll come upon Lake Chetlo. It is a nice size lake and is clear and blue. Winchester Ridge Trail #3596 exits going north. Beyond Lake Chetlo, Wahanna Trail ends at a "T" intersection with Salmon Lakes Trail #3585. Overall the west portion of Wahanna Trail #3583 is a rolling path with 2 creeks to cross, one of which can be a bit muddy.

Deer

Waldo Lake #3590

Distance:	22 Miles
Altitude:	5300'-5500'
Map:	Waldo Lake Wilderness
Difficulty:	Moderate

Directions: Read the beginning of this chapter for more information to get to Harrelson Horse Camp, this trail starts near camp.

Connecting Trails: 4364 (4363), 3593, 3664, 3586, 3572, 3551, 3576, 3585, 3583, 3555

Horse Camping: See the map at beginning of this chapter for more information.

Trail Description: Waldo Lake Trail #3590 circles Waldo Lake and is described clockwise starting from Harrelson Horse Trail #4363. Charlton Lake Trail 33593 exits first, going left (east). Waldo Lake Trail #3590 begins in the timber and heads south, it runs parallel between Waldo's east shoreline and Forest Service Road 5897. For 6.1 miles the path is flat and you never even see Waldo Lake. Excellent footing through this section. The trees vary from being lush and jam-packed with moist undergrowth to tall and spindly. Betty Lake Trail #3664 merges from the left (southeast). Traveling around the south tip of Waldo Lake you attain views across the lake of the Three Sisters Mountains. There are a series of bridges to cross and small emerald green meadows and ponds to see. The rustic South Waldo Shelter sits in a little meadow, and South Waldo Trail #3586 exits, going south. Riding around to the west shore of Waldo Lake, you are now headed north. Travel in dense forest with vistas here and there of gigantic Waldo Lake. Waldo Lake Trail #3590 changes and gets a bit rougher, with some rocky spots and ups and downs (mostly downs). You'll pass High Divide Trail #3572, Black Creek Trail #3551, Koch Mountain Trail #3576, then Salmon Lakes Trail #3585 all spaced about 2 miles from each other. The west shore of Waldo Lake Trail #3590 has a few short, steep places and some flat areas as well. Watch for big toads crossing your path. The whole ride is laced with bear grass, which was in bloom in late July when Sandy and I visited. Huckleberry bushes are everywhere! The next section of trail has some narrow spots and a drop-off area. (If you want to avoid this section you may consider a small detour using Salmon Lakes Trail #3585 and Wahanna

108

Trail #3583.) After riding the narrow section and rock slide area, you'll pass Wahanna Trail #3583, which heads left (west). Continue riding as the path bends around and heads east, on the north shore of Waldo Lake. The trail goes over a bridge near Dam Camp. The other end of Wahanna Trail #3583 departs going left (north). The north section of Waldo Lake Trail #3590 is partly in the burnt area of 1996 and partially in the trees. Scan the horizon across the spectacular Waldo Lake and you'll see a snow-white triangle, that's Diamond Peak to the south. Be sure to keep off the hiker-only trails that go a little closer to the lake than the horse trails. You may want to hike down to the sandy shore to take a peek. The north rim of the lake can be hot in the exposed burnt area in mid summer. Rigdon Lakes Trail #3555 heads left (north). The "sock water" sign is near the end of this loop; this goes to Waldo Lake. Cross the unimproved Road 514, and continue on to reach Harrelson Horse Trail #4364. Turn left (east) to go to camp. This is a loop and a marvelous trail. Most of the east shore of Waldo Lake is not inside the Wilderness, so be watchful of quiet running mountain bikes.

*HINT- On a camp out you may want to pool together and split up who tows horses and who hauls camp supplies. This is a nice way for the horses to keep each other company, and the camp supplies are easier to load and unload.

Whig & Torrey Way #3581

Distance:	2 Miles
Altitude:	5000'-5000'
Map:	Waldo Lake Wilderness
Difficulty:	Moderate

Directions: The trailhead is off of unimproved, dirt Forest Service Road 514 north of Harrelson Horse Camp. You can ride to it easy enough. It is a 4-WD type of road and I'm not advising to trailer across it, due to boulders imbedded in the road. Read the beginning of this chapter for more information.

Connecting Trail: 3583

Horse Camping: Harrelson Horse Camp is nearby.

Trail Description: Whig & Torrey Way Trail #3581 begins from Forest Service Road 514, where there is a small pull-off at the signed trailhead. The trail goes down from a knoll to greet three lakes, leading northwest. The path runs along the southern shorelines of Torrey and Whig Lakes. Winding its way around, the trail goes along the north shore of Wahanna Lake. Here you can get your livestock a drink. Taylor Butte is to the north. Whig & Torrey Way Trail connects to Wahanna Trail #3583 at its end. This trail is all in the burn area of 1996 and you can see how the inferno has cleaned the forest floor and it is making a fresh start with tiny plants. It is a stark trail and can be dusty with lots of fascinating lakes. The contrasting colors range from the deep blue hues of the water, to the rich black and tans of the sand. Watch out for roots and holes in the baked soil. The map shows Fields Lake Trail #3579 near Whig & Torrey Lakes. Nonetheless the burn destroyed the south end of the trail and there was no evidence of a trail left. You can ride the north end of Fields Lake Trail, but the Forest Service says that it will not connect to Whig & Torrey Way Trail. Before riding any of the trails in the burn area, call the Forest Service for trail conditions.

BOX CANYON HORSE CAMP
Three Sisters Wilderness & Waldo Lake Wilderness

Box Canyon Horse Camp is located in South Central Oregon on the west side of the Cascade Mountains. There are several lake basins to aim for here. The trails are in the "Moderate" rating and the footing is excellent. There are neighboring views of the Three Sisters Mountains and surrounding hills, ridges and deep hollows to appreciate. The reason that there are two chapters in my book highlighting Waldo Lake Wilderness is due to the forest fire in 1996. Prior to the fire, Taylor Burn Road was probably accessible to truck and trailer rigs, now however, it is a rough jeep road. To make things more practical I'm using Taylor Burn Road as the boundary for the Waldo Lake Wilderness and the Box Canyon Horse Camp Chapters. I am sure there are hardy riders or perhaps packers that will go in from either place. I encourage you ride all of the trails described in both of these chapters.

There is an excellent horse camp, and a cozy cabin for rent. It was not very busy and my friend Sandy and I were able to pull right in to camp. I have included a description of the hot springs that is down the road. I hope you go and enjoy this area, I bet it will make you want to ride the rest of Waldo Wilderness and more of the Three Sisters Wilderness Areas. I have found it is fun to take a day off from riding occasionally. Especially since I am usually gone for 1-2 weeks at a time camping. On my day off I frequently hike or do nothing but rest and eat a lot. I have noted several hikes that are either on hiker-only trails or the trailhead is not suitable for trucks with trailers. Included are two trails that I feel you would enjoy knowing about. Be sure to check out the table in the back of this book for more trails in the area, listed under Three Sisters Wilderness.

Terwilliger Hot Springs: For a minimal fee, you can visit Terwilliger Hot Springs, located about 20 miles north of Box Canyon Horse Camp on Road 19, towards Cougar Reservoir. It is about a ½ mile hike on a wide trail into the hot springs. The setting is beautiful, a lush green forest with huge trees. There are 5 rock-lined pools. The top one is the hottest, then cools as each tear is made going down to the coolest. There is a small waterfall leading from one pool to the next. Bathrooms and a rack to hang your clothes on are available. Be sure to bring your pay-stub, there may be someone checking to see that everyone there has paid. Call the McKenzie River Ranger District for current regulations. Clothes are optional here!

Directions to camp: To reach Box Canyon Horse Camp, drive on Highway 126 west of the town of Mckenzie Bridge and turn south onto Aufderheide Road (Forest Service Road 19). This is the turnoff for Cougar Reservoir. Forest Service Road 19 is about 5 miles west of McKenzie Bridge and about 4.5 miles east of the town of Blue River. Drive about 25.5 miles to the Box Canyon Horse Camp, which is on the right hand side of the road. If you're coming in from Highway 58, you'll need to take the Westfir exit. Go past the covered bridge, straight to Forest Service Road 19. After the steep grade to the top of the pass, is Box Canyon Horse Camp, you'll drive past the exit from camp and around the corner you'll find the entrance on the left side of the road. Camp is about 28 miles from Oakridge. The use of both Three Sisters and Waldo Lake Wilderness maps are in order.

Box Canyon Horse Camp: The elevation is about 3,750 feet. There is a 14-day stay limit. It has 11 sites, fire rings, garbage service, corrals, tables, and toilets. Livestock water is available in a wonderful wooden trough equipped with a spigot. It is used to refill the trough or fill your buckets. Bring potable water. (The Forest Service says, folks should bring water in case the spigot isn't working, water can be brought down from Skookum Campground for both human and horse use, see Erma Bell Lakes Trail for directions to Skookum Camp.)There was a camp wheelbarrow and rake for our use while Sandy and I visited. Manure bins are across the Street on Forest Service Road 1957. The camp is set under tall timber. It is remarkably beautiful! No fee was being charged as of 2002. There is a cute little cabin across the street from camp that has a corral and a "2 roomer" with a wood stove. To rent, call the McKenzie River Ranger District for more information. For more information on trails in the Three Sisters Wilderness Area check out the trail table in the back of this book.

*NOTE: The Forest Service would like everyone to know that in general, most trailheads are for short-term use and are not suitable for long-term camping. This way there will be ample parking for day users.

Northwest Forest Parking Passes are available at Forest Service offices, they are required at designated trailheads.

Re-energize your spirit in the Wilderness...

McKenzie River Ranger District
State Highway 126
McKenzie Bridge, OR 97413
541-822-3381

Middle Fork Ranger District
46375 Highway 58
Westfir, OR 97492
541-782-2283

Willamette National Forest
211 E.7TH Ave.
P.O. Box 10607
Eugene, OR 97440
541-465-6521

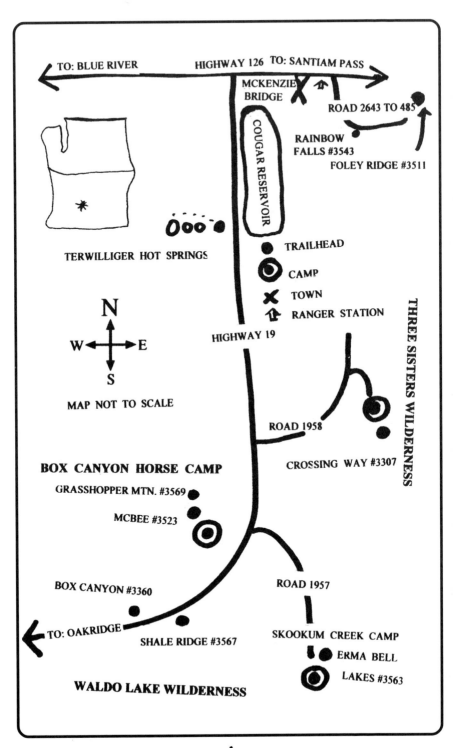

TO: BLUE RIVER

HIGHWAY 126   TO: SANTIAM PASS

MCKENZIE
BRIDGE

ROAD 2643 TO 485

RAINBOW
FALLS #3543

FOLEY RIDGE #3511

COUGAR RESERVOIR

TERWILLIGER HOT SPRINGS

● TRAILHEAD

◎ CAMP

✗ TOWN

⇑ RANGER STATION

N
W ← → E
S

HIGHWAY 19

MAP NOT TO SCALE

THREE SISTERS WILDERNESS

ROAD 1958

CROSSING WAY #3307

BOX CANYON HORSE CAMP

GRASSHOPPER MTN. #3569

MCBEE #3523

BOX CANYON #3360

ROAD 1957

TO: OAKRIDGE

SHALE RIDGE #3567

SKOOKUM CREEK CAMP

ERMA BELL

LAKES #3563

WALDO LAKE WILDERNESS

114

Chucksney Mountain #3306

Distance:	6 Miles
Altitude:	3750'-5760'
Maps:	Waldo Lake Wilderness
	Three Sisters Wilderness
Difficulty:	Moderate

Directions: Use Grasshopper Trail #3569 to reach Chucksney Mountain Trail #3306. Day parking is available as well as camping. For more directions on how to reach camp see the introduction to this chapter.

Connecting Trail: 3569

Horse Camping: Box Canyon Horse Camp, see the introduction to this chapter for details.

Trail Description: Chucksney Mountain Trail #3306 begins .3 mile up Grasshopper Trail #3569. This trail is a loop, meaning it begins and ends from Grasshopper Trail. (Box Canyon Trail #3360 (3660) (see note below) departs first off of Grasshopper Trail, then Grasshopper and Chucksney Trails split from each other.) Riding from camp, the complete loop is around 10 miles. Chucksney Mountain Trail #3306 will be described going counter-clockwise. Leaving Grasshopper Trail #3569, head north (right) on Chucksney Mountain Trail #3306 you begin riding in deep old-growth forest. As you traverse up the slope rather steeply, you'll notice the foliage is made up of Douglas fir, and the ground is laced with sword ferns, Oregon grape plants, and small star shaped flowers. The trail turns to climb around to the north slope with one semi-open spot to ride over. The trail levels a bit to cross a seasonal wet area, here you may find some water for hard working horses or mules to drink. Rolling trail with an occasional wash area takes you to an open meadow that has views of the Three Sisters, Bachelor Butte, and Broken Top Mountains. Back to the trees we go. Switchback up on a rocky area, the path horseshoes around and is now headed south. Ride to the crest of Chucksney Mountain and get out your camera at an open spot with panoramic views. This makes a great spot for lunch. Here you'll see the mountains listed before, plus Grasshopper Mountain, as well as many neighboring hillsides and gullies. The trail wades down through a peaceful grass covered slope, with hemlock trees and bear grass outlining the trail. Continue down in to cool timberland and meet up with the sign-less "T" intersection with Grasshopper Trail #3569. If you're heading back to camp turn left here. For more details on this loop, see Grasshopper Mountain Trail #3569, I'm sure you'll find this trail worth going on, especially if its clear weather.

*NOTE: The Three Sisters Wilderness Map shows Box Canyon Trail as being #3360, and the Waldo Wilderness Map shows it as #3660.

"GRASSHOPPER RIDGE IS ON FIRE"

Check in at the Ranger Station near the area where you are staying, they can tell you any news pertaining to the region. If we hadn't known ahead of time that Grasshopper Ridge was on fire and was contained, we would have freaked out when we saw the plume of smoke and burned trees through the viewfinder on the video camera, from atop of Chucksney Mountain!

Josie

Lower Erma Bell Lake

Crossing Way #3307

(To McFarland Lake)

Distance:	6 Miles
Altitude:	4500'-6300'
Maps:	Waldo Lake Wilderness
	Three Sisters Wilderness
Difficulty:	Moderate

Directions: To reach Crossing Way Trailhead from Box Canyon Horse Camp, go north of camp on Road 19 towards the reservoir. One-half mile from camp, you'll turn onto a gravel logging road, number 1958, which heads up, and to the east. Follow the one lane road for 3 miles, being careful of logging traffic. A CB radio may be helpful. At the 3 mile-point, there is a guiding sign pointing you toward the trailhead and turnaround. For more details on how to reach camp, see the map for this chapter. No fee here.

Connecting Trail: 3523

Horse Camp: There are 4 spots to camp with hitching' rails. They are all drive through parking spots, graveled nicely, and day parking area with a dirt bank for unloading livestock. There are fire pits made of rock circles, although you need to check before hand to see what the fire conditions are before attempting a fire. It's a very secluded spot to camp.

Trail Description: Sign in at the Three Sisters Wilderness box at the Crossing Way Trailhead. This trail connects with Irish Mountain Trail #3588, and may or may not be cleared beyond McFarland Lake. Sandy and I, had a great ride and gained a wonderful panorama of the huge McFarland Lake, ate lunch and called it a victory and headed back to camp. The trail is maintained by the "Longears Club", there is a sign at the trailhead reading such. It is a rolling pathway through forest and intersects McBee Trail #3523 at about the ½ mile-point. There are loads of huckleberry and blueberry bushes along the trail, full and meaty in late summer. Climb gradually in and out of timber, with areas full of broken off snags lining the trail. There are young trees sprouting to replace the old dying ones. Lots of rocks to deal with from here on to the lakes. The trail stays mainly in the forest with very little feed. Cross several waterless streams. The footing is rocky and sandy at the same time. Pass a rocky knoll and mossy trees, this is the Wilderness boundary. Climb up the three "R's" of trail riding, roots rocks and ruts! A quick glimpse of the Three Sisters Mountains, Bachelor Butte, and Broken Top Mountain are in your rear-view mirror. Ride up between boulders here and there, then up some more. The path levels a bit after a dry wash, then through some low brush and bear grass. The tread is kind of rocky here and pretty abrupt. Meet Piper then Smith Lakes. There is a nice spot to water your horses. Dragonflies skim the surface and edge of the lakes for a mosquito meal and buzz you for dessert. There is a campsite at the far end of one of the lakes.

Ride through a mossy open area to a level area in deep forest. Ride onward through a somewhat brushy area by a pond. Going up in stages. Either step-up onto and over some nasty sharp rocks with ruts. Or we found that riding to the right of the trail was much easier. Clamber up and peek over a bowl to view the huge McFarland Lake. It looks like there is no way to access the shoreline. Hope your ride will be as interesting as we found ours to be. Sandy watched a mink romping around on some rocks while she held the horses and I took some snaps of the lake. The total mileage of this trail is 6 miles and it connects to Irish Mountain Trail.

Terri says it's time to saddle up

Elk Creek #3510

(From Trail #3523 to Trail #3537)

Distance:	. ,8 Mile
Altitude:	4700'-4800'
Map:	Three Sisters Wilderness
Difficulty:	Moderate

Directions: Access this trail from McBee Trail #3523, near Mink Lake.

Connecting Trails: 3523, 3537, 4334

Horse Camping: Box Canyon Horse Camp or Crossing Way Trailhead are the closest camps. See the Crossing Way Trail description for its camp or the introduction to this chapter for more details on Box Canyon Horse Camp.

Trail Description: This trail goes towards Mink Lake, all in forest. Beginning from McBee Trail #3523 the path goes east, on a trail that looked unmaintained, we found quite a few downed logs, luckily we were able to make our way over and around them to the next intersection. It travels up slightly to meet with Packsaddle Mountain Trail #4334 and Starwano Trail #3537. The total mileage of this trail is 8.6 miles. We only needed a fragment of it to complete our loop this trip.

Erma Bell Lakes #3563

Distance:	4.2 Miles
Altitude:	4500'-5000'
Maps:	Waldo Lake Wilderness
	Three Sisters Wilderness
Difficulty:	Moderate

Directions: From Box Canyon Horse Camp and Road 19, drive to gravel Road 1957, which you'll find across the road from camp. The Erma Bell Lakes Trailhead is 3.6 miles up dead end Forest Service Road 1957. There is a very large space at the end of the road, most any size rig would be able to turn around here. It has an outhouse. This is a "walk-in" type of camp for people only, named Skookum Creek. Skookum means "powerful", in this case it is the name of the creek running beside the camp. For more details on how to reach camp see the introduction to this chapter.

Connecting Trails: 3588, 3575, 3589

Horse Camping: Box Canyon Horse Camp is nearby. See the map.

Trail Description: To start Erma Bell Lakes Trail #3563, register at the Waldo Lake Wilderness permit box. Walk through a few feet of Skookum Camp to cross a wide sturdy bridge with handrails, there is no way to ford this one. In .6 mile, you will intersect with Irish Mountain Trail #3588, which leaves to the left. (The signs are destination signs, so Irish Mountain Trail #3588 is toward Otter Lake.) Erma Bell Trail continues on, traveling south and is a gradual trend upward. There are hardly any rocks and it is a very wide trail, people in wheel chairs can even use it! Follow the hillside above a hazy deep valley with the hidden Middle Fork Willamette River below. Cross another wide hand-railed bridge, this time the far side has access to stock water, it is an outlet from Otter Lake. Ride up a switchback and along a hillside with Lower Erma Bell Lake below. You can hear, but not see a rushing waterfall that cascades between the Lower and Middle Erma Lakes. Ride up to see Middle Erma Bell Lake, then ride on a rolling trail lined with rhododendron plants. Pass a small lily padded pond as the trail flattens a bit. Still easy footing for the horses. Ride by Upper Erma Bell Lake. (You may miss Upper Erma Bell Lake when the trees and bushes are in full foliage, the user trail is about ¼ mile past the pond on the right hand side of the trail.) Two long switchbacks take you up, wind along a hillside passing a seasonal creek with a culvert. Cross a wash that has been filled with rocks to make it easy to cross. You'll see where Judy Lake Trail #3575 exits downhill from Erma Bell Lakes Trail, coming into view is a lovely vast meadow. Pass Mud Lake, then the trail bends around to the east (left) to meet up with Williams Lake Trail #3589. Continue on and cross a narrow side-less bridge over a seasonal creek (dry in late summer). Ride over several comparable bridges on level terrain, then head up and over a rocky area with a culvert next to a small gully. Ride ½ mile more to Taylor Burn Road and to the end of this trail. The road to this trailhead is not recommended for truck and -trailer rigs! It is a rough jeep road. Loops possible, the most popular loop is with Williams Lake Trail and a portion of Irish Mountain Trail.

"IN HONOR OF"

Erma Bell was a Forest Service bookkeeper that perished in an automobile crash in 1918 in the town of Troutdale. Erma Bell Lakes are named in her honor. May she rest in peace.

Josie

Josie and Ali crossing a bridge

Foley Ridge #3511

(To lookout site)

Distance:	4 Miles
Altitude:	4000'-5600'
Map:	Three Sisters Wilderness
Difficulty:	Moderate

Directions: From Highway 126 turn onto a one lane paved Foley Ridge Road (Forest Service Road 2643) located one-quarter to one-half mile east of McKenzie River Ranger Station near the town of McKenzie Bridge. This road is pretty steep in places. Drive uphill for about 7.5 miles, then the road becomes gravel, there are turnouts along the road. Follow the road up a razor back ridge to the end, turn around here, then park alongside the road. You'll probable find it crowded with other horse users and their rigs. It is a popular spot to reach the Pacific Crest Trail #2000.

Connecting Trail: Substitute Point (lookout site)

Horse Camping: Primitive camping along Foley Ridge Road at the trailhead area. There is a hitching rails and rock rings for fires. The camps are along the road before the trailhead.

Trail Description: Foley Ridge Trail #3511 stays in deep forest. It goes all the way to the Pacific Crest Trail #2000, however we were only interested in going to the old lookout site at Substitute Point, so only 4 of the 9 miles will be described. Foley Ridge Trail #3511 begins by going slightly downhill. Cross a small bridge and enter the Three Sisters Wilderness. This is a rolling trail that travels along with over-all nice footing with some rocks here and there. It is a steady uphill trek to the turnoff to the lookout, rugged boulders with moss on them are beside the trail. Reach a pond, the banks were to muddy to water the animals here. There is and an old camp at about the 3-mile point. Go around the north side of Substitute Point cross a rock slide and ride up to the turn-off for the old lookout site. For more details on the trail up to the lookout site see Substitute Point in this chapter. Go for it!

*NOTE: For more details on the other end of this trail by the PCT, see the table in the back of the book it is listed under Three Sisters Wilderness.

Grasshopper Mountain #3569

(To the far end of Chucksney Mountain Trail)

Distance:	4 Miles
Altitude:	3750'-5500'
Maps:	Three Sisters Wilderness
	Waldo Lake Wilderness
Difficulty:	Moderate

Directions: The Grasshopper Trailhead is near camp space number one, which is next to the entrance of Box Canyon Horse Camp. Day parking is available as well as camping. For more directions on how to reach camp, see the introduction to this chapter.

Connecting Trails: 3306, 3360 (3660)

Horse Camping: Box Canyon Horse Camp, for more data, read the map.

Trail Description: Use the access trail from Box Canyon Horse Camp near space number one to reach Grasshopper Mountain Trail #3569. This 4 mile-section of Grasshopper Trail was used to make the popular loop to Chucksney Mountain. It will be described from camp, however, if you're making the loop I think going counter-clockwise works best, I like to go up the steeper side and come down the more mild routes when possible. The entire loop is only 10 miles. From camp ride left from the access trail onto Grasshopper Mountain Trail #3569. The trail stays in timberland the entire time. You will pass Box Canyon Trail #3360 that departs to the left. Continue on to a fork in the trail and stay left. Ride along a slope headed west across a wide, but rocky mossy creek that may be a bit slippery. Hop up and out of the brook bed along a fern covered grade. Lots of switchbacks take you up, steadily climbing. There are few rocky spots. Pass black-eyed Suzan flowers, small meadows and seasonal wash areas. Ride out and around a knob where some water may be found for the animals. Switchback uphill to cross a flatter spot. Merge with the other end of Chucksney Mountain Trail #3306. The Grasshopper Mountain Trail continues on to Grasshopper Mountain and beyond, explore and be happy.

*NOTE: The Three Sisters Wilderness Map shows Box Canyon Trail as being #3360, and the Waldo Wilderness Map shows it as #3660.

*HINT- Bag Balm rubbed onto an imbedded tick will make it back out of its hole.

Wide trail and nice footing

Helen Lake #3577

Distance:	.3 Mile
Altitude:	4900'-5000'
Maps:	Waldo Lake Wilderness
	Three Sisters Wilderness
Difficulty:	Moderate

Directions: Even though this trail starts off of Taylor Burn Road it is not a road that is passable for trucks with trailers. It is a rough jeep road. Access this trail from the Waldo area or from Erma Bell Lakes Trailhead by Skookum Creek Camp.

Connecting Trail: 3579

Horse Camping: There is a horse camp at both Waldo Lake and Box Canyon. The Box Canyon one is described in the introduction of this chapter and the Waldo camp is in the Waldo Lake Wilderness Chapter.

Trail Description: Helen Lake Trail #3577 begins off of Taylor Burn Road 514 and heads downward to the north. On the other side of Taylor Burn Road is Fields Lake Trailhead #3579 (the description of this trail is in the Waldo Lake Wilderness Chapter). At first Helen Lake Trail appears to be an old road, then becomes a definite trail as it switchbacks down and levels by the sumptuous hidden Helen Lake. There is a good spot to water your animals on a stable south shoreline. Rock outcroppings make this an interesting lake to visit.

Irish Mountain #3588

(From Erma Bell Lakes Trail to 1 mile beyond Jack Pine Way Trail)

Distance:	3.5 Miles
Altitude:	4500'-5800'
Maps:	Waldo Lake Wilderness
	Three Sisters Wilderness
Difficulty:	Moderate

Directions: From Box Canyon Horse Camp and Road 19, drive to a gravel road across the road, which is number 1957. The Erma Bell Lakes Trailhead is 3.6 miles up this dead end road. Irish Mountain Trail #3588 begins .6 mile up Erma Bell Lakes Trail. There is a very large space at the end of the road. Most any size rig would be able to turn around here and there is an outhouse. Here is a "walk-in" type of camp for people only, named Skookum Creek. Skookum means "powerful", in this case it is the name of the creek running beside the camp. For more details on how to reach the nearby horse camp, see the introduction to this chapter.

Connecting Trails: 3563, 3589, 3587

Horse Camping: See introduction to this chapter for Box Canyon Horse Camp.

Trail Description: Irish Mountain Trail #3588 exits Erma Bell Lakes Trail #3563 at the .6 mile-point and heads east (left). The sign at the intersection is a destination sign, go towards Otter Lake, this is the start of Irish Mountain Trail. Ride slightly uphill there are some roots, rocks and meadows along the path and it is all nice, cool forest. Go gently downhill to reach Otter Lake on the left. Ride along the south shoreline. Breathe deeply, can you "smell that smell" is it "otter"? Sandy and I were sure we heard them frolicking in the water on the other side of the lake. Loads of rhododendron plants here. Cross the outlet to the lake, this is a good watering hole. Here we found the mud teaming with tiny frogs, and some nursery trees that had 2-3 saplings taking root in them. Intersect with Williams Lake Trail #3589 just past the outlet, keep to the left to stay on Irish Mountain Trail #3588. There is another small meadow just up from Otter Lake. Begin your ascent toward the top of Irish Mountain, view Otter Lake through the lacy limbs of fragrant timber. The next sector of trail is less traveled to say the least, we found out why later. The tread is covered with pine needles. Begin your ascent toward the top of Irish Mountain. Jack Pine Way Trail #3587 departs 1.1 miles from the last intersection with Williams Lake Trail #3589. Climb up, then up more, find your way around re-routes of trail in soft ground and downed logs until you can go no more. Too bad it wasn't cleared all the way to the Crossing Way Trail #3307 on the other side of the mountain. It would have made a cool point-to-point ride. I read somewhere that you can see Waldo Lake from on top of Irish Mountain, maybe you'll have better luck when you visit we were several miles short of reaching the top. The total mileage of this trail is 5.3 miles.

"THE TRAIL MARE"

Handle her with care,
For it's an honor to ride a mare,

Jumping the logs,
Through the bogs,

Her body's intact as the day she was born,
She'll run all night and into the morn,

Galloping swiftly, hoofs glide effortlessly through the air,
Crossing the river, water splashes and her nostrils flare,

Her mane flies as her speed increases,
She makes my heart soar and I love her to pieces!

"THE BROOD MARE"

Her senses make her so keen,
Protecting her young, she **will** get mean,
Driven by instincts, old as dirt,
She'll kick em' in the head and the blood will spurt!

Josie

Jack Pine Way #3587

(From Irish Mountain to log-jam)

Distance:	5 Miles
Altitude:	5050'-5500'
Maps:	Waldo Lake Wilderness
	Three Sisters Wilderness
Difficulty:	Moderate

Directions: Access this trail from Irish Mountain Trail #3588.

Connecting Trail: 3588

Fields Lake Trail

Horse Camping: Box Canyon Horse Camp is the closest camp. See details in the introduction of this chapter.

Trail Description: Jack Pine Way Trail #3587 leaves Irish Mountain Trail #3588 at its 2 mile-point and heads south. Jack Pine Trail is a delightful rolling path in the timber. Unfortunately, due to manpower needed to help in forest fire fighting, the trail was only cleared for 2 miles. Maybe the trail will be open all the way for you, the Forest Service encourages you to call ahead before your trip to check on trail conditions. This trail was relocated since the fire of 1996, because of all the downed wood, and has been cleared several times since the fire. The total mileage of this trail is 5 miles, and loops are possible with the use of Taylor Burn Road.

"PRIORITIES"

The year of 2002 was dry and the forests were tinderboxes. Sandy and I found a Forest Service worker's blue hard hat stuck in between 2 trees on the ground where the last log was cleared. Of course we realized the priority is fighting the fires, or maybe we caught the workers between cleanings of this trail. We jumped several logs and were closing in on an old burn area and knew riding this trail was a lost cause. We were able to access the other end of Jack Pine Trail on Taylor Burn Road at a later date, only to discover that the trail was completely buried with old, burned and bleached trees. Massive acres of rotting trees are down in the area and more are toppling with each windstorm. It was pretty awesome to see and we were glad to have been witness to it.

Let's hear it for the hard working forest fire fighters and Forest Service workers clearing out our trails! The Forest Service has a huge job trying to keep up with the continual falling burned trees in this area, and I was informed that the trails were cleared the year I visited. They clear them only to find more have fallen down in a short period of time.

Josie

Judy Lake #3575

Distance:	.8 Mile
Altitude:	4800'-5000'
Maps:	Waldo Lake Wilderness
	Three Sisters Wilderness
Difficulty:	Moderate

Directions: This trail can be accessed from Erma Bell Lakes Trail #3563. Although it does come out into Taylor Burn Campground (Forest Service Camp), Taylor Burn Road is too rough for trucks and trailers to drive on.

Connecting Trail: 3563

Horse Camping: Nearby camping at Box Canyon Horse Camp, see the introduction of this chapter for details.

Trail Description: Judy Lake Trail #3575 will be described from Erma Bell Lakes Trail #3563 going south to Taylor Burn Campground. Head downhill with some rocks, roots and overhanging branches to deal with. Cross the outlet creek from Judy Lake. Ride along on rolling trail, all in forest. Judy Lake is on the right side of the trail. Now the trail gets into a more serious climbing phase. We found bear scat along the path. The trail pops out onto a two-track road and finishes the climb, reaching its end at Forest Service Camp (Taylor Burn Campground). Located at the end of Taylor Burn Road. Loops possible using Taylor Burn Road.

Martin Way #3525

Distance:	.7 Mile
Altitude:	5000'-5000'
Map:	Three Sisters Wilderness
Difficulty:	Moderate

Directions: Access this trail from McBee Trail #3523, near Mink Lake.

Connecting Trails: 3523, 3525, 3537

Horse Camping: Box Canyon Horse Camp or Crossing Way Trailhead are the closest camps. See Crossing Way Trail description or the introduction to this chapter for more details.

Trail Description: This trail goes towards Mink Lake, all in forest. Beginning from McBee Trail #3523 follow the path with the destination sign "Mink Lake" it goes east, to the west shoreline of Mink Lake. It travels up slightly to cross a seasonal wash. Pass Martin Lake on the right side of the trail, which was a glassy-green when we were there. Mink Lake is straight ahead, there is a good watering spot at the outlet. We came to an intersection where we found more destination signs, we turned right toward Elk Creek, as we were making a loop. The total mileage of this trail is 2.2 miles and goes to the shelter at Mink Lake.

*Note: The Three Sisters and the Waldo Wilderness Maps have opposite ideas as to which is Trail #3525 and which is Trail #3526 around Waldo Lake. I used the Three Sisters Wilderness Map. For this area it would be wise to rely on destinations signs rather than count on the trail numbers to guide you.

Josie and her horse at Mink Lake

McBee #3523

(To Mink Lake)

Distance:	10.9 Miles
Altitude:	3750'-5000'
Maps:	Waldo Lake Wilderness
	Three Sisters Wilderness
Difficulty:	Moderate

Directions: McBee Trailhead is at Box Canyon Horse Camp, near the water trough, which is next to the entrance to Box Canyon Horse Camp. Day parking is available as well as camping. For more directions on how to reach camp see the introduction to this chapter.

Connecting Trails: 3307, 3510, 3525

Horse Camping: Box Canyon Horse Camp, see the introduction of this chapter for details.

Trail Description: For McBee Trail #3523 you'll need the Three Sisters Wilderness Map for sure. The Waldo Wilderness Map is helpful to have too, but the end of the trail runs off the top of the map. The Three Sisters Wilderness sign-in box is in camp. McBee Trail wanders away from Box Canyon Horse Camp and crosses Forest Service Road 19 headed east. It is fairly level with some rocks, this lower section looks like it may have been a road at one time. Switchback up, it makes its way along a slope, crossing a couple of roads with bike symbols on them and an overgrown logging road. Pass over several seasonal creeks, one had some water it in late August. Bear grass, rhododendron plants and beautiful pines line your way. Sandy and I spotted a black bear an hour from camp. There are a few rocks here and there on a rolling trail with a stray switchback. Peek at the Three Sisters Mountains through the trees. The trail contours a hill on its north face to meet with Crossing Way Trail #3307, which travels north and south. Nice signs. On the bushes there are lots of big juicy huckleberries and blueberries in late summer. Here is the Wilderness boundary. The trail intermittently travels up, then down and around slopes with a few small glimpses of the Three Sisters and Bachelor Butte, which are all above the 9,000' level. The trail is in great shape and is wide with few rocks. There is a clearing and lake off to the left with a path, marked by a horseshoe sign in a tree. Cross a few rocky washes (dry in Aug.). View Packsaddle

Mountain in front of you. Meander across small bridges and ride next to a little seasonal creek, and small clearing. The trail bends, heading north. The signs in this area are destination signs, keep going toward Mink Lake. Elk Creek Trail #3510 crosses your path. McBee Trail will bend again; heading east there is a nice spot to water your animals up ahead by a bridge. Junction Lakes are on the left and Shipper Lake is on the right, it has islands. A big meadow area is alongside the path as well. Another intersection with destination signs, this is where this trail description ends as we took a right onto Martin Way Trail #3525 to make a loop. McBee Trail #3523 does continue on. The total mileage of this trail is 16.1 miles, to read a brief description of another section ridden on this trail see the table in the back of the book, listed under Three Sisters Wilderness.

*Note: The Three Sisters and the Waldo Wilderness Maps have opposite ideas as to which is Trail #3525 and which is Trail #3526 around Waldo Lake. I used the Three Sisters Wilderness Map. For this area it would be wise to rely on destinations signs rather than count on the trail numbers to guide you.

Shale Ridge Trail

"BERRIES IN YOUR EARS"

Sandy and I are on our first ride out of Box Canyon Horse Camp on the McBee trail. One hour from camp we screeched to a halt when my mare "Ali" froze in her tracks. I could feel her heart beating under the saddle. She stood quietly and I looked right between her ears. As "Ali" scoped the meadow she closed her sights in on a massive bramble of huckleberry bushes. Low and behold the mystery unfolded before our eyes. Decisions were made, yes, the camera not the gun this time. It is a small black bear, just 10 yards from us. After several snaps were attained, Sandy and I were ready to move on. Only problem was the little tyke hadn't even given us the time of day yet, we were unbelievably close and the big cub was so busy eating it didn't hear us. So we proceeded to cautiously make some noise. First a puckered whistle was tried, nope, nobody home. Next we tried clapping, hooting, then giggling and finely Sandy let loose with her "finger in the mouth whistle". Well, that did it! When "blackie" looked up the sight of us scared it so much, it ran away. It was about as big as a Saint Bernard dog & a half. We suspected that mom was in the meadow that "Ali" had so keenly scoped earlier. We were grateful for our cool calm mounts this day. The picture I took turned out too dark to see the bear very well.

Josie

One of the Sister Mountains and McFarland Lake

Rainbow Falls #3543

(Hike)

Distance:	2 ¼ Miles
Altitude:	2300'-2400'
Map:	Three Sisters Wilderness
Difficulty:	Moderate

Directions: Starting from the town of McKenzie Bridge on Highway 126 drive east. Just past McKenzie River Ranger Station, you'll turn south on Foley Ridge Road (Forest Service Road 2643), which is one-quarter to one-half mile east of the ranger station. Go up this paved road to the trailhead on the right (south). We found room for our rigs to park here, as we were on our way from another horse ride in the area. This is a "hiker only" trail.

Trail Description: Rainbow Falls Trail #3543 is marked with a nice sign along Foley Ridge Road. It begins by going over several berms, and is an old road for about ½ mile. The road heads downhill slightly in dense timber and undergrowth. The trail begins at another sign, it reads Rainbow Falls Overlook 1 ¾ miles. Hike down to a cliff, then the trail turns to the left along a deep, narrow canyon with a steep drop-off, you can hear the falls a long way off. Follow this to the rock outcropping. The vista is of the far off Rainbow Falls. The backdrop for this scene is of the Sisters Mountains or at least one of them. The trail is so overgrown with coastal foliage, we had to duck through several spots of heavy moss-laden branches, and pillow size fern fronds. Boulders were hardly recognizable with the green carpets of moss on them. This was a delight to experience, Sandy and I are having even more fun on our horse trips now that we are allowing extra time to do these little hikes that we can't do on horseback. Enjoy the wilds.

"IT IS AN EVERGREEN"

Sandy spotted a grove of Pacific Madrone trees on the slope below Rainbow Falls Trail. They are a broadleaf flowering evergreen. They are very beautiful with glossy foliage and when it's in bloom it has large clusters of tiny white flowers and orange-red fruit, the bark is reddish and it peels off easily. Sandy's mom used the bark like paper to write letters to her kids while hiking. The Indians from California used the fruit to eat and either ate it raw or cooked. This may cause cramps if overeaten. The flowers contain honey and the birds and deer like to consume the fruit.

Josie

Hot Springs

Shale Ridge #3567
(Hike to Skookum Creek)

Distance:	2.1 Miles
Altitude:	3000'-3000'
Maps:	Waldo Lake Wilderness
	Three Sisters Wilderness
Difficulty:	Moderate

Directions: From Box Canyon Horse Camp, drive toward Oakridge on Forest Service Road 19. Go to the bottom of the first hill, about a mile, the parking is in a small area in the trees on a hairpin curve of the road. There is a hiker symbol on a sign. See the introduction of this chapter for directions to Box Canyon Horse Camp.

Trail Description: Just for an evening stroll, Sandy and I drove from camp to check out this trailhead and ended up hiking for a couple miles. We found the trailhead was too small for a truck and trailer to park, and the trail was geared more for hikers, too many low branches. It felt wonderful to stretch out our legs, after long days in the saddle. It's a level path with lovely old-growth timber, thick cool air and huge trees. The sunlight coming through the big green leaves on the vine maple was beautiful; the moss grows thick as a carpet, don't step on the slugs. There are hemlock, fir and lots of cedar trees, some over 200' tall, with the trunks of the trees being as big as 6 to 7' in diameter. Although you're alongside the Wilamette River, you cannot see it, the river is on the other side of the valley and hidden by a marsh. We turned back at the Skookum Creek crossing because of the daylight factor. Enjoy your day off! The total mileage of this trail is 5.5 miles, we only used part of it for our hike.

*Note: This trail goes for 5.5 miles to end at the Blair Lake Trail, the Forest Service does not recommended it for livestock travel beyond the 3.5 mile point at the crossing of the North Fork Willamette River.

Starwano #3537

(Near Mink Lake)

Distance:	1.8 Miles
Altitude:	4600'-5000'
Map:	Three Sisters Wilderness
Difficulty:	Moderate

Directions*:* Access this at Martin Way Trail #3525 by Mink Lake, or from Elk Creek Trail #3510 (near McBee Trail #3523).

Connecting Trails*:* 3525, 3510, 4334

Horse Camping: Box Canyon Horse Camp or Crossing Way Trailhead are the closest camps. See the Crossing Way Trail description for its camp or the introduction to this chapter for more details on Box Canyon Horse Camp.

Trail Description: Starwano Trail #3537 connects Mink Lake's west shoreline (on Martin Way Trail #3525) to Elk Creek Trail #3510. Begin by riding in the timber, traveling to the west, go down several short steep sections, cross a meadow and creek to meet up with Elk Creek Trail #3510 and Packsaddle Mountain Trail #4334. We used this trail for making a small loop; it is less traveled than some and was worth exploring.

*Note: The Three Sisters and the Waldo Wilderness Maps have opposite ideas as to which is Trail #3525 and which is Trail #3526 around Waldo Lake. I used the Three Sisters Wilderness Map. For this area it would be wise to rely on destinations signs rather than count on the trail numbers to guide you.

Substitute Point #3511

(Lookout)

Distance:	1 Mile
Altitude:	5600'-6344'
Map:	Three Sisters Wildemess
Difficulty:	Moderate

Directions: The trail to Substitute Point Lookout has the same trail number as Foley Ridge Trail. Access it from Foley Ridge Trail #3511.

Connecting Trail: 3511 (Foley Ridge)

Horse Camping: Nearby primitive camping at Foley Ridge Trailhead, see Foley Ridge Trail #3511 for more details.

Trail Description: Substitute Point Trail #3511 begins at the 4 mile-point up Foley Ridge Trail #3511 at the 5,600' level, and rises for close to a mile to the summit. Both trails have been assigned the same number for some reason. This trail is in trees most of the way to the old lookout site. The trail contours and switchbacks up the mountain. It is seldom traveled, by the looks of the tread. We went over several small logs and were able to attain our objective. *Warning*-at the only flat spot on the trail you will need to dismount and either tie or take turns holding the animals as the other one scrambles up to the old lookout on foot, a horse would not be able to go beyond this point. The tread is treacherous even to a two-footed creature. Clamber your way on hands and knees towards the top over the rocks, to reach the lookout. On a clear day you get a grand view of the South Sister Mountain. Unfortunately, I only saw a picture of the view, as it was socked in with clouds the day we went.

"WHAT'S IN A NAME?"

In 1916 Substitution Point won the war with Proxy Point for the right to have the lookout tower for the triangulation station, and was named by the survey party. At the summit you'll find names and dates scratched into stones by lookout post workers in 1939 and 1940. I don't know about you, but I get a thrill to stand in the same spot where the old lookout towers once stood. The Three Sisters Mountains are only 6 miles away, "as the crow flies".

Josie

Hot Springs

Williams Lake #3589

Distance:	3 Miles	
Altitude:	4500'-5000'	
Maps:	Waldo Lake Wilderness	
	Three Sisters Wilderness	
Difficulty:	Moderate	

Directions: Access Williams Lake Trail #3589 from either Irish Mountain Trail #3588 or Erma Bell Lakes Trail #3563.

Connecting Trails: 3563, 3588

Horse Camping: Box Canyon Horse Camp is nearby, for details see the introduction to this chapter.

Trail Description: Williams Lake Trail #3589 will be described from the intersection with Irish Mountain Trail. Williams Lake Trail goes south leaving Irish Mountain Trail. Head up on rolling terrain, then switchback once. The path flattens out to reach a huge meadow with lots of feed, splattered with Indian paintbrush flowers and purple asters. When we visited the area in the late summer, the grass was rolling over on itself it was so long. You'll pass meadow areas and cross over periodical washes and ride through deep-forested areas, with ferns and moss. There are some rocky spots. Some of the rock is flat slabs, which you ride across. One wash had a lot of big rocks and a deep severe bank. Sandy and I found a better route around, off trail to the left (east). Up ahead there is a spot to water the horses. Next is a short segment of trail that is rutty, lots of flowers and some sandy footing. Ride through a bushy section and adjacent to a seasonal streambed. Reach Williams Lake, it is quite lengthy and beautiful. More meadows and brush take you to a long bridge and the end of the trail as you "T" intersect with Erma Bell Lakes Trail #3563.

MOUNT WASHINGTON WILDERNESS AREA

The Mount Washington Wilderness Area is located in Central Oregon west of the towns of Sisters and Bend, and covers over 52,500 acres of the Oregon Cascade Mountain Range. Mount Washington is 7,802' high and is a sharp core of an old volcano. He juts from the ground with charcoal color plains of lava surrounding him. The trails in the region are "Moderate" in their difficulty. Belknap Crater is a cinder-and-ash cone that is 6,872 high, and is located the middle of this Wilderness, the area around it is known as the "Black Wilderness". The Pacific Crest Trail #2000 serpentines through this region and is described in the Pacific Crest Trail chapter of this book under the heading of "Mount Washington Wilderness Area". With the exception of the lava flow by McKenzie Pass, most of the footing on the paths is surprisingly soft; given there are over 75 square miles of lava flows, and volcanic terrain. The wildlife that inhabit the area include black-tailed deer, elk, mule deer, black bear and a few cougar, along with a lot of the usual smaller animals in the forest. If you enjoy riding to lakes and viewing huge volcanoes and their geological remains, this will be a spot you'll want to spend time in. Primitive camping is free at the trailheads described. The Forest Service would like people to understand that camping at trailheads in general, are for short-term use and are not suitable for long-term camping. This is an isolated environment with no quick stops for food or gas, so come prepared. I rode this territory with my friend Madeleine, we had a memorable time here and it is a sure bet you will also. We used three different camp areas to access the area.

Santiam Pass/Big Lake- Drive 40 miles west of the town of Sisters on Highway 20, near Santiam Pass. From Highway 20 turn south on paved Forest Service Road 2690, follow the signs almost to the end of the paved road and Big Lake. Old Santiam Wagon Road 810 goes to the west (right) and is a sandy dirt road. Road 811 is also a sandy dirt road and goes to the east (left). There are spots to park alongside these roads, be aware, the terrain is sandy and you may get stuck if you pull off too far.

Santiam Camp- There are primitive camp spots and day parking is available all along Santiam Wagon Roads 811 and 810, some are in tree lined grassy meadows. Bring potable water, livestock water is at Big Lake or if you're camped at the meadow just to the west of the PCT #2000, you'll find a trail that goes to a small lake where you can water your horses.

Robinson Lake Trailhead- If you're coming from the town of Mckenzie Bridge, drive northeast about 16 miles on Highway 126 to Robinson Lake Road 2664. If you're coming from Highway 20, near Santiam Pass, take Highway 126 going south and between mile markers 8-9 you'll reach Robinson Lake Road 2664. After reaching Road 2664, turn east and drive almost 5 miles to reach the end of the gravel road and Deer Butte Trail. There are 6 spots to park in a big circular drive. The map reads Robinson Lake Trailhead.

Robinson Lake Camp- This trailhead is a beautiful spot for primitive camping, it has six spaces. Some have rock lined fire pits. Surrounded by blueberry bushes, brush-bunnies and deep woods drenched in wildflowers, it is extremely peaceful. Bring potable water, livestock water is .7 mile up the trail at Robinson Lake. It is a circle drive and a Northwest Forest Pass is required.

Scott Lake Camp- Drive on Highway 242 (Old McKenzie Highway), which has a 35 foot length restriction for rigs, measure from the front bumper to the back of the horse trailer. The road has hairpin turns that are tight! Turn west on paved Forest Service Road 260 (between milepost 71 and 72) the sign reads Scott Lake turnoff. Turn west on paved Forest Service Road 260 to the end, where you'll find a small parking area in an old shale pit. Benson Trail #3502 shares this trailhead with Hand Lake Trail #3513. This can be an active area in the summer; it is wise to visit on the weekdays.

Let's tack up and hit the trail...

McKenzie River Ranger District	Sisters Ranger Station
State Highway 126	P.O. Box 249
McKenzie Bridge, Or 97413	Sisters, OR 97759
503-822-3381	541-549-7700

Deschutes National Forest	Detroit Ranger Station
1645 East Highway 20	HC60 Box 320
Bend, OR 97701	Mill City, OR 97360
503-388-2715	503-854-3366

Bend Ranger Station	Willamette National Forest
1230 NE 3rd Suite #A262	211 E. 7th Ave., P.O. Box 10607
Bend, OR 97701	Eugene, OR 97440
541-388-5664	503-465-6521

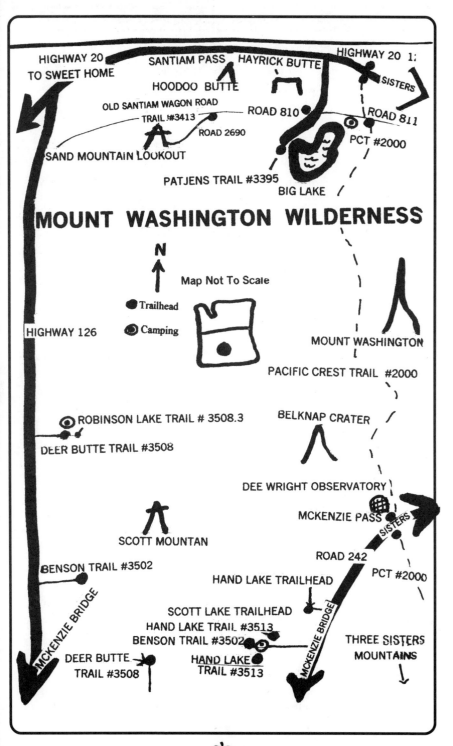

Benson #3502

Distance:	5.5 Miles
Altitude:	4000'-5400'
Map:	Mount Washington Wilderness
Difficulty:	Moderate

Directions: Use the Scott Lake Camp directions at the beginning of this chapter. Benson Trail #3502 can also be accessed from the east end by driving Forest Service Road 640. The parking is nil at the east trailhead and the trail signs are behind the bushes, all you can see from Forest Service Road 640 is a hiker picture on a post. On closer examination, you then find the wooden Wilderness permit box, and beyond that you will see the Benson Trail #3502 sign. The destination sign reads Tenas Lakes, and it is in the Mount Washington Wilderness. The map shows this as the Benson Trailhead.

Connecting Trails: 3513, 3502.3(C), 3513.4(D), 3508

Horse Camping: Primitive camping at the Scott Lake trailhead. See the introduction to this chapter.

Trail Description: Benson Trail #3502 will be described from the east trailhead by Scott Lake going toward the Hand Lake Cutoff Trail. Hand Lake Trail #3513 leaves from the same trailhead going both north and south. Benson Trail #3502 is the middle trail. Start by riding on a wide path that travels through cool shady forest. There are a few rocky spots here as you ascend gently next to a small gully on the right of the trail. Cross over a seasonal creek as the draw meets the trail. Continue up the path, riding beside huckleberry bushes, with camp-robber birds calling to each other above in the boughs of the evergreens. Small ponds abound near Benson Lake, however some of them were dried up when we visited in August, and had become little meadows. Ride up and over a boulder-sprinkled hillside, with the use of 1 switchback. Benson Trail #3502 levels out only to rise again, this time to view a tobacco colored pond. The trail flattens once again to intersect with Tenas Lakes Trail #3502.3(C), departing to the west. Ascend again to more boulders, as the trail reaches another bench. Descending slightly, you can spot some of the Tenas Lakes peeking thorough the timber. Scott Mountain is in plain sight, high above you. At about the 2 mile-point you'll reach an intersection with Hand Lake Cutoff Trail

#3513.4(D) at the 5,400' level. The destination signs read: The Knobs, Scott Mountain and Tenas Lakes. Follow The Knobs goal, and continue, still on Benson Trail #3502. The trail continues for about 2.7 miles (that I didn't have a chance to ride, but I did ride a portion at the far end of the trail on a separate ride). Here is what I found on that separate ride, the last ½ mile of Benson Trail #3502 exits the intersection with Deer Butte Trail #3508, where the destination signs read: Robinson Lake, Road 2649, Trailhead and Tenas Lakes. Follow in the direction of the destination marked "Trailhead". Heading down to reach Forest Service Road 640, you'll ride through a clearing and down a switchback. Cross a spring, it is wild with waist-high ferns and flowers that vary in color from purples, white, yellows and reds. Benson Trail #3502 ends at gravel Forest Service Road 640.

Hand Lake Trail and the 3 Sisters Mountains

Deer Butte #3508

(To Benson Trail)

Distance:	9.2 Miles
Altitude:	3900'-4600'
Map:	Mount Washington Wilderness
Difficulty:	Moderate

Directions: Use the Robinson Lake Trailhead directions at the beginning of the chapter. The map reads Robinson Lake Trailhead, although Deer Butte Trail is the trail that leads out of this parking area and then connects to Robinson Lake Trail #3508.3(C). This trail can be accessed from Forest Service Road 676-2649, on the southern end of the trail.

Connecting Trails: 3508.3(C), 3513, 3502

Horse Camping: See the introduction to this chapter under Robinson Lake Camp.

Trail Description: Deer Butte Trail #3508 will be described from the north end, out of Robinson Lake Camp. The destination board at the trailhead reads Robinson Lake, just beyond that there is a trail signifying Deer Butte Trail #3508. A nice path takes you .3 mile to intersect with Robinson Lake Trail #3508.3(C), which leaves to the left. Continue up a slight incline, passing several seasonal ponds. Rhododendron plants and mossy boulders abound here. Cross a big gully, which was dry when we visited in August. There is a good size lake, Lake Kuitan, hidden just a few feet from the trail to the east. (To find the path, start looking for it past the deep gully, 4-5 beach ball size rocks, all in a row, mark the turn off to the lake. Be aware that there are logs down over the small path with no upkeep done to this trail, the shoreline is very brushy and the lake is lovely.) At the 3 mile-point Hand Lake Trail #3513 exits toward the southeast (left). This trail has ideal footing to this point. Deer Butte Trail #3508 climbs a mere 500' in the first 3 miles. The next 3.7 miles to Benson Trail #3502 rolls along, gaining several hundred feet more to reach the high-point of the trail at 4600'. Deer Butte Trail #3508 intermittently levels, climbs and descends passing in and out of the Mount Washington Wilderness Boundary. There are a few rocks in this section. The trail passes over several wash areas. Be watchful for holes in the trail. You can see where root-wad holes have claimed pieces of the trail, then laid to rest down the hillside, leaving behind narrow slices of trail to scale across. Next, a peaceful lake awaits you to water your trusty mount. We used this for a relaxing spot to lunch, the horses enjoyed it also, as the grass was thick, and the mosquitoes were NOT! The trail skims along the side of the lake with vague tread. Continue riding, passing bear grass and large timber, to attain view from atop a knoll of some mountains to the west. A long bridge over a mud area takes you to where Benson Trail #3502 crosses Deer Butte Trail. The signposts are destination signs, continue following the route that reads "Road 2649". The other two directions read "Trailhead" and "Tenas Lake" these are both Benson Trail #3502. To continue, be sure to add 2.5 miles to your ride, this section was not ridden on our trip. The trail ends at Forest Service Road 676, which is a small road off of Road 2649. Loops can be made in this area.

*HINT: Plan one night to have a potluck.

Sand Mountain Ride with Mount Jefferson in the backdrop

Hand Lake #3513

(From Hand Lake Trailhead north to Deer Butte Trail)

Distance:	7.4 Miles
Altitude:	4400'-5200'
Map:	Mount Washington Wilderness
Difficulty:	Moderate

Directions: To find the directions to this trailhead, look in the introduction to this chapter under Scott Lake Camp.

Connecting Trails: 3502, Hand Lake Shelter, 3513.4(D), 3508

Horse Cam ping: Primitive camping at a small turnaround at the trailhead, See Scott Lake Camp.

Trail Description: Hand Lake Trail #3513 goes both north and south from the trailhead, it was ridden to the north only for 7.4 miles ending at the intersection with Deer Butte Trail #3508. Ride in forest and along the west end of the massive Scott Lake. Lots of feed here. Ride through two meadows that were full of tiny little frogs when Madeleine and I visited in mid August. Then pass a third big meadow and ride in to the trees where you'll find a path marked with a destination sign, reading Road 242, with an arrow pointed to the east, this is Hand Lake Shelter Trail. Continue on to view a huge mud flat toward the east (right) it is the seasonal Hand Lake. It was a mere puddle in August. Wander along a forest made up of sticks, lined with bright green bear grass to reach the edge of a gigantic lava field. Go uphill slightly and cross a rocky wash area. The footing for the horses is a mixed bag of sand and lava rock. The views are behind you, so turn around and start clicking the camera. The Three Sisters Mountains names are Faith, Hope and Charity. There are many other mountains dwarfed at their feet. Go gently uphill and enter the timberland again, you will find a trail departing to the southwest in a sandy clearing. It had no sign when we rode this trail. A quick look at the map revealed it as Hand Lake Cutoff Trail #3513.4(D). Follow the arrow marked Bunch Grass Ridge still on Hand Lake Trail #3513. It becomes a less traveled trail from here on. I found this to be a delightful surprise. Heading up to reach the high-point of the trail atop a bench at 5,200'. A small depression may be wet and filled with tender green grass and insects. The mossy trees in this area have been sheared off by the stress of severe weather. I can't imagine why this wonderful little trail is so untouched by travelers. Ride 4-5 switchbacks down to pass some boulders as the trail rolls gently next to a rock wall off to the north. The path may be thick with low slung limbs in the next section. Head down slightly with tons of bear grass almost so thick that it claims the trail. Hand Lake Trail #3513 ends as it reaches a "T" intersection with Deer Butte Trail #3508. Loops available.

Josie n' Madeleine at Robinson Lake

Hand Lake Cutoff #3513.4(D)

Distance:	2.7 Miles
Altitude:	5200'-5800'
Map:	Mount Washington Wilderness
Difficulty:	Moderate

Directions: No trailhead. Access from either the north end, off Hand Lake Trail #3513, or from the south end, off Benson Trail #3502. See the directions to Scott Lake Camp in the introduction to this chapter for the closest access.

Connecting Trails: 3502, Scott Mountain Trail, 3513

Trail Description: Hand Lake Cutoff Trail #3513.4(D) can be ridden from either end. It will be described from the south end headed to the north end. Leaving the intersection of Benson Trail #3502, Hand Lake Cutoff Trail #3513.4(D) goes north. This trail leads up gently towards Scott Mountain Trail, over a ridge and back downhill gently to its end at the "T' intersection with Hand Lake Trail #3513, it is mostly in the forest. The trail begins on flat terrain in a small meadow, then ascends for a short way on rocky tread with a seasonal pond on the left. A switchback will take you higher with another pond and meadow to enjoy. Here you'll find skinny weathered trees. Climb another switchback and around some boulders, now on an open hillside, ride across a well-placed trail made of red lava cinders. Look over your right shoulder to see the Three Sisters Mountains toward the southeast. Next you'll see

Scott Mountain Trail going west, this is the high-point of the trail at 5,800'. The next 1.7 miles is a steady downward trek, passing open areas with several ponds, rocks, huckleberry bushes and grassy patches. The switchbacks are mild and are not shown on the map. Ride by even more ponds and the path mellows out to reach a "T" intersection with Hand Lake Trail #3513, which goes southeast and northwest. Here the destination sign reads, Bunchgrass Ridge, with an arrow toward the west, and Hand Lake with an arrow toward the east, there is no sign indicating Hand Lake Cutoff Trail #3513.4(D), but since you just rode it, you know where it goes!

View of Mount Washington through the observatory window

Old Santiam Wagon Road #3413 (Road 810)

Distance:	3 Miles
Altitude:	4600'-4600'
Maps	Mount Washington Wilderness
Difficulty:	Moderate

Directions: Use the directions to Santiam Pass in the introduction to this chapter.

Connecting Trails: Sand Mountain Lookout Ride
   Horse Camping: Use the directions to Santiam Camp at the beginning of this chapter.

Trail Description: This 3-mile section of the Old Santiam Wagon Road Trail #3413 (Road 810) will be described going west from Forest Service Road 2690, near Big Lake and ends on the north side of Sand Mountain. Be advised that this can be a very busy place teaming with motor bikes and quad runners, as well as equestrians, especially on the weekends in mid-summer. In August Madeleine and I found the area very dry, sandy and sunny. This is a rolling road with views of Hayrick Butte (looks like he got a crew-cut hair do), Hoodoo Butte (ski area), Sand Mountain (old lookout site), Mount Washington and the Three Sisters Mountains. You'll travel through some old clear--cut areas and lots of sand, ranging in colors from tan to black. You will pass a road and wooden sign leading to the Sand Mountain Lookout ride. If it's a hot day, consider going in the early morning or perhaps make it an evening ride, thus avoiding the heat, as this ride has hardly any shade.

Josie watches some swimmers at Tennas Lake

Scott Mountain Trail with the 3 Sisters Mountains in the background

Deer Butte Trail – Josie and Ali enjoy the tall pines

Patjens #3395

Distance:	5.5 Miles
Altitude:	4644'-4800'
Map:	Mount Washington Wilderness
Difficulty:	Moderate

Directions: Use the directions to Santiam Pass at the introduction to this chapter. At the end of Forest Service Road 2690, follow the signs to Big Lake and Patjens Trailhead. There is a small turnout on the right to park, although it is usually full of boat trailers. I suggest you ride your horse to this trailhead via the connecting roads. Just before the lake, you can turn either way onto the Old Santiam Wagon Road 810 or Road 811 (both ways are dirt roads). There are spots to park alongside these roads, be aware the terrain is sandy and you may get stuck if you pull off too far.

Connecting Trails: 3522 (abandoned), unmarked trail to youth camp

Horse Cam ping*:* See Santiam Camp listed at the introduction to this chapter.

Sand Mountain Lookout Ride, Mount Washington in the background

Trail Description: Patjens Trail #3395 is a 5.5 mile loop. It is located on the west edge of Big Lake, it goes around two small mountains. It will be described from the north end. At the Patjens Trailhead, you can catch a glimpse of Mount Washington towards the south, sticking out of the ground like an old apple core. This trail is all in timber with tons of bear grass on the forest floor. At the trailhead you'll probably hear a roar emanating from powerboats on Big Lake. This trail has excellent footing with hardly any rocks or roots. Patjens Trail #3395 starts above the "people" campground for Big Lake, the first ¼ mile takes you to the loop's beginning, turn right (west). On the side of the trail, there sets a big green swampy meadow that stretches lazily. The path climbs slightly, then down to intersect the unsigned abandoned, Pocket Way Trail #3522. Begin a short climb where the trail has been lined with water bars, placed across the tread to help with erosion. The path levels a bit as it reaches the Mount Washington Wilderness Boundary sign and a reminder sign (a picture of a bike with a line across it meaning "NO BIKES"). Continue up to a saddle for a quick view of one of the Three Sisters Mountains. Ride down the south side of the saddle on a deeply worn trail, crossing a field of emerald green ferns and then flatting out to meet the first of the Patjens Lakes on the right. Madeleine and I were able to get our horses a drink here. The shore may be a bit soggy. The forest has a mixture of snags and evergreen trees. Approach a second lake as the trail smoothes out with a big meadow on the left. The biggest lake is situated with a nice watering spot on its stable rock shoreline. This section of Patjens Trail #3395 has sandy footing. Ride slightly uphill to leave the solitude of the Wilderness and reach the immense Big Lake. There is an unmarked path that exits to the right (east) and goes to the youth camp. Views of Mount Washington towards the south can be seen from this angle along Big Lake's sandy shore. Depart from the lake's shoreline, a switchback takes you down, then levels only to go up again on several more switchbacks to reappear at the beginning of your loop. Retrace your hoof prints back to the trailhead. This is a delightful stroll.

Lookout tower at Sand Mountain

Robinson Lake #3508.3(C)

Distance:	¼ Mile
Altitude:	3900'-3900'
Map:	Mount Washington Wilderness
Difficulty:	Moderate

Directions: No trailhead. Access from Deer Butte Trail #3508. Use the Robinson Lake Trailhead directions listed at the beginning of this chapter.

Connecting Trails: 3508

Horse Cam ping: See Robinson Lake Camp listed at the introduction to this chapter.

Trail Description: Robinson Lake Trail #3508.3 can be located .3 mile from Deer Butte Trailhead. The trail is only ¼ mile long. It is all in forest and climbs slightly to reach Robinson Lake. There may be some logs down over the trail. Have a refreshing swim, the water is warm and the sun feels good on a hot August day after a long ride. During the week you can get some solitude. The shoreline may be receded enough to walk around the entire lake.

*HINT: Use a magnetic "Hide-A-Key" with trailer and truck keys hidden at the rig case of emergency.

Big Lake with Mount Washington in the back

Madeleine and Josie ride the trail

Monarch butterflies migrating

*Top of Dee Wright
Observatory*

*Bottom – Base Camp near
Big Lake at Santiam Pass*

Sand Mountain Lookout

Distance:	1.5 Miles, then hike for 1.3 Miles
Altitude:	4600'-5459'
Map:	Mount Washington Wilderness
Difficulty:	Moderate

Directions: I'm not recommending the Old Santiam Wagon Road Trail #3413 (Road 810) be driven to its starting point, due to deep sand and bumps in the road. Access by riding the Old Santiam Wagon Road to Road 810-2690, there is a wooden sign describing the Sand Mountain Lookout Area at this crossroads. Ride the Old Santiam Wagon Road Trail listed for this chapter to reach this point.

Connecting Trails: 3413 (Road 810)

Trail Description: Sand Mountain Lookout is a ride and hike adventure. From the intersection of Old Santiam Wagon Road #3413 (Road 810), take Road 810-2690 it is flat at first, then climbs on a one lane road to the parking area that is fenced to keep horses and motorized vehicles out. The footing for your horses is nice and soft, it is a sand and dirt mix to ride in, to reach this parking area. Either take turns holding the animals to finish the adventure by hiking around the crater and lookout, or tie up your mounts and go for the hike. Do not attempt to take your horses into this area for the lookout is manned and they <u>are watching</u>! The hike goes up a couple hundred feet on an old road and becomes trail to reach the tower. Another trail will take you south to a fenced view area, go through a designated opening in the fence and begin a trip around the crater that is over 1,500 feet deep. The trail makes a circle around the rim and then goes back down to catch the old road again (at a different spot than you came up) travel back to the parking area. The views are awesome and the crater is surprisingly deep and is made of cinder. The surrounding mountains are the Three Sisters, Hoodoo and Hayrick Buttes, Mount Washington and Mount Jefferson. This is a "must see" for this region.

Scott Mountain

Distance:	½ Mile
Altitude:	5800'-6116'
Map:	Mount Washington Wilderness
Difficulty:	Moderate

Directions: No trailhead. Access from Hand Lake Cutoff Trail #3513.4(D). The closest trailhead is Scott Lake. For more information read Scott Lake Camp listed in the introduction to this chapter.

Connecting Trails: 3513.4(D)

Trail Description: Scott Mountain Trail begins from Hand Lake Cutoff Trail #3513.4(D) and goes west to the top of Scott Mountain and the old lookout site. Ride up the path through a small field of flowers mixed with boulders. The trail begins its ascent to the top by way of switchbacks. The trail evens out for a while and climbs again. The trees are weathered here. Stop to see the view of Three Fingered Jack Mountain, switchback again to a level area on a knoll, with trees and an open area. Go the final grunt to the grassy top and the old lookout site. Here you'll get a panorama of a portion of the Cascade Mountain Range. There is excellent footing, although I'd bet it's slick when it is wet. The amount of mountains to identify from the top of Scott Mountain is endless. Here are a few we saw: The Three Sisters, Husband, Mount Washington, Three Fingered Jack, Belknap Crater, Twin Craters, Yapoo Crater, Little Brother, Sand Mountain, Hoodoo Butte, Mount Jefferson and possibly Mount Hood (it was pretty smoky with nearby forest fires when Madeleine and I visited). You can also see the huge lava fields, McKenzie Pass and McKenzie River drainage, and a lot of lakes below. Scott Mountain Trail is an exhilarating experience.

Madeleine and her mare

Dee Wright Observatory

Mount Washington

Tenas Lakes #3502.3(C)

Distance:	1 Mile
Altitude:	5400'-5400'
Map:	Mount Washington Wilderness
Difficulty:	Moderate

Directions: No Trailhead. Access from Benson Trail #3502. The closest trailhead is Scott Lake, look under Scott Lake Camp in the beginning of this chapter for more information.

Connecting Trails: 3502

Trail Description: Tenas Lakes Trail #3502.3(C) is a short side trail that leads towards the most beautiful lakes. The edge of the first lake is a rocky ledge, there were people swimming in the deep aquamarine pool below, it was so hot we wanted to join them. We continued on our trek and let them have their peace and quiet. If you are in the area, these lakes are worth the few feet off the trail to come to see. Tenas means "little" and they are truly little gems of the forest.

*Note: On the map Tenas is spelled two ways, Tennas and Tenas.

Otter

The Ochoco National Forest is located in Central Oregon. The word "Ochoco" has many possible meanings. It may mean the Indian word for "willow", another thought is, that it refers to a Snake Indian or Northern Paiute chief. Others say it was in reference to Chief Ochoco, because Ochoco Creek is located near where his camp use to be. I think it means "Time to ride". The canyons and rocks are filled with rich history of long ago camps, sacred grounds, old wagon roads, mines and cabins as well as old lookout sites. These are fragile things that must be respected at all times. There are an overflow of streams, and reservoirs for fishing and swimming. The creeks may be low in the late summer and fall due to the desert climate. This is where the mule deer and the antelope play, as well as the elk. There is a wild horse range not too far from Bandit Springs area. Bandit Springs is the region I will be describing for you. There are loads of trails to ride on from base camp, the endurance riders have a 30 mile loop and a 25 mile loop going out from this camp. Also, there are several Wilderness and National Forests close by, with regular Forest Service Trails to ride. I rode this area in the early fall with two close friends, Terri and Judy. All of us have ridden endurance races before and were interested in riding some of the current trails. Often times we have gone to a territory where an endurance race has been held and followed their tracks and sometimes their ribbons!

Directions to Bandit Springs Camp: Drive from Highway 97 at Madras and turn southeast on Highway 26, it is about 50 miles to camp from here. Go through the town of Prineville, and pass Ochoco Reservoir. In about 6 miles or so, the road splits with Road 23, stay to the left, still on 26, and go uphill. Just beyond mile-marker 48 is your turn. Turn right onto gravel Road 2630 (Marks Creek Sno Park). You are about 28 miles from Prineville. Drive 2 miles to a big meadow with an old pole fence around it. Go in on a small Road 201 (the number is vertical on the little sign) and park on the far side of the old fence at the back of the meadow. The road ends here, beyond the meadow it becomes a trail. This is a wide-open spot. Park where it feels good and level.

The Camp: The setting is under the boughs of huge ponderosa pine and in a big long meadow. The camping is primitive, bring water, there is a stream at the entrance to the meadow for stock water, but I would suggest you bring some in case it is dry for some reason. Check ahead for fire restrictions, and as always spread the manure thin so it will blow away, and pack out all garbage.

Northwest Forest Parking Passes are available at Forest Service offices, they are required at designated trailheads.

Ride your horses hard, treat them right and enjoy the rewards...

| Prineville Ranger District |
| 3160 NE 3rd Street |
| Prineville, Oregon 97754 |
| 541-416-6500 |

Fall ride

Bandit Springs

Distance:	6 Miles
Altitude:	5100'-5400'
Map:	Ochoco National Forest/
	Crooked River National Grassland
Difficulty:	Moderate

Directions: Follow directions given in the introduction to this chapter for Bandit Springs Camp.

Horse Camping: See the introduction to this chapter for information.

Trail Description: This trail is not on any Forest Service map as of yet. It is a small taste of the trail that the endurance riders use for their races. The trail is pretty well used and is not hard to spot, but there are cattle ranging in the area and they have their own ideas about trails so there are many crisscrossing paths in the area. We had a limited time to explore here and so this is just a sample to get you started. Go up the main gravel Road 2630, to the right, out of camp past the meadow you are camped in. Ride about ½ mile and turn left, at the 2nd old two-track road. Stay on this two-track for 1 mile or so. When the road bends to the left you'll see a trail on the right, take it. Ride on the trail through the woods and across a wet area, skirt meadows and ride slightly uphill and cross a gravel road. Continue on the trail on the far side of the road and to a cattle guard (If he is sleeping, wake him up!). Go through a gate and hang to the right, still on trail. At the next old road, cross it and then ride left on another old 2-track road, ride it for ¾ mile, then proceed to the right on a trail. Keep going until you see a little creek, cross it, stay on the trail and go right at a two-track. Cross a paved road and go to a gravel pit, you'll find water at the end of the pit. Ride around to the right side of the willows and up a gravel trail to meet a dirt trail. We had to turn around at this point due to daylight. If you want to continue, follow these directions. Hang right onto a dirt road. Stay on this road for 1 ¾ mile. Watch for a trail to the left, you are now in the wild horse area, the trail is light in this area, but will take you out to a road, this is where the first vet check is held when there is a race being held. We were told later that this is where the scenery starts to get wonderful, I guess we'll just have to go back to ride the rest of the 30-mile loop!

"WHAT IN THE... HAPPENED HERE?"

My friends, Judy, Terri and I, were tacking up to go on a ride. Just before we left, I remembered that I would need another bale of hay open for the night's feeding. I decided to climb up on my horse trailer and let a bale bounce down. You never can tell it may be dark when we return. We saddled up and rode our ride. Upon returning we noticed a lot of cattle had come to camp. Well, they not only came; they had eaten the entire bale of hay! It is a good thing to bring extra hay, sometimes it gets wet, other times it may bounce off the truck and now I know UN-invited guests may even eat it! We had some good laughs over this one as we had to watch our step around camp; they had left some cow patties for dessert!

Josie

Camp

171

Terri waters her arab

Rabbit

Snake

Owl

Coyote

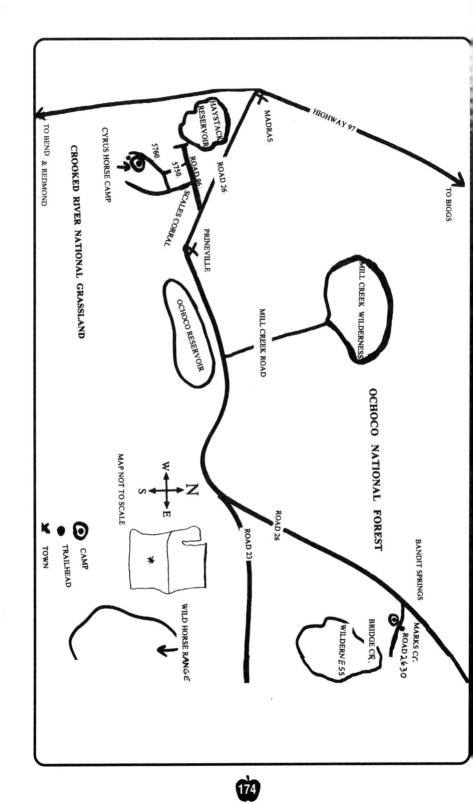

CROOKED RIVER NATIONAL GRASSLAND
Cyrus Horse Camp

Cyrus Springs is located in the Grassland of Central Oregon. My friend Judy and I found the riding here astounding. It is a combination of cross-country, unmarked trails and old roads. There are gates to go through and water troughs to visit. The panorama of the Cascade Mountain Range is splendid. The Three Sisters, Mount Jefferson, Three Finger Jack, Bachelor Butte, and Broken Top are the largest mountains you'll see. Also visible are Haystack Reservoir, Haystack Mountain, and Gray Butte. Some wildlife includes antelope, deer, coyote, and last but not least slow elk (cattle). If you're not sure where to start to ride in this wide-open country there is usually a fellow camper around waiting for you to pick their brain. Or just start out to the south of camp by the gate, and head around the hill, towards the south, I don't think you could get lost here. There are days of riding in this area. Some people come here to drive their buggies or carts, as the roads are sloped gentle enough for this. Others exercise their endurance horses. There is an abundance of trail riders, and of course there are those who just bask in the lawn chair. Volunteer efforts by equine groups, The Prineville Ridge Riders and The Columbia Gorge Back Country Horsemen of Oregon keep this camp "fee free" so be sure to pack all garbage out and move droppings to the manure site.

Directions to Camp: Drive from Highway 97 at Madras and turn southeast on Highway 26 to just beyond milepost 11. Turn right on a gravel Road 96 where the sign reads Gray Butte TH, Scales Corral, Haystack Reservoir and Haystack Mountain. Go past Scales Corral, turn left at the next road, which is at the 2.8 mile point, onto dirt Forest Service Road 5750. Stay on Road 5750 for 1.1 mile more. Watch for a small brown sign with white lettering, "Cyrus Horse Camp" is on the left side of the road.

Cyrus Horse Camp: There is no real set place to park, just pull in where you want, if it is hot, head for the trees! There are 5 corrals, one camp has 3 and the rest have 4 stalls to a set. There is a water spigot in a fenced area with a trough. Bring potable water. It is a spacious camp with scrub pine and tall deciduous trees. Of course there is lots of grassland and sagebrush in this area, and you can see forever. The camp makes a big loop. There are picnic tables, an outhouse, and take your garbage home with you.

Map: Ochoco National Forest & Crooked River National Grassland

Northwest Forest Parking Passes are available at Forest Service offices, they are required at designated trailheads.

Find joy in the small things in life...

Crooked River National Grassland
813 SW Highway 97
Madras, Oregon 97741
541-416-6640

Judy on a trail behind Cyrus Horse Camp

Fawn

MOUNT SAINT HELENS AREA

The Mount Saint Helens territory is located in the southwest corner of Washington State in the Gifford Pinchot National Forest. A figure "8" of main trails were ridden by my friend Sandy and I in the fall of 2002. All of the trails are in the "Moderate" rating and are in timber, except for the viewpoints and there are an abundance of those! Also ridden were a couple of ski trails that worked grand for trail riding and one other trail leading to an old lookout site to the northeast of Mount Saint Helens. Time ran short so the 8.5 mile Cinnamon Peak Trail wasn't ridden this trip. A new trail was getting its finishing touches (rock blasting) and will be open soon. It is called "Fossil Trail". Expect to ride over sand, volcanic rocks, lava fields, dried mudslide areas, and rushing creeks. Along the trails you'll see waterfalls, old growth forests, lakes and great views of the blown volcano of Mount Saint Helens, she stands at 8,363' tall. After a large earthquake the mountain erupted Sunday morning May 18, 1980. Fifty-seven people died or were missing. Part of the north side of the mountain fell into Spirit Lake. Once she popped, ash and hot gas rose up to 15 miles above the earth, walls of cement-like mud flowed, laced with huge rocks ripping apart everything in its path. Hundreds of homes were lost, over 50 thousand acres of land was leveled and 230 square miles of timberland was knocked over. Mount Saint Helens Mountain shrunk 1,300 feet and lost tons of weight that day! Some of the surrounding hills look as though it happened just yesterday, barren and bleak. On the other end of the spectrum, a lot of the area is covered with new growth trees, tall plants and animal life abounds. The Backcountry Horsemen of Washington and The Washington Trail Riders Association volunteers made the Kalama Horse Camp become a reality. There are two nice loops. The newest is the lower loop, it was dedicated in 2000 in honor of Lorri Bisconer who worked with the U. S. Forest Service. Honored in the top loop is Wayne Parsons, who worked at the Gifford Pinchot National Forest for 14 years. The camp is the most beautiful camp I have ever seen. It is secluded from civilization in a cave of deep evergreens, moss and ferns with fragrant mountain air! The only sounds are of laughter and chitchat of like-minded horse enthusiasts, as only horse camping is permitted here.

Kalama Horse Camp-There are two large paved loops with the majority of spaces being drive-through, the island in the middle of each loop is designed for single rig, back-in sites. Over 20 spots are available to camp at, and there are two water troughs, one at each loop. A horse "rolling area", complete with hitching rails is located at the top loop by the trailhead. Next to that is a horseshoe pit, try it out just for fun. Big group areas are equipped to accommodate several rigs with high-line hitches, and there is a day parking area near the horseshoe pit and trailhead. There are assisted mounting areas, nice clean outhouses, and fire pits with grates and tables. A massive log cabin that has lots of windows sets in the middle of the top loop. Inside you'll find a cozy wood stove and a large wood picnic table. Each site has corrals topped with a line you can drape a tarp on for cover from the elements for those hard working steeds. There is a stock ramp. Manure dump areas are abundant, complete with camp wheelbarrows and rakes. The Kalama River runs behind camp. The camp setting is under tall timber and has thick undergrowth; it is cool and calming.

Directions to camp-If coming from the west off of I-5, you'll turn at the town of Woodland and take Highway 503, head east toward the town of Cougar. Then drive up Forest Service Road 81 (8100) to Kalama Horse Camp. If you are contemplating coming in from the northeast through Randle, you'll be better off taking Highway 12 all the way to I-5. It is easier than coming in from Road 25 and 90, then to 81/8100 to camp. It is very winding and slow! I suggest the same advice for coming from the south or east. Take Highway 14, drive west along the Columbia River to I-5 north and up, it is much quicker. I have researched every way in and out.

Northwest Forest Parking Passes are available at Forest Service offices, they are required at designated trailheads.

Get the camera ready....

Cowlitz Valley Ranger District	Mt. Adams Ranger District
10024 U.S. Highway 12	2455 Highway 141
P.O. Box 670	Trout Lake, WA 98650
Randle, WA 98377	509-395-3400
360-497-1100	

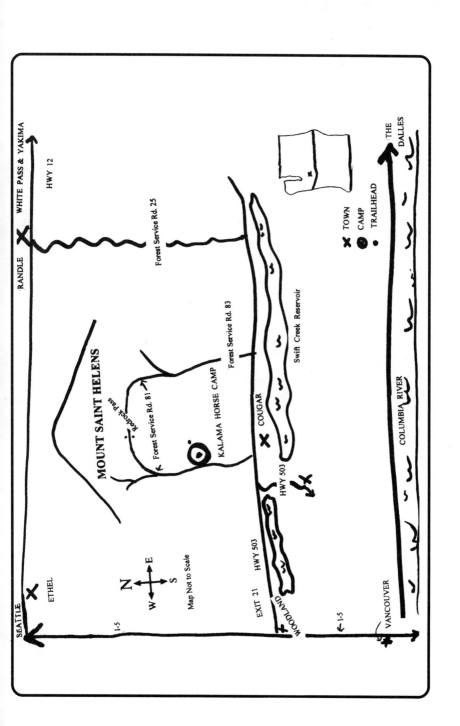

Sandy on Toutle Trail

View of Mount Saint Helens from Blue Horse Trail

Blue Horse #237

Distance:	5.5 Miles
Altitude:	2300'-3800'
Map:	Gifford Pinchot National Forest
Difficulty:	Moderate

Directions: Blue Horse Trail #237 begins from Toutle Trail #238.

Connecting Trails: 238, 231

Horse Camping: Kalama Horse Camp, see description of camp at the beginning of this chapter.

Trail Description: Blue Horse Trail #237 starts off of Toutle Trail #238, approximately 3 miles from Kalama Horse Camp. Leave Toutle Trail #238 and the Kalama River on an old road, which is the way Blue Horse Trail #237, begins. Ride north straight as an arrow for a mile or so, through an incredible old growth area with 300' tall noble fir trees, cross Forest Service Road 8100, there are trail signs here. Now the trail narrows to become a trail. The footing on the path is a variation of rock and sand, to deep sand. The trees go from enormous to sparse, skinny, lodge pole pines. There is a "V" in the trail and we stayed to the main looking one on the left and found we were on track, another trail joined later, Sandy and I suspected that it was the other end of the stray trail, however we can't say for sure. Cross Kalama Ski Trail #231, which is also signed. Continue north, rocks and ashes are what

Ali gets set to cross a rigid lava flow

you ride over here as the trail continues up through sparse, thin trees. Crossover Toutle Trail #238, the trail is rolling with more volcanic ash and some stony spots. Pass lots of huckleberry bushes that have cranberry red coloring in the fall, they cover the hills. Come to a somewhat challenging dry mudflow area with a small stream. Time for the camera! Here is an excellent area to water your livestock, then cross the water to meet a maze of large boulders. Make your way up, then across, (not straight across) this gray landscape. The views of Mount Staint Helens will take your mind off of the task of getting over this rock-mound graveyard. Follow the rock cairns, not the ribbons, (those are for boulder--jumping hikers) the prize is getting out of this colossal wash and back into the forest, off the rocks. I am sure your horse will be grateful too. We were thankful to whoever put up the rock cairns to guide people across this wash. Blue Horse Trail #237 never touches the shore of Blue Lake, although it is close by. Rise up on 1 switchback to a saddle in the mountain, then lower down on 1 switchback to an overgrown road and turn north (right), (left dead ends). There is no sign to guide you here. Ride up this old road. Notice the soft slouchy edges of the path with the trees suspended off the side, dangling by the hair of their roots. An odd sight in the woods, is a solar panel on a long pole in amongst the timber. There is a small clearing at the next "T" Intersection. This is Huckleberry Pass and the end of Blue Horse Trail #237. Here there is a destination sign. To the left it reads Blue Lake Trailhead 2 miles, to the right it reads Sheep Canyon ¾ mile. This is Toutle Trail #238. Loops are possible using this connecting trail.

River crossing

Kalama Ski #231

(To Blue Horse Trail)

Distance:	3 Miles
Altitude:	2300'-2600'
Map:	Gifford Pinchot National Forest
Difficulty:	Moderate

Directions: Kalama Ski Trail can be accessed from either Toutle or Blue Horse Trails.

Connecting Trails: 238, 238.2(B), 237

Horse Camping: Kalma Horse Camp, see description of camp at the beginning of this chapter.

Trail Description: Kalama Ski Trail #231 and Toutle Trail #238 have the same trailhead and share the first few feet of trail. Kalama Ski Trail exits Toutle Trail a few minutes from Kalama Horse Camp. The trailhead is located on the east side of the horse camp, by the day parking area and water trough. Head down and cross a small bridge over a creek, Cinnamon Trail #238.2(B) departs to the right. Kalama

Josie and Ali on Blue Horse Trail

Ski Trail #231 leaves to the left; there are ski symbols in the trees to mark the route. Ride above the Kalama River on a ridge, although you won't be able to see the river. Meet back with Toutle Trail #238 at an unmarked "Y" in the trail. It gets a bit confusing here. Your first option is to ride up taking the trail to the right, which is the closest path to the river, this is Toutle Trail #238, follow it. Then at an intersection that has a sign for Kalama Ski Trail #238, turn left. The second option is, continue on this path furthest from the river, to the left at the unmarked intersection and follow the path along a small ridge in dense forest. Eventually the 2 portions of the ski trail connect to become one trail. Cross an old road, then cross Road 8100. Proceed to a large parking area and you'll find the trail to the far right. Going uphill gradually, this trail becomes an old road that is a pleasure to ride. The trail becomes thinner again and connects to Blue Horse Trail #237, where you'll find a sign. Kalama Ski Trail #238 keeps going, however, it looked like it was not being used by equestrians, no hoof prints. We turned here to make a loop anyway.

View of a waterfall from Sheep Canyon Trail

Blue Horse Trail, Mount Saint Helens recovering mud slide area

Blast area from Sheep Canyon Trail

Sheep Canyon #240

(To waterfall view)

Distance:	½ Mile
Altitude:	3700'-3800'
Map:	Gifford Pinchot National Forest
Difficulty:	Moderate

Directions: Use Toutle Trail #238 to reach this point.

Connecting Trail: 238

Trail Description: Sheep Canyon Trail #240, goes to a view of a waterfall and is only ½ mile long or so, and is well worth seeing. From the intersection of Toutle Trail #238 head left (downhill) to a small rock outcropping that you can see from above. Follow next to a deep gully on the right-hand side with rushing white water spilling into Sheep Canyon. The river is quite loud here. Ride along a hillside that is in open brush. The trail is good and the view is superb of both the falls and the canyon below, you'll also be able to see Mount Saint Helens above the falls. Her volcanic blast area is in front of you on the next set of stark ridges. Take note that Sheep Canyon Trail #240 is open only in this direction to livestock and you are allowed to ride down to the trailhead if you wish. We turned around after taking a video and snaps of the area.

Lava field

Strawberry Lookout Ride #220

Distance:	7 Miles
Altitude:	2200'-5464'
Map:	Gifford Pinchot National Forest
Difficulty:	Moderate

Directions: West of the town of Randle on Highway 12, take Road 25 south. Between milepost 17 and 18 turn onto Forest Service Road 2516, either park along Road 25 or drive ¼ mile up to the end of the pavement to a small turnout. The road past this point has big swells that are not recommended for trailers.

Connecting Trails: Old and new Strawberry Mountain Trail #220

Horse Camping: Primitive camping at the turnout.

Trail Description: Strawberry Mountain Lookout Ride is a combination of road and part of the old Strawberry Mountain Trail #220, and the Lookout Spur Trail. Ride the rough Forest Service Road 2516 for 6 of the 7 miles. It is a pleasant ride with lots to see. You'll ride up 3,200 feet total from the parking area. The road is primitive for the most part and the footing is pretty good. The views along the road are of Mount Adams and the blast areas of Mount Saint Helens. At about the 5 to 6 mile-point you will find a small parking area. This is where Strawberry Mountain Trail #220 comes across the road. The newly routed trail goes downhill on an old logging road, marked with a sketch and poem on a post, forget this trail. Continue up on the road, pass an old sign that reads "ROAD CLOSED", it is half buried in debris. Here you can see why the road is closed to motorized traffic. The road is deteriorating off the shelf it was originally put on. The trail begins on the right side of this road, it is marked by logs used to reinforce the trail keeping it where it belongs! There is an old sign in the tree. A single switchback takes you up to a ridge on nice wide and smooth trail. The forest is deep and quiet here. The snow level in the winter can be measured by looking at the distance between the ground and where the moss is hanging from the tree. I would estimate it to be about 15 to 20 feet of snow in the winter. Ride this ridge that offers a few re-routes here and there to an open saddle. The old trail continues on an open ridge to the east and south. This is where you go west, (right) uphill to the old lookout site on top of the knoll on the Lookout Spur Trail. Views are of Mount Hood, Mount Adams, Mount Saint Helens and Mount Rainer, as well as Strawberry Lake below. The lookout trail climbs in stages from this point. At the top of the first level you'll find a flat area with two old blue propane tanks. You can either hike the rest, or continue on a scramble up a brushy, sandy soft hill to reach the old lookout. The old lookout site has a panoramic view of the area. Way below you, you'll see where the new re-routed trail goes to Strawberry Lake. I think it looks boring compared to this trail. You can also see the old trail clinging to the razor back ridge to the east and south from this perspective. The red bushes truly do resemble strawberries from here. Bring a saw and call ahead for trail information. This location is marked on the map and reads as "Strawberry Mtn. Viewpoint"

"THERE IS A SHELF LIFE"

After returning from Strawberry Mountain, I was reviewing the pictures that Madeleine and I had taken on my digital camera. They were awesome, the day was crisp and clean and we had several pictures that the hikers had snapped for us, with Mount Saint Helens, Mount Rainier and Mount Adams in the backdrop. I turned off the camera and when I returned to open the floppy to print the pictures, it wouldn't open! Turns out that there is a shelf life on floppy discs (zip discs too) this was news to me. **Pass it on**, burn your pictures onto a CD, it is much safer to store that way!

Josie

"Weasel"

Toutle #238

Distance:	10 Miles
Altitude:	2300'-3800'
Map:	Gifford Pinchot National Forest
Difficulty:	Moderate

Directions: Use the directions to camp in the introduction to this chapter.
Connecting Trails: 238.2(B), 238.1(A), 237, 231, 240

Horse Camping: Kalama Horse Camp, see description of camp at the beginning of this chapter. Or camp at primitive spots along Road 81-8100.

Trail Description: Toutle Trail #238 and Kalama Ski Trail #231 have the same trailhead and share the first few feet of trail. The trailhead is located on the east side of the horse camp by the day parking area and water trough. Head down and cross a small bridge over a creek. Cinnamon Trail #238.2(B) departs to the right. The Kalama Ski Trail #231 exits left cross a small bridge over a seasonal flow. Follow the path going eastward alongside the Kalama River in dense forest with soft easy footing for the horses. Switchback up to meet one of the trail options to ride Kalama Ski Trail again, which is unmarked at this point also. Keep on the trail closest to the river and be on your way, for this is Toutle Trail #238. Ride the ridge above the Kalama River. Go over some rocks here and there on rolling terrain with a steep slide area next to you. Kalama River is noisily scurrying along below (a section of the old trail is abandoned now and has been re-worked farther from the slide area). Here is another trail option to catch Kalama Ski Trail #231, it has a sign this time. Ride behind some camps, which are located off Road 81-8100, as the trail parallels this road. Cross Road 8122, still in deep woods with sandy gray ash footing. There is a spot along the river to get your horses into for a drink. Blue Horse Trail #237 exits on an old road to the left at about the 3 mile-point, and is signed. Ride the opposite way on this same road (to the right) and cross a big culvert to catch the trail again on the left side of the road. Ride along with the river now on your left-hand side. The first views of Mount Saint Helens await you as you come closer to Mc Bride Lake. This next 1 ¾ mile of trail is somewhat more challenging, as it climbs it will cling to the mountain with steep terrain below. After riding the south side of McBride Lake you'll encounter some wet spots and small

189

culverts to cross. Meet with Cinnamon Trail #238.2(B) as it descends from above you and head down to cross Road 81-8100. This area is known as Redrock Pass, there is a small parking spot here. Enter another world as you switchback up onto a lava flow frozen in time. Ride across the pumice stone. The ground sounds hollow and a bit mysterious as your steed's hooves make their way safely across the moonscape. I think this is the best spot, on this trail for a picture of Mount Saint Helens! Have no fear, the trail is good and solid ground is just ahead in a bear grass meadow filled with huckleberry bushes, draped with red and purple berries. The leaves are brilliant in the fall with rich ruby, gold and green colors. Continue straight at the next 4-way intersection that has a big sign. (If you were inclined to wander off the trail here, you would find that one of the trails to the left is the **old** Toutle Trail. There is an old wooden sign in a tree, it is now a ski trail (maybe it is the far end of Kalama Ski Trail?), anyway, it has lots of logs down and by the looks of it, it is rarely used and we don't recommend it. All the other trails dead end.) Continue on Toutle Trail #238 now headed north. Still in forest, the trail goes around a knoll and down to cross a seasonal wash and up again using 1 switchback. Blue Camp Trail #238.1(A) departs to the right (east). Ride up on a mound of cinder and note the gray ash here on the hillside left over from Mount Saint Helens eruption,

no doubt. Cross a couple water spots and another culvert. Rolling terrain, and views of surrounding mountains take you onward through a brushy, rocky wash area, with a nice view of the mountain. The trees grow straight out of the rocks; it's so amazing. Do you think they'd do that if you tried planting them like that at home? NOT! Go slightly downhill as Blue Horse Trail #237 crosses here. This is about the 7 mile-point. It can be dry and dusty on this section of trail. There are a few rocks here also. In ½ mile you reach the Blue Lake Trailhead, which most any size rig can fit in, it is huge with lots

Sheep Canyon

of room to negotiate. Catch the trail on the far side of the parking lot. The next 3 miles are in lush green forest, with great footing. The views of Mount Saint Helens are excellent. There are some drop-off spots, although the trail is wide enough for any seasoned trail horse. First ford Cold Springs Creek. In the fall this area looks like it has snowed yellow from the shedding needles of the tamarack trees limbs above. Ride above Blue Lake, which looked mighty green to us. Contour around several draws, cross a culvert. Meander along with a stop in a small meadow for a rest or a photo session with Mount Saint Helens. Ride up on gentle terrain to intersect with Blue Horse Trail #237 at Huckleberry Pass (the signs here are destination signs), continue straight towards Sheep Canyon, Toutle Trail is not done yet. Go down ¾ mile next to a gully with the help of 1 switchback to reach another intersection, and a camp, and the end of the description of Toutle Trail #238. This is where Sheep Canyon Trail #240 "T" intersects and is "hiker only" going towards the right. You may turn left riding on Sheep Canyon Trail #240 to view a waterfall in less than a ½ mile, see Sheep Canyon Trail for details. (There is a way across the canyon on a bridge, although it is a "hiker only" trail also.) A figure "8" using Blue Horse Trail #237 is a favorite ride for a lot of horse enthusiasts.

Madeleine at Mount Saint Helens

TIETON AREA

My friend Sandy and I delved into the Tieton Area one summer looking for trails to ride. It is located in Central Washington, near Rimrock Lake. From White Pass, go east on Highway 12 to reach Rimrock Lake. From Yakima, travel west on Highway 12 toward White Pass to reach Rimrock Lake. I found this part of the Tieton area to be pretty quiet during the week. It offers some rugged country to ride. Some of the old trails are now 4-wheel drive roads. They are quite a challenge to ride. The 4-wheelers must winch themselves up some steep cliff areas; it's a scramble on the horses. Be prepared to ride cross-country when the paths are impassable. This is not an area to bring beginner riders, unless you stick to the main Forest Service roads to ride. We took note of the available primitive camp spots along the roadside. It was a hoot!

Northwest Forest Parking Passes are available at Forest Service offices, they are required at designated trailheads.

Make tracks to the trailhead...

Naches Ranger District
10237 Highway 12
Naches, WA 98937
509-653-2205

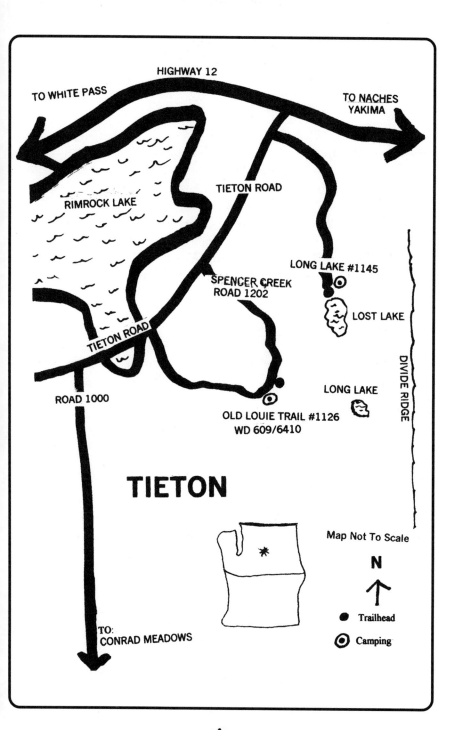

TO WHITE PASS

HIGHWAY 12

TO NACHES
YAKIMA

TIETON ROAD

RIMROCK LAKE

LONG LAKE #1145

SPENCER CREEK
ROAD 1202

LOST LAKE

TIETON ROAD

LONG LAKE

ROAD 1000

OLD LOUIE TRAIL #1126
WD 609/6410

DIVIDE RIDGE

TIETON

Map Not To Scale

N

● Trailhead

◉ Camping

TO:
CONRAD MEADOWS

Long Lake #1145

Distance:	1.9 Miles
Altitude:	3800'-4300'
Map:	GTM 304 Rimrock
Difficulty:	Moderate

Directions: If coming from Western Washington, drive Highway 12 over White Pass headed east, passing Rimrock Lake. Turn right on Tieton Road (Forest Service Road 1200). If coming from Eastern Washington, drive Highway 12 near Yakima, and turn towards White Pass. It's 17.3 miles more after leaving the intersection of Highway 410 to reach paved Tieton Road. Turn left, onto Tieton Road, cross the bridge and turn left again on the first road: you'll see a sign that reads Lost Lake. Drive to Lost Lake. This is one way to access Long Lake Trail #1145. Roadside parking only.

Connecting Trail: 1126 (4W609 -6410)

Horse camping: Primitive camping at Lost Lake, or pack-in to the shelter at Long Lake.

Trail Description: Long Lake Trail #1145 starts at the 3,800' level at Lost Lake and ascends going south to Long Lake. Maybe you'll see some fishermen trying their luck. A small creek follows you as you ride a mini ridge up towards Long Lake. There are some rocky spots along the trail and a dirt road to cross. Old Louie Trail #1126 meets at the shelter by Long Lake. This is a nice trail to add on to the Old Louie Trail #1126 (4W609-6410). Views from Long Lake Trail #1145 are of Divide Ridge toward the southeast and Bethel Ridge toward the north.

*HINT- Are your feet cold in the chilly weather? Insert a hand warmer on the topside of your feet between 2 pair of socks. They are activated by air, shake and bake!

Old Louie #1126 (4W609-6410)

Distance:	3.6 Miles
Altitude:	3400'-4800'
Map:	GTM 304 Rimrock
Difficulty:	Moderate-Challenging (Steep short climbs)

Directions: If coming from Western Washington, drive Highway 12 over White Pass headed east, passing Rimrock Lake. Turn right on Tieton Road (Forest Service Road 1200). If coming from Eastern Washington, drive Highway 12 from Yakima and turn towards White Pass. It's 17.3 miles more, after leaving the intersection of Highway 410 to reach paved Tieton Road, turn left on Tieton Road, cross the bridge and drive 2.7 miles and turn left onto gravel Spencer Creek Road 1202. Drive 3 miles on Spencer Creek Road (be aware of a hairpin turn that has some moguls-go slow around them!). Reaching a spot that has a pond on each side of the road, be on the lookout for the Old Louie Trail #1126, which is signed as 4W609, it is on the left (east) side of the road. Parking is available in a large meadow near the trailhead, or at one primitive camp spot alongside of Spencer Creek Road 1202. The camp spot is located on a curve just past Old Louie #1126 (4W609-6410) Trail.

Connecting Trails: 1145, 4W1127

Horse Camping: Primitive camping alongside Spencer Creek Road 1202.

Trail Description: Old Louie Trail #1126 has been turned into a 4-wheel drive route to Louie Way Gap, which is on top of Divide Ridge. There are several spots in which the Old Louie Trail #1126 (not maintained) is easier to ride than the newer jeep trail! The trail goes toward the east, passes a pond on the right side, and continually rises and falls with rutty spots and some mud. Going mostly up through meadows, over a bridge (or ford). There are views of Strobach Mountain and Divide Ridge. The first of many steep spots is easiest to ride by going on a small game trail up between the Old Louie Trail #1126 and the jeep trail 609. Next you'll see another pond. A steep section brings you to a big meadow, then an old clear-cut area. A road is in the clear-cut, take it to the left, (north) watch for an old triangle and old blazes in the trees marking the Old Louie Trail #1126, the trail goes off toward the right (east). Keep in mind the trail is not maintained; skirt Pickle Prairie Meadow (marked with a wooden sign that's only readable if coming from the other direction). Low branches may hinder or intrigue you, depending on what type of ride you like. Look for a mile marker "2" on a tree. Cross a creek and meet Forest Service Road 1201; turn left within a few feet to reach a sign that reads 4W6410. You can see Mount Rainier in the distance. Follow 4W6410 to Long Lake, there is a shelter and the old wooden signpost under a tree signifying the intersection of Long Lake Trail #1145. This is a great place for some pictures of Long Lake with Divide Ridge in the backdrop. (You may notice a remnant of Pickle Prairie Trail #1125 near the shore of Long Lake.) Follow 4W6410 up to Louie Way Gap, sometimes using the Old Louie Trail #1126, depending on which path is easier to ride. You'll cross over a creek; the next hill we found the old trail was easier. But, on the following hill, the jeep trail was easier. It is STEEP here! Ride through a rocky, level area. The next section is extremely steep to the top of the hill, where you'll get views of distant Mount Rainier. The path levels a bit to Louie Way Gap. Here is a 4-way intersection of 4-wheel drive tracks; to the south is WD613, north is Old Jumpoff Trail #1127 (which used to go both directions) and straight ahead, east is Reynolds Creek Road. This trail is mostly trees and meadows.

*NOTE: Use the GTM 304 Rimrock for general guide, the map reads 608 4X4 and the middle section of this trail is not shown on the GTM. To find this portion of trail on the map, draw a line from Long Lake to 4W608.

*HINT- Use battery heated socks for keeping your toes snug as bugs on cool weather riding days.

"DON'T GIVE UP LITTLE ONE"

One early spring day, my friend Sandy and I were riding up a local canyon north of Ellensburg. We found a tiny newborn hereford calf in a slight gully. At first glance we thought it was dead, upon further inspection I saw its rusty soft hair moving slightly up and down with the shallow breaths it was taking. We looked around and found the mom across the fence, she had long ago stopped calling for her baby. She was still standing near the fence; her utter was very full. I tried to rouse the calf, but to no avail, its huge liquid brown eyes staring up at me. Sandy and I would need to work together on this one; we tied our horses to the sagebrush. Sandy got the front legs and I grabbed the rear ones- on the count of three, ugh… the little calf was pretty heavy and we were going uphill. Next we decided to drag it, we pulled and grunted and were able to get the limp calf to the fence line, the little one had no struggle left in it at all, it had given up on life totally. It was weak, and it wouldn't stand on its own so we held it up and started to push it through the fence. Then the big break came, mom came toward the fence bellowing and the baby let out a groan and perked up. It squirmed out of our hands and finished getting through the wire on its own and was re-united with mom! We watched as the baby started to nurse and the cow took her calf away from us. She looked back as if to say thanks! This area is crawling with coyotes and cats, what a meal it would have made after a long winter. We think we saved the day and were light-hearted about our encounter with the pair.

Josie

197

Long Lake

Lost Lake from Long Lake trail-Josie and Ali

GOAT ROCKS WILDERNESS/ CONRAD MEADOWS

The Goat Rocks Wilderness/Conrad Meadows areas are located in Central Washington, southwest of Rimrock Lake off of Highway 12. These areas are picturesque, views of the icy mountains that make up part of the Goat Rocks Wilderness can be seen everywhere. There are ample meadows with crystal clear streams, and dark emerald green lakes. Be on the lookout for mountain goats! Remember to keep food safe in bear-proof containers. A lot of horse clubs use the Conrad Meadows area for camping because it is so big, has water, and lots of trails. The setting is in a wide-open meadow, lined with trees, any level of rider can have fun here. Ten Day Trail #1134 was not ridden, I left it for you to ride and perhaps tell me about some day. Madeleine, Sandy and I have had nice trips to these areas.

Directions to Conrad Meadows: If coming from Western Washington, drive Highway 12 over White Pass headed east, passing Rimrock Lake. Turn right on Tieton Road. If coming from Eastern Washington, drive Highway 12 near Yakima and turn towards White Pass, it's 17.3 miles more after leaving the intersection of Highway 410 to reach paved Tieton Road, turn left. Once on Tieton Road, cross the bridge and drive around the east tip of Rimrock Lake to reach Forest Service Road 1000, turn left onto it. There is a sign here that reads: "Conrad Meadows 14 miles". The first 7 miles is paved, one lane, with turnouts. The last 7 miles is gravel and is narrow in places. Follow the signs to Conrad Meadows. There is a lot of parking in this expansive meadow. Bear Creek Mountain Trail #1130 leaves going uphill on the right-hand side of the road, and South Fork Tieton Trail #1120 heads downhill after the gate on the left-hand side of the road, both trailheads are at the far end of camp.

Conrad Meadows Camp: It is a spacious tree lined area, skirting the babbling Tieton River. There are outhouses. People with most any size rig can come enjoy this camping area. Circle around and park where it feels right. No fee was charged when we visited. The elevation of camp is 4,000 feet.

*****NOTE:** The Forest Service informed me that Conrad Meadows is actually on private land.

Northwest Forest Parking Passes are available at Forest Service offices, they are required at designated trailheads.

Taste the smile on your face...

| Naches Ranger District |
| 10237 Highway 12 |
| Naches, WA 98937 |
| 509-653-2205 or 509-664-2791 |

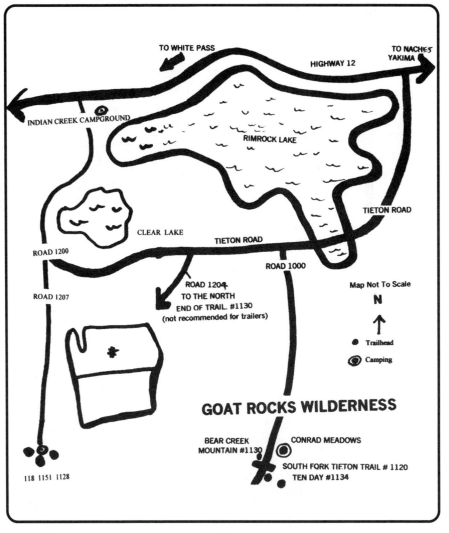

Ali rests while Josie takes a snap at Bear Creek Mountain Lookout

Bear Creek Mountain

Bear Creek Mountain #1130

Distance:	7.1 Miles (see note at bottom of trail)
Altitude:	4000'-6400'
Map:	GTM 303 White Pass
Difficulty:	Moderate-Challenging (Steep climbs)

Directions*:* Follow the directions given for Conrad Meadows in the introduction to this chapter.

Connecting Trails: 1120, 1130.1(A), 1128

Horse Camping: See the introduction of this chapter for camp information.

Trail Description: You might want to warm up your mount's muscles before heading up this one! Bear Creek Mountain Trail #1130 begins by the gated road and climbs steeply on a wide, dusty path for 2 miles. South Fork Tieton Trail #1120 leaves on the opposite side of the gated road. There are some rough and rocky spots to negotiate. You attain views of Conrad Meadows and your camp spots below. The trail switchbacks here and there taking you up this mountain. Lots of Mount Saint Helens ash is lingering at your feet as you climb along the forested trail. The trail flattens a bit to reach the 5,600' level. Go down the other side of the mountain and ride along a rock wall and follow the rolling trail, fording creeks with the cool damp feel of the north slope of the mountain on your face. There may be a few muddy spots by the creeks. Here Bear Creek Mountain Trail #1130 offers nice footing for the animals. Ride along a hillside for awhile on sturdy trail, down to a small meadow in a flat area. Cross a stream and climb again on steep terrain, which will bring you into sub-alpine vegetation, stubby trees and low lying plants. You'll see views of Bear Creek Mountain, it had snow patches when Madeleine and I visited. This brings you to the intersection of Bear Creek Mountain Lookout Trail #1130.1(A) now you're at the high-point of the trail at 6,400'. The trail travels down and rolls in and out of meadows with little streams. There is one difficult creek crossing in a gully that has steep, soft, unstable edges with a boulder in the center. Next you'll intersect Tieton Meadows Trail #1128 departing toward the west. Continue riding slightly downhill 2.9 miles further, to the end of the trail to Forest Service Road 1204. Forest Service Road 1204 is a very rough, rutted narrow road, leading to this end of Bear Creek Mountain Trail #1130. It is not suitable for trailers.

*NOTE: The Forest Service says the mileage is 7.1 and the GTM reads that it is 8.4. The GTM shows the last .9 mile as being Minnie Meadow Trail #1129, that has been change to be part of Bear Creek Mountain Trail #1130.

*HINT-When the ground wasps or bees are on the trail it is best to run out of their territory as quickly and safely as possible.

"WHO IS IN THE TENT?"

After climbing to the lookout at the top of Bear Creek Mountain. We found a tent and a large dog, the dog was barking and the tent was flapping against the gale force wind. Thank goodness the horses were calm. Finally a voice, a man slithered out of the tent, his hair all a muss, he was as surprised to see us as we were to see him. He has camped here every summer and usually spends a week on top of the mountain, and had never seen a horse on the top before. We chatted a while, he was low on water and since we had refillable water bottles, we gave him some of ours. His name is Mike and he loves to go to the lookout where he and his dad came hiking as he was growing up, maybe he'll be there when you go, also.

Josie

View of the Goat Rocks

Bear Creek Mountain Lookout #1130.1(A)

Distance:	1 Mile
Altitude:	6400'-7337'
Map:	GTM 303 White Pass
Difficulty:	Challenging

Directions: No Trailhead. Access from Bear Creek Mountain Lookout Trail #1130. See the directions to Conrad Meadows for a starting place, found in the introduction to this chapter.

Connecting Trails: 1130

Trail Description: Bear Creek Mountain Lookout Trail #1130.1(A) begins in sub-alpine terrain at the intersection of Bear Creek Mountain Trail #1130. It has sandy footing at first and quickly passes a coral pink rock slide. Clamor on as the trail turns into rock slabs with sharp edges that have many tricky spots, such as narrow openings going between boulders, flat slick rock and it's very steep in places. Bear Creek Mountain Trail #1130.1(A) is all on open hillsides. You may pass big patches of snow or small glaciers, whichever way you want to classify them. Luckily for us, the snow wasn't on the trail. The trail flattens several times at small meadows. This is a good place to give your horse a breather and look up towards the towering ridge above. Get ready to ride as the path ascends again. We speculated where the trail would be placed on the hillside, because it was virtually invisible from our perspective. Now begins the relentless climb on switchbacks to the old lookout site. The trail gets steeper with a few more rocks, but they are easier to contend with than the ones below. After all, it is the Goat Rocks! Reaching some dwarfed trees, you get your first glimpse of Mount Adams. As you swing around the mountain, the sky opens up in all its glory. Level out at the top on a rocky ridge, where you'll see the most fantastic views, looking at Mount Adams to the south, Mount Rainier to the north and the fabulous Goat Rock Mountains in between. The panorama is breathtaking. See if you can find the white plastic tube with a sign-in sheet inside to make your mark, it may be in the nooks and crannies of the rocks. This trail is "Short n' Dirty" and has a "Sweet" ending, you're at the 7,337' level. This is the highest point you can ride to in the Goat Rocks and is only slightly lower than the tip-top of Old Snowy Mountain. If you come from a low elevation, you may want to acclimate for a day or two before pressing to this higher elevation.

"WE GRAB SOME TAIL AND PULL OURSELVES UP THE TRAILS"

Once in a while my friend Madeleine and I practice the art of "Tailing Up", this is a technique that the endurance riders use sometimes on cross-country 50-100 mile courses. A cool spot to do this is up a real steep incline, so you will get the full benefit of the PULL. I enjoy a hike and sometimes it feels good to get off and stretch my limbs. Madeleine's Arabian mare doesn't mind it at all when I tail up on her. It is like getting pulled up on a towrope on a ski lift; sort of, only you have to move your feet. It is fun to do and adds excitement to our rides. (Madeleine has done the same on my mare's tail, on other occasions.) I got pulled up a portion of Bear Creek Lookout Trail on this day. I am not recommending this to anyone who isn't sure of the horse's temperament that they are tailing. The hikers were looking at us like we were nuts, they also said we'd never make it to the top!

Josie

Full scope of the Goat Rock Mountains

North Fork Tieton #1118

Distance:	4.9 Miles
Altitude:	3300'-4800'
Map:	GTM 303 White Pass
Difficulty:	Moderate

Directions: From Highway 12 east of White Pass or west from Yakima, turn on Forest Service Road 1200, the sign reads Clear Lake. Go south on a paved road for about 3 miles. Reach a fork in the road by a sno-park; take a right on Forest Service Road 1207. Drive about 4 miles more on gravel road to the end of the road where you will find the trailhead for North Fork Tieton Trail #1118. The turnaround is big enough for most rigs and it has a stock ramp.

Connecting Trails: 1128, 1117, 61, 2000

Horse Camping: Primitive camping with an outhouse and stock water is in the nearby North Fork Tieton River.

Trail Description: Madeleine and her friend rode this trail, and Madeleine is sharing their adventure with us.

"North Fork Tieton Trail #1118 starts out with a bad bridge. We forded the creek instead (see note at bottom of page). The trail is nice and wide to the first intersection with Tieton Meadows Trail #1128. North Fork Tieton Trail #1118 turns to the right and narrows. After 1.6 miles you'll pass Hidden Spring Trail #1117 on the right. Ride the hillside, passing a few draws here and there with creeks. Through the openings in the trees you can see Bear Creek Mountain it is 7,337'. You can ride

PCT in the Goat Rocks

207

to the top of Bear Creek Mountain Lookout from Conrad Meadows Area. The jagged edges of Devil's Peaks and the beginning of the Goat Rocks Mountains with Old Snowy Peak at 7,930' are peeking above a mountain range to the south. The last 2 miles gets steep in places. North Fork Tieton Trail #1118 ends at Tieton Pass at 4,800' and meets the PCT #2000 going north and south and Clear Fork Trail #61 going to the west. For a loop you can ride north to Hidden Springs Trail #1117 back to camp."

"We rode a little further- Riding south on the PCT #2000 for about 3 miles. The trail is a little narrow with soft edges. In 1.6 miles you'll reach Old Army Trail #1151 (Which is hard to find, not recommended for stock, removed from the Forest Service "system" and has not been maintained for years.). Riding on, the trail gets steeper. We arrived at a small lake and watered the horses. Continuing up, the trail gets steep as it switchbacks on a hillside in sub-alpine terrain. At this point you can get a glimpse of Mount Rainier to the north. Above the tree line after the switchbacks, you'll see all the mountains that were peeking at you earlier from the North Fork Tieton Trail. McCall Basin is seen below as well. Lack of daylight forced us to turn around. Remember to allow the same amount of time for your return trip."

Full scope of the Goat Rock Mountains

*NOTE: The Forest Service informed me that the bad bridge has been rebuilt. The Forest Service wants you to note that Hidden Springs is a steep challenging trail!

Madeleine

*HINT-When low branches are met on the trail, lift up on them a little as you duck under, instead of catapulting the limb sideways. This prevents the rider behind you from getting whacked in the face with the bough.

Bear Creek Lookout Trail with white sand and snow

Full scope of the Goat Rock Mountains

South Fork Tieton #1120

Distance:	11.4 Miles
Altitude:	4100'-5600'
Map:	GTM 335 Walupt Lake
Difficulty:	Moderate

Directions: Follow the directions given for Conrad Meadows in the introduction to this chapter.

Connecting Trails: 1130, 1134, 1131 (not maintained)

Horse Camping: For information on camping at Conrad Meadows read the introduction to this chapter.

Trail Description: South Fork Tieton Trail #1120 starts at the far end of the camping area by the gated road. Bear Creek Mountain Trail #1130 leaves uphill by the gate and South Fork Tieton Trail #1120 begins by going downhill just beyond the gate. Be aware that cattle are grazing all over this area, you may see the catching pens set up. Ford 2 streams

Little Bey and Madeleine take on the elements

and the trail enters into a massive meadow to intersect with Ten Day Trail #1134, which exits to the left. View Gilbert Peak in the distance straight-ahead through the next string of meadows. There are several "V's" in the trail, most come back to each other. If you end up on a road, with no trail across the other side (like the map shows) turn left on the road and head down until you meet the trail again. The sign-in box for the Goat Rock Wilderness is in sight from the road. Pass Tieton Peak Trail #1131 (not maintained), it departs going north. Next is a stream, ford or cross on a bridge, there is a rather tricky set of rocks to clamor over on the other side of the creek (see note on the bottom of page). Weave your way through trees, meadows and ride the rolling trail. Again ford or cross another bridge on the next stream. The loop begins going 2 directions. I will describe it from the north end going around, and coming down the south end. Turn to the right and head up a rocky spot and switchback, then flatten out and switchback again passing small meadows. Cross a somewhat narrow spot on an open hill, with a drop-off. Ride around to alpine meadows with gray boulders and lots of water for your animals to drink. There are views of Gilbert Peak and glaciers all over this area. This is the high-point of the trail at 5,600'. Head down and around a knoll and be surprised by Surprise Lake, it is a majestic lake with aquamarine colored water. Lots of Mount Saint Helens ash found here. Down, down and more down on switchbacks, there are a few creeks here and there. At one point you'll notice you're between two deep draws and will be amazed at how well the trail has been placed. Cross 1 final creek on a bridge (no ford) and ride on flat ground to meet the place where your loop began. This trail is very interesting with varied terrain and beautiful views of the Goat Rock Mountains. The south end of South Fork Tieton Trail #1120 to Surprise Lake is easier and traveled more than the north end, even though it is steeper.

*NOTE: The Forest Service has advised me that this section has been worked on for easier passage.

*HINT-When crossing a swift stream, head for the other bank upstream from where you want to come out, in case you get swept a bit.

Monarch Butterfly

Alpine flowers

Surprise Lake near Conrad Meadow

WILLIAM O'DOUGLAS WILDERNESS AREA

The William O' Douglas Wilderness Area is located in Central Washington. The region described in this chapter is reached from either Highway 410 east of Chinook Pass on Bumping River Road past Bumping Lake (This is the back door of White Pass.), or from Highway 12 near White Pass. There are also some trailheads just east of White Pass described in this chapter. Several horse camp areas are available. There is a horse camp at White Pass and 2 camps, 1 at each end at the trailheads for Indian Creek Trail. Some of the trails in this chapter are in the Gifford Pinchot National Forest, and some are in the Wenatchee National Forest. These territories offer deep forests on meandering trails through flat mountain meadows filled with an array of brilliant green grasses and plants. The hills are speckled with flowers in a rainbow of colors and tons of icy cold alpine lakes. The vivid blue fall skies with stark white clouds make a perfect post card setting for taking pictures. The Pacific Crest Trail in this area is described in the Pacific Crest Trail chapter under William O'Douglas Wilderness Area. This is one of my favorite places to ride. With all the water and occasional muddy spots it's natural that mosquitoes are attracted here to make their homes, so bring repellent. Madeleine, Sandy and I, all love this area and when we are not on a mission to research new trails we may be found here! Remember that you should be at least 200' from any water source when tying, staking, or hobbling your animals.

White Pass Horse Camp: There is a road on the north side of Highway 12 that leads to the horse camp and Leech Lake. It is hard to spot this road, it is east of the ski area. Look for a small sign. The camp has several camp spots, tables, fire pits, an outhouse, and a large day parking area.

Indian Creek (South end) & Little Buck Trailheads: Drive Highway 12 east of White Pass, near Rimrock Lake, and turn onto Indian Creek Road, which is opposite the Indian Creek Camp. Go to Forest Service Road 1308 and turn left. Drive to the end where you'll find a spacious parking area at Indian Creek Trailhead (north end), Little Buck Trail #1147 leaves a few feet up Indian Creek Trail #1105.

Indian Creek (South end) & Little Buck Camp: Primitive camping is at the trailhead, with an outhouse. Bring potable water. Water for the livestock is in Indian Creek, which is to the southwest of the camp. No fee was charged (a Northwest Forest Pass is required to park at this trailhad). This is a delightful spot to camp with lots of trees and the babbling river. Call ahead for any updates on Forest Service Road 1308, sometimes it can be washed out and too rough to drive on.

Indian Creek (North end), Twin Sister and Twin Sisters Spur Trailheads: From Yakima, drive west on Highway 12, to Highway 410. Drive Highway 410 to the Bumping Lake turn-off, which is Forest Service Road 1800, continue for 11 miles on paved road. After reaching Bumping Lake, the road turns from pavement to a gravel road, at a fork in the road take Forest Service Road 1808 left (south) (old maps read Road 395). Drive to Deep Creek Horse Camp listed below, and ride a mile or so up the Spur Trail to reach Twin Sisters Trailhead. The Forest Service wants me to tell stock users that the Deep Creek Camp at the end of the road is for hikers only. If you miss the Deep Creek Horse Camp you can turn around at the Deep Creek "people" Camp, there is a large turnaround. This is where Twin Sisters Trailhead is, use the access trail from the horse camp reach this trail.

Indian Creek (North end), Deep Creek Horse Camp: This camp is located 1.2 miles before the end of Forest Service Road 1808, drive down a hill to the left, in to the trees to find the camp and Indian Creek Trailhead and Twin Sisters Spur Trail. This camp has about 6 sites, an outhouse and 1 table, use creek water for the animals. No fee was charged (Northwest Forest Pass is required).

Northwest Forest Parking Passes are available at Forest Service offices, they are required at designated trailheads.

Get off your rear and grab your gear...

Naches Ranger District
10237 Highway 12
Naches, WA 98937
509-653-2205 or 509-664-2791

Packwood Ranger District
Packwood, WA 98361
206-494-5615

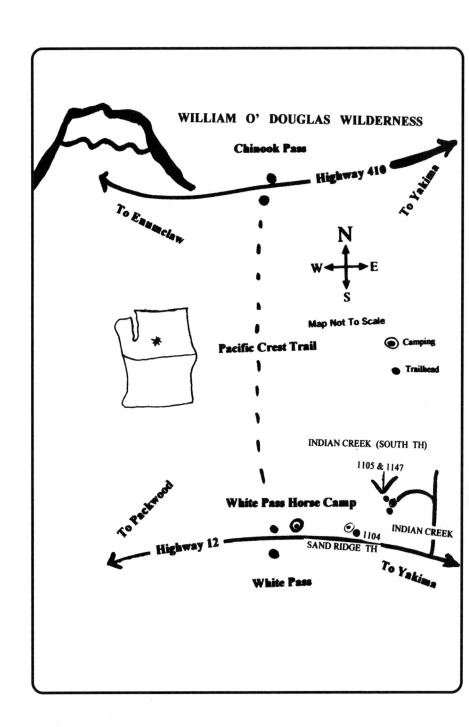

WILLIAM O' DOUGLAS WILDERNESS

Chinook Pass

Highway 410

To Yakima

To Enumclaw

N

W ← → E

S

Map Not To Scale

Pacific Crest Trail

◎ Camping

● Trailhead

INDIAN CREEK (SOUTH TH)

1105 & 1147

White Pass Horse Camp

INDIAN CREEK

To Packwood

◎ ◉ 1104

Highway 12

SAND RIDGE TH

To Yakima

White Pass

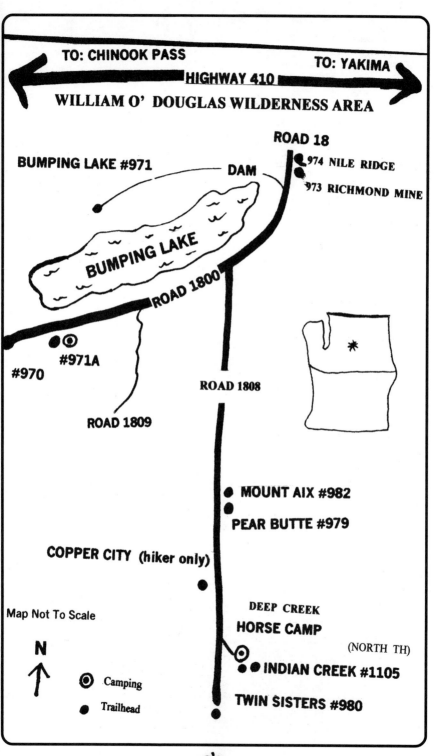

Cowlitz #44

(PCT #2000 to Trail #41)

Distance:	1.5 Miles
Altitude:	4800'-5100'
Map:	GTM 303 White Pass
Difficulty:	Moderate

Directions: Access from the connecting trails listed below. For the nearest trailhead see the directions to Indian Creek (north end) listed in the introduction to this chapter.

Connecting Trails: 45, 41, 2000

Trail Description: This small portion of the Cowlitz Trail #44 was used to make loops in the William O' Douglas Wilderness Area. Beginning at the PCT #2000, Cowlitz Trail #44 is pretty flat as it passes Penoyer Lake on the north side of the trail. It drops swiftly around the top of a gully and travels through forest to meet with Pothole Trail #45 and Crossover Trail #41.

*NOTE: The Forest Service noted that the PCT is the division for the name of Trail #44. On the east side of the PCT in the Wenatchee National Forest it is known as "Tumac" and on the west side in the Gifford Pinchot National Forest it is "Cowlitz".

*HINT- Horse clumsy? Maybe your cinch is too tight!

Elk

Cramer Lake #1106

Distance:	4.3 Miles (see note)
Altitude:	4200'-5100'
Map:	GTM 303 White Pass
Difficulty:	Moderate

Directions: Drive Highway 12 towards White Pass, just east of the pass you'll turn north towards Dog Lake Campground. This is Cramer Lake Trailhead.

Connecting Trails: 1107, 1156, 1142

Horse Camping: Nearby camping at White Pass Horse Camp. See the introduction to this chapter.

Trail Description: Cramer Lake Trail #1106 will be described from Dog Lake north to the intersection with Shellrock Lake Trail #1142. Leaving Dog Lake, the trail meets with Dark Meadows Trail #1107, which departs to the west (left). As big as Dog Lake is you would think you would get a nicer view from the trail, it is deeply forested here. Spiral Butte is to the east across a small wash. The trail meanders along and crosses a rock slide area, and you'll need to ford a creek, which can be deceivingly deep with mud. Climb up 400' where the trail levels a bit as it continues next to Cramer Lake and turns sharply to the right passing Dumbell Lake Trail #1156, then Otter Lake. Cramer Lake Trail #1106 ends as it merges with Shellrock Lake Trail #1142. You can make some time on this trail, the footing is nice for most of the way.

*NOTE: The Forest Service says the mileage is 4.3, the GTM reads 5.4 miles

*HINT-When you turnaround on a narrow trail point the horses nose to its hip bone, and give a firm steady command, it doesn't matter if you turn in to the hill or turn to the outside.

Crossover #41

Distance:	1 Mile
Altitude:	4400'-4800'
Map:	GTM 303 White Pass
Difficulty:	Moderate

Directions: No trailhead. Access from any of the trails listed below. For the nearest trailhead see Indian Creek (North end) in the introduction to this chapter.

Connecting Trails: 43, 44, 45

Trail Description: Crossover Trail #41 will be described from east to west. From the intersection of Cowlitz Trail #44 and Pothole Trail #45 the trail heads downhill. This is a gentle trail that travels through old growth trees, and mossy earthen smells are thick in the air. Crossover Trail #41 crosses over (get it?) several water drainage areas that cut deeply into the terrain. This was the only challenge we had on the trail. In the fall they're probably going to be dry. On a sunny day the lighting underneath the timber is fused and it feels as if you are riding inside a huge green tent. Crossover Trail #41 meets with Jug Lake Trail #43, Sandy, Madeleine and I used this trail for making a loop.

Yvonne and her gelding enjoy a break

Dark Meadows #1107

Distance:	1.8 Miles (see note)
Altitude:	4200'-4500'
Map:	GTM 303 White Pass
Difficulty:	Moderate

Directions: No trailhead. Access from the connecting trails listed below. The closest trailhead is at White Pass.

Connecting Trails: 2000, 1106

Horse Camping: Nearby camping at White Pass Horse Camp. See the introduction to this chapter for more information.

Trail Description: Dark Meadows Trail #1107 will be described from the PCT #2000 to Cramer Lake Trail #1106. Leaving the PCT #2000, head gently down a pine needle covered trail into very dark forest, with great footing for the horses. The trail was not cleared very well when Madeleine and I visited, be sure to call ahead whenever you're planning a trip. This is a marvelous little trail through the woods it connects to Cramer Lake Trail #1106 in a short 1.8 miles.

*NOTE: The Forest Service says the mileage is 1.8 miles, the GTM reads 1.5 miles.

*HINT-Horse overly excited about a trail obstacle say a bridge, mud or log? Unhook the reins from the bit and hook on the halter, or use a long small rope (some people carry clothesline ropes just for such occasions). Then stretch it out, with you well ahead and to the side of the obstacle and have someone behind the horse send him on across on his own.

Dumbell Lake #1156 (see note)

Distance:	1.5 Miles (see note)
Altitude:	5000'-5100'
Map:	GTM 303 White Pass
Difficulty:	Moderate

Directions: No trailhead. Access from the connecting trails listed below. This trail is in the center of the area described and can be accessed from any of the trailheads listed in the beginning of this chapter.

Connecting Trails: 2000, 1142.1(A), 1106

Trail Description: Dumbell Lake Trail #1156 parts from the PCT #2000 and goes to the east, then south, skirting Cramer Mountain. You'll pass Long John Trail #1142.1(A), then ride the shore of Dumbell Lake and pass lots of other lake pots. It is a flat trail and this area can be muddy. This trail ends as it connects to Cramer Lake Trail #1106.

*NOTE: There are two ways listed pertaining to the spelling of Dumbbell Lake. On the front of the GTM, Dumbell is listed with two "b's", on the back of the map they only use one "b". Also the GTM shows Dumbell Lake Trail #1156 listed in two spots since it is split on the boundary line of two National Forests. The back of the map has it listed twice, a small portion is in the Gifford Pinchot National Forest and the rest is in the Wenatchee National Forest.
The Forest Service says the mileage is 1.5 miles, the GTM reads 1.1 miles.
The Forest Service says the number for this trail is 1156, the GTM reads 56.

*HINT-The climax of a trail may not be the top of the mountain with a breathtaking view. It may be an forest animal's antics or a strange outcropping of rocks with a funny face imbedded into it or perhaps a water crossing with silver waves that stirs your soul.

Indian Creek #1105

Distance:	8 Miles
Altitude:	3400'-5200'
Maps:	GTM 303 White Pass
	GTM 271 Bumping Lake
Difficulty:	Moderate

Directions: Indian Creek Trail #1105 has two trailheads, the north and the south. See the introduction to this chapter for more information.

Connecting Trails: 980, 1105.1(A), 1104.1(A), 1148, 1114, 1109, 1105.2 (B), 1147

Horse Camping: Read the introduction to this chapter for details of Indian Creek Trailheads, north and south.

Trail Description: Indian Creek Trail #1105 will be described from the north trailhead to the south. Beginning from the south end of Deep Creek Horse Camp, ride the trail a few feet and when the trail forks, stay to the left (to the right is what I call the Twin Sisters Spur Trail). Indian Creek Trail #1105 is rather rocky at first, as it crosses huge seasonal run-off gullies. The trail climbs away from the rocks and has nice footing as it steadily treks onward and upward. The Forest Service workers were in full swing fixing the trail, putting in water bars (logs

Chinook Pass

223

wedged in the ground and across the trail to help divert runoff water to the side of the trail rather than down the trail, which may end in nasty ruts). The trail flattens in a long meadow where invisible fingers bend the grasses and Mount Rainier's white head peeks up. Some distant snowy peaks are seen as well as the closer baldheaded Tumac Mountain. At Blankenship Meadows, Round Lake Trail #1105.1(A) leaves to the west (right). Follow the meadow to reach Sandy Trail #1104.1(A), which also exits west (right). Continue on flat trail through Indian Creek Meadow passing Pear Loop Trail #1148 (you'll pass it again on the other end of its loop, see note). Then Rattlesnake Trail #1114 intersects from the east (left). Head down on a rougher section of trail to meet McAllister Trail #1109, which departs to the west (right). Here you will notice that you're following Indian Creek. It becomes a bit steeper here as you work your way downhill, cross a bridge, or ford Indian Creek, then go up on a somewhat narrow tread, Indian Creek Mine Trail #1105.1(A) connects, going uphill (not maintained). Cross a gully, then the trail becomes wide like an old road. Little Buck Trail #1147 forks to the south (right). Indian Creek Trailhead (South) and camp is straight ahead.

*NOTE: The Forest Service says the name is Pear Loop Trail, the GTM reads Pear Lake Trail.

Mount Rainier near the William O' Douglas Wilderness

Jug Lake #43

(From Trail #41 to Trail #2000)

Distance:	2.2 Miles
Altitude:	4400'-4800'
Map:	GTM 303 White Pass
Difficulty:	Moderate

Directions: No Trailhead. Access from the connecting trails listed below. The closest trailhead area is listed under Indian Creek (North) in the introduction to this chapter.

Connecting Trails: 41, 42, 2000

Trail Description: This section of Jug Lake Trail #43 will be described going north from Crossover Trail #41 to the PCT #2000. Leaving the intersection with Crossover Trail #41, Jug Lake Trail #43 switchbacks up a hillside on a nice wide trail in very deep old growth timber. The path levels out quickly. You'll pass huge meadows with tall hellebore plants growing in the moist ground. Fryingpan Lake is on the east side of the trail. Kincaid Trail #42 departs shortly after to the west (left) we could see lots of logs over Kincaid Trail #42. In just over ½ mile the PCT #2000 "T" intersects, where this section of Jug Lake Trail ends. We used this path to make loops in the area.

*HINT- Water repels on your nylon saddle bags or pommel bag when a wood sealant is applied to the bags. Do at least a week before use, and let it dry outside.

Twin Sister Mountain with Tumac Mountain in distance

Little Buck #1147

Distance:	9 Miles
Altitude:	3400'-3700'
Map:	GTM 303 White Pass
Difficulty:	Moderate

Directions: Read the trailhead directions for Little Buck Trail in the introduction to this chapter under Indian Creek Trailhead (South). Or read Sand Ridge Trail for another trailhead access.

Connecting Trails: 1104, 1105

Horse Camping: Read the introduction to this chapter under Indian Creek & Little Buck Trailheads and camping.

Trail Description: Little Buck Trail #1147 departs to the southeast from Indian Creek Trail #1105. Ford Indian Creek, which by the looks of its wide gravel and rock bed must be a churning mess in the spring. Ride up the other side and begin the .9 mile trek to the crown of the hill on thin tread, with roots here and there and quite a drop-off on the side of the soft trail. Meet up with Sand Ridge Trail #1104 on top. This trail is used to make loops in the area.

Indian Creek Trail with Mount Rainier in the backdrop

Long John #1142.1(A) (see note)

Distance:	7 Mile
Altitude:	5200'-5200'
Map:	GTM 303 White Pass
Difficulty:	Moderate

Directions: No trailhead. Access from the connecting trails listed below. This trail is in the center of the area described and can be accessed from any of the trailheads listed in the beginning of this chapter.

Connecting Trails: 1142, 1156

Trail Description: Long John #1142.1(A) is a short little trail that goes west from Shellrock Lake Trail #1142 by Long John Lake, to Dumbell Lake Trail #1156 (see note). It is level and has pockets of water next to the trail, with meadows. The path emerges at the large Dumbell Lake, which is at the foot of Cramer Mountain. Lots of loops from here!

*NOTE: There are 2 ways listed pertaining to the spelling of Dumbell Lake. On the front of the GTM, Dumbell is listed with two "b's", on the back of the map they only use one "b". The Forest Service says it is correctly spelled with one "b".

The Forest Service says the name of this trail is Long John, the GTM reads Dumbell.

The Forest Service says the number of Dumbell Trail is 1156 the GTM reads 56.

Thimble Berry

McAllister #1109

Distance:	2 Miles (see note)
Altitude:	4400'-4700'
Map:	GTM 303 White Pass
Difficulty:	Moderate

Directions*:* No trailhead. Access from connecting trails listed below. This trail is closest to Indian Creek Trailhead (South), which is listed in the introduction to this chapter.

Connecting Trails: 1104, 1105

Trail Description: McAllister Trail #1109 connects Sand Ridge Trail #1104 to Indian Creek Trail #1105. This is a mild little trail in spots and can be muddy and rocky in others. It stays in the timber. There are several short switchbacks to ride. It goes downhill as it reaches Indian Creek Trail #1105.

*NOTE: The Forest Service says the mileage is 2 miles, the GTM reads 1.9 miles.

*HINT-Above 4,000' it is easier to get dehydrated, so drink lots of water even if it's cold or wet. If you're feeling dizzy or nauseated, drink some water and see if that helps.

Twin Sisters Lake with Tumac Mountain in the background

Nile Ridge #974

Distance:	5.9 Miles (see note)
Altitude:	3200'-6300'
Maps:	GTM 271 Bumping Lake
	GTM 272 Old Scab Mountain
Difficulty:	Moderate-Challenging (Climbing)

Directions: The Nile Ridge Trailhead is near Highway 410, east of Chinook Pass. From Yakima, drive west on Highway 12, to Highway 410. Drive Highway 410 to the Bumping Lake turn-off, which is paved Forest Service Road 1800. The trailhead is just past Bumping Crossing Campground. It has a nice big parking area. The road is a little steep from the Forest Service Road to the parking lot. This is a shared trailhead with Richmond Mine Trail #973.

Connecting Trails: 696, 985

Trail Description: My friend, Donna Evans has graciously consented to write this trail she rode with her husband, Dean.

"Nile Ridge Trail #974 starts out along Bumping River through timber. The path has good footing all the way to the top and slight elevation differences. The trail is vague in places and we lost sight of it for a while. In about 2 miles, the trail turns southeast and starts climbing through open timber. Nile Ridge Trail #974 skirts Old Scab Mountain's south side. At first the climb is gradual, but after going along some sidehills it really starts to climb. It ranges from the 3,200' level to 6,300' in 4.3 miles, with few real switchbacks. When you finally get to the top you ride along the north side of the ridge a short way, with a nice view of American Ridge to the northwest. Then you pop out onto the south side of the ridge with a view of mountains to the south and southeast toward White Pass. The trail levels out for about .5 mile, and then gently climbs through an open meadow on a hillside to Clover Springs area. Here you meet Mud Spring 4x4 Trail #696 going southeast, Road 1600 leaving to the north, and Windy Ridge Trail #985 going to the south."

Donna

*NOTE: The Forest Service says the mileage is 5.9, the GTM reads 6.4 miles.

Pear Loop #1148 (see note)

Distance:	2.5 Miles (see note)
Altitude:	5000'-5100'
Map:	GTM 303 White Pass
Difficulty:	Moderate

Directions: No trailhead. Access from the connecting trails listed below. The closest trailhead is listed in the introduction of this chapter under Indian Creek Trailhead (North).

Connecting Trails: 979, 1105

Trail Description: Pear Loop Trail #1148 makes a horseshoe loop off of Indian Creek Trail #1105, connecting to and from Indian Creek Meadows. This trail will be described from the west to the east. Leaving the intersection with Indian Creek Trail #1105 ride gently up toward the north and meet Pear Butte Trail #979 (see note). Continue to the east (right) as Pear Loop Trail #1148 bends across a meadow area. The trail goes through a serene swamp like area, crossing the outlet from Apple Lake. Beautiful meadows with thick grasses are what you'll find here. Then the path passes Pear Lake and descends back to Indian Creek Trail #1105.

*NOTE: The GTM on the back of the map shows Pear Butte Trail #979 connecting to Indian Creek Trail #1105. It connects to Pear Loop Trail #1148.

The Forest Service says this trail's name is Pear Loop, the GTM reads Pear Lake.

The Forest Service says the mileage is 2.5 miles, the GTM reads 2.7 miles.

Peek-A-Boo moss covered root-wad

Pot Hole #45

Distance:	1.5 Miles
Altitude:	4800'-4900'
Map:	GTM 303 White Pass
Difficulty:	Moderate

Directions: No trailhead. Access from the connecting trails listed below. The closest trailhead to this trail is listed at the beginning of this chapter under Indian Creek Trailhead (North).

Connecting Trails: 2000, 41, 44

Trail Description: Pot Hole Trail #45 is only 1.5 miles long and can be used for making loops in the William O'Douglas Wilderness Area. It is pretty flat and at the north end, it connects to the PCT #2000. On its south end, it collides with Crossover Trail #41 and Cowlitz Trail #44. The middle part of the path has a nasty mud crossing. Here I felt it better to let the horse jump across at a narrower part, rather than chance getting hurt with the unseen remits of an old bridge at the wide part, camouflaged by goopy sticky mud. Pot Hole Trail #45 visits several meadows as it meanders along, there is a nice camp spot, next to the mud (stream) crossing.

Pear Lake Trail, outlet for Apple Lake

Richmond Mine #973

(From Bumping Crossing Camp to Windy Ridge Trail)

Distance:	5.6 Miles
Altitude:	3400'-6000'
Maps:	GTM 272 Old Scab Mountain
	GTM 271 Bumping Lake
Difficulty:	Challenging

Directions: The Richmond Mine Trailhead is located near Highway 410, east of Chinook Pass. From Yakima, drive west on Highway 12, to Highway 410. Drive Highway 410 to the Bumping Lake turn-off, which is paved Forest Service Road 1800. The trailhead is just past Bumping Crossing Campground, good parking area, although it is a little steep from Forest Service Road to the parking lot. This is a shared trailhead with Nile Ridge Trail #974.

Connecting Trail: 985

Trail Description: Richmond Mine Trail #973 begins at a shared trailhead with Nile Ridge Trail #974. Donna Evans critiques this trail.

"My husband Dean and I rode this trail. Starting from the parking area the first mile of trail is good. The next section is tough, I'm not sure it is maintained at all because we had to negotiate 12 downed trees, some of which were quite difficult to get around. In places the trail is gutted badly, and it is brushy. You can't get out of the trail easily to avoid the rocks. The trail winds through boulder fields and heavy timber. I am not recommending this section for livestock. The terrain is extremely rough going and Richmond Mine Trail #973 ascends very rapidly up steep sidehills with few switchbacks. Climb away from the Bumping River side of the mountain to the 6,000' level. A steep descent takes you to the small, but pretty Richmond Lake. In 2.7 miles you'll reach Windy Ridge Trail #985. The trail descends through dense forest quite rapidly here. This trail continues from this intersection, however we were on a quest to make a loop, so you'll have to discover the rest of Richmond Mine Trail #973 for yourselves."

Donna

*NOTE: The Forest Service informed me this trail is on a rotating maintenance schedule.

*HINT-If you can't take the heat. Try out a cowboy hankie, the ones with the little pellets in them that swell up when dipped in water. It will keep you cool all day. Remember to soak it in clean water a couple hours ahead of your ride, and keep your hat on to block the sun.

Sand Ridge Trail, Madeleine and Falinka

Distance:	1 Mile
Altitude:	5200'-5300'
Map:	GTM 303 White Pass
Difficulty:	Moderate

Directions: No Trailhead. Access from the connecting trails listed below. The closest trailhead is Indian Creek Trailhead (North), see the introduction of this chapter.

Connecting Trails: 1104, 1105

Trail Description: Round Lake Trail #1105.1(A) connects Sand Ridge Trail #1104 with Indian Creek Trail #1105. It travels east and west through mountain pines that can be drenching to horse and rider if they are wet. It is kind of an overgrown trail with low branches. The trail can be greasy slick when muddy. You'll pass the small Round Lake on the north side of the trail. The east end of the trail connects with Indian Creek Trail #1105 at Mosquito Valley, and Blankenship Meadows.

Indian Creek Trail, Sandy and her Appy gelding, Chris

Sand Ridge #1104

Distance:	8.9 Miles (see note)
Altitude:	3400'-5400'
Map:	GTM 303 White Pass
Difficulty:	Moderate

Directions: Sand Ridge Trailhead is located in Central Washington, off Highway 12, east of White Pass. There is no sign on the road indicating the trailhead, it is on the north side of the highway, west of Indian Creek Corrals. The trailhead is a few feet off the highway and is out of sight behind thick trees, near some bends in the road and guardrails. There is an outhouse here and lots of room to turn around. Northwest Forest Pass required here.

Connecting Trails: 1147, 1142, 1109, 1104.1(A), 1105.1(A), 44, 980

Horse Camping: Primitive camp, although the highway is very close and is quite noisy. Bring water.

Trail Description: Sand Ridge Trail #1104 starts at the far end of the parking area. Fill out your Wilderness permit and head up the trail, long switchbacks take you to a ridge, where Little Buck Trail #1147 exits, now head northwest on a soft, sandy, and wide trail, which can be

Big Horn Sheep

quite dusty in the dry season. This trail is under huge ponderosa and mixed pines stays in the timber almost the entire time. When the trail bends to the north on a bench, you can see Mount Rainier, and surrounding hills, buttes and ridges. Shellrock Lake Trail #1142 heads off to the west (left). The next trail you'll meet is McAllister Trail #1109, it departs down to the northeast (right). Ride on, slightly downhill, then back up again on a great mountain trail, with the 3 "R's" of trail riding (rocks, ruts and roots) and maybe a log or two depending on the year. Tumac Mountain is on the left side of you now. Pass the highest point of Sand Ridge Trail at the 5,400' level, where Sandy Trail #1104.1(A) hooks in. Ride a short 1.2 miles, passing a clearing to reach Round Lake Trail #1105.1(A), it joins from the east (right). In .2 mile, you'll see Tumac Trail #44 (see note), it leads to Tumac Mountain. In sight is one of the Twin Sisters Lakes. Sand Ridge Trail ends as it "T" intersects with Twin Sisters Trail #980. This is a grand trail with oodles of possibilities for loops.

*NOTE: The Forest Service says the mileage is 8.9 miles, the GTM reads 8.5 miles. The Forest Service noted that the PCT is the division for the name of Trail #44. On the east side of the PCT in the Wenatchee National Forest it is known

One of numerous lakes in the William O' Douglas Wilderness

as "Tumac" and on the west side in the Gifford Pinchot National Forest it is "Cowlitz".

*HINT- Do you bring the dog with you when you ride? When there is no water along the trail, I use a plastic bag to give my dog a drink out of, just make sure you still have enough water left for yourself.

Twin Sisters Trail

Sandy #1104.1(A)

Distance:	1 Mile (see note)
Altitude:	5200'-5400'
Map:	GTM 303 White Pass
Difficulty:	Moderate

Directions: No trailhead. Access from the connecting trails listed below. This trail is closest to the Indian Creek Trailhead (North) listed in the introduction to this chapter.

Connecting Trails: 1105, 1104

Trail Description: Sandy Trail #1104.1(A) is a 1 mile stretch that connects Sand Ridge Trail #1104 to Indian Creek Trail #1105. It runs east and west through meadows and past Blankenship Lakes, which are gorgeous. They look like a scene on a post card, and they could be, if you remember to bring your camera!

*NOTE: The Forest Service says the mileage is 1 mile, the GTM reads .8 mile.

Jug Lake Trail, Josie n' Sandy ride in the mist

Shellrock Lake #1142

Distance:	6.5 Miles (see note)
Altitude:	4600'-5200'
Map:	GTM 303 White Pass
Difficulty:	Moderate

Directions: No trailhead. Access from the connecting trails listed below. The closest trailheads is Sand Ridge Trailhead, read that trail description for more details.

Connecting Trails: 1104, 1108, 1106, 1142.1(A), 44

Trail Description: Shellrock Lake Trail #1142 connects Sand Ridge Trail #1104 with Cowlitz-Tumac Trail #44 (see the note at the bottom of the page). The path runs diagonally northwest to southeast and will be described starting from Sand Ridge Trail #1104. The trail follows the base of Spiral Butte. There are a few rocky sections here. Spiral Butte Trail #1108 leaves going up Spiral Butte (hiker only because of boulders, see note). Continue riding passing Shellrock Lake, slightly uphill, the trail meets with Cramer Lake Trail #1106. After seeing numerous small lakes, you'll notice Long John Trail #1142.1(A) exiting

Rock slide area

to the left (see note), and finally Shellrock Lake dead ends at Cowlitz Trail #44 (see note). As usual, this area offers tons of loops to entertain you.

*NOTE: The Forest Service says the mileage is 6.5 miles, the GTM reads 4.4 miles. Spiral Butte Trail is shown as Big Peak Trail on the GTM. Long John Trail is shown as Dumbell on the GTM.

The Forest Service noted that the PCT is the division for the name of Trail #44. On the east side of the PCT in the Wenatchee National Forest it is known as "Tumac" and on the west side in the Gifford Pinchot National Forest it is "Cowlitz".

Creek crossing in the Wilderness

Twin Sisters #980

Distance:	4.4 Miles (see note)
Altitude:	4500'-5200'
Maps:	GTM 303 White Pass
	GTM 271 Bumping Lake
Difficulty:	Moderate

Directions: Read the introduction to this chapter under Indian Creek Trailhead (North) and Deep Creek Horse Camp.

Connecting Trails: Twin Sisters Spur, 1104, 980.1(A), 2000

Horse Camping: Read the introduction to this chapter under Indian Creek Trailhead (North), Deep Creek Horse Camp.

Trail Description: Twin Sisters Trail #980 starts from the end of Forest Service Road 1808, although you need to park at Deep Creek Horse Camp to access this trailhead. The Forest Service wants us only to use the horse camp to park at, because horses are not allowed to be in the people camp area, and the horse camp has easier parking too. The trail I call "Twin Sisters Spur Trail" leaves the horse camp, ride it to the northeast for a little over a mile to reach the Twin Sisters Trailhead. Fill out your Wilderness permit and head up the trail, which switchbacks up for over 1-mile on nice wide tread and excellent footing. At the top of the ridge you'll see the 1st of the 2 huge Twin Sisters Lakes, the sun reflecting off the surface sheds light on the underside of the limbs that hang over her. Sand Ridge Trail #1104 leaves to the south (left). This is the high-point of the trail at 5,200'. You'll pass the 2nd of the Twin Sisters Lakes and Big Twin Trail #980.1(A) (hiker only). Head east on rolling trail, riding slightly downhill through meadows and past small ponds. The end of Twin Sisters Trail #980 is at the intersection with the PCT #2000. Many loops are possible to ride from this area.

*NOTE: The Forest Service says the mileage is 4.4 miles, the GTM reads 4.2 miles.

Twin Sisters Spur

Distance:	1.2 Miles
Altitude:	4000'-4500'
Map:	GTM 271 Bumping Lake
Difficulty:	Moderate

Directions: Read the introduction to this chapter under Indian Creek (North), Twin Sister, Twin and Sister Spur Trailheads. Park at Deep Creek Horse Camp to access this trail.

Connecting Trails: 1105, 980

Horse Camping: Read the introduction to this chapter under Indian Creek (North) Trailhead, Deep Creek Horse Camp.

Frying Pan Lake, Josie and Madeleine

Trail Description: Twin Sisters Spur Trail starts at the far end of the camp and travels through the trees and gains 500' in 1.2 miles to reach Twin Sisters Trail #980. Indian Creek Trail #1105 exits a few feet from the start of the Twin Sisters Spur Trail near the horse camp.

*HINT-Are your bottles of water too small? Use the new type of bottle that has a filter inside of it and refill it as much as you need along the trail out of streams, lakes or even puddles. When it is time for a new one it will get hard to squeeze the water out, some last for 5-7 seasons.

Judy fording a river

Windy Ridge #985

> **Distance:** 3.2 Miles
> **Altitude:** 4400'-6300'
> **Map:** GTM 272 Old Scab Mountain
> **Difficulty:** Moderate

Directions: No Trailhead. Access from either Nile Ridge Trail #974 or Richmond Mine Trail #973.

Connecting Trails: 973, 974, 696 (4WD Rd,)

Trail Description: Donna Evans wrote this trail, she and her husband Dean are avid trail riders and friends of mine.

"Windy Ridge Trail #985 leaves the Intersection with Nile Ridge Trail #974, Road 1600, Mud Springs 4x4 Road 696, going south up and out over an open rocky hillside, then descends quite fast. The trail is rocky and a little steep in places. Once down in the bottom the trail undulates through timber and open meadows and it is very peaceful here. In about 3.5 miles from the Clover Springs area the trail ends at the junction with Richmond Mine Trail #973."

Donna

TABLE MOUNTAIN
Haney Meadow & Lion Rock

The Haney Meadow and Lion Rock areas are located in Central Washington, north of Ellensburg and south of Blewett, Swauk Pass off of Highway 97. Its cool high elevation and natural springs make for an oasis in the hot summer. Most of the trails are in the "Moderate" range, which entice many families and clubs to ride here; there is something for everyone. You'll find a major horse camp at Haney Meadow and primitive camping toward Lion Rock. The road to Haney Meadow from Blewett, Swauk Pass is a bit on the steep and narrow side and has pullouts here and there. The route to Lion Rock from Ellensburg is even steeper, with pullouts, and is a one lane paved road. It is paved for a good reason, if it weren't you would probably never get enough traction to get up to the top. On the down side, the pavement makes for quick running tires, be very, very sure you have low enough gears to crawl back down safely. Remember one of the steepest parts of the road is near the bottom, where it becomes straight and you get a false sense of being down off the mountain. Haney Meadow and Lion Rock areas are connected by Forest Service Road 35, which crosses over Table Mountain. This road may be too rough for most rigs to maneuver over safely. I recommend that you check it out on a dry run before tackling it with a full load. You can easily weave the two areas together by day riding. There is lots of feed in the big meadows. Some of these trails are closed to motor bikes and some are not. Read the back of the maps listed in each trail description for information if it is a concern to you. I think its fun to be able to drive the ups and ride on top all day. Judy, Donna, several other friends and I like this area a lot, for us it is our backyard. Be sure to use bear-proof food containers for food storage.

Directions to Haney Meadow: From Highway 97 off Blewett, Swauk Pass, follow the signs to Haney Meadow. Drive south on Forest Service Road 9716, which begins as a paved one lane road and turns into a steep gravel road to Forest Service Road 9712, which is also steep and narrow in spots. It's about 11 miles or so from Highway 97. Camp is at the 5,600' level.

Ken Wilcox Horse Camp: Ken Wilcox Horse Camp has around 20 sites with fire rings, picnic tables, outhouses and tie rails. No fee was charged as of 2001. Bring potable water, stock water is in the stream at the south end of

Haney Meadow. Elk often visit the meadow in the evening and early morning hours, and seem to like the quiet of mid week.

Directions to Lion Rock Area: From I-90 at Ellensburg's west interchange, exit 106. Drive towards Ellensburg and go past the DQ and over the railroad track overpass to Reecer Creek Road, turn left (north). (You will not go into Ellensburg.) Drive about 22 miles to reach the trailheads. When Reecer Creek Road becomes Forest Service Road 35 it is a one lane paved road. It's approximately 10 miles more to reach Lion Rock, the last several miles are gravel and uphill. (This is a very steep road, be sure you have the proper gears to get you back down safely.) At a 4-way intersection, where the sign reads Lion Rock to the left, turn right. Drive a few feet to find a small turnout on the left that leads to an open spot with a primitive camp, it has a big area to turn around. Another idea for parking is to turn left (follow the signs toward Lion Rock). Before Lion Rock there is a road to the left that leads out on a knoll, this is a grand place to park, especially if you're planning to camp.

Camp at Lion Rock Area: Bring your own potable water. Water for your stock may be found several places; there is a small stream in the draw to the east of the knoll described above. There is also a water trough at Lion Rock people camp to the west of the knoll; it is located down the hill from the fenced camp.

Northwest Forest Parking Passes are available at Forest Service offices, they are required at designated trailheads.

Tread lightly and camp friendly...

*NOTE: The GTM 211 Wenatchee is written on the edge of GTM 210 Liberty, as in the connecting map to the east. Although it has yet to be announced when this map will become available, so use the Wenatchee National Forest Map for general use as well as the GTMs listed.

Cle Elum Ranger District	Leavenworth Ranger District
803 West 2nd	600 Sherbourne
Cle Elum, WA 98922	Leavenworth, WA 98826
509-674-4411	509-782-1413

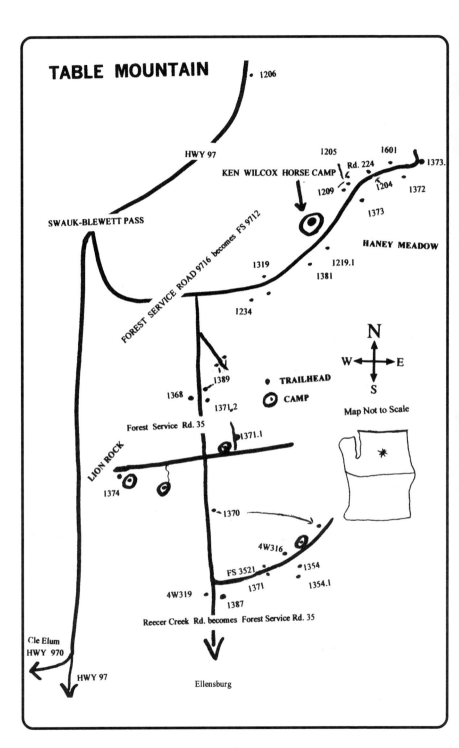

TABLE MOUNTAIN

1206

HWY 97

1205   1601

KEN WILCOX HORSE CAMP   Rd. 224   1373.

SWAUK-BLEWETT PASS   1209   1204   1372

1373

HANEY MEADOW

FOREST SERVICE ROAD 9716 becomes FS 9712

1319   1219.1

1381

1234

N
W ← → E
S

1389

TRAILHEAD

1368   CAMP

1371.2

Map Not to Scale

Forest Service Rd. 35

1371.1

LION ROCK

1374

1370

4W316

FS 3521   1354

4W319   1371   1354.1

1387

Reecer Creek Rd. becomes Forest Service Rd. 35

Cle Elum
HWY 970

HWY 97

Ellensburg

Access Trail

Distance:	1.5 Miles
Altitude:	5500-5600
Map:	GTM 210 Liberty
Difficulty:	Moderate

Directions: Read the directions to Haney Meadow in the introduction to this chapter. Access Trail leaves from camp on the south end.

Connecting Trails: 1381, 1209, Road 224, 1204

Horse Camping: Ken Wilcox Horse Camp is listed in the introduction to this chapter.

Trail Description: Access Trail connects surrounding trails so riders do not need to ride on Forest Service Road 9712. Go south out of camp, the trail takes you through the forest a short way to Naneum Creek #1381. To the north, the Access Trail travels to several trails: the first of which is Table Mountain Trail #1209, then Road 224, and finally to Tronsen Ridge Trail #1204. The north section of Access Trail winds around and up and down. Cross a few sage hills to get to Tronsen Ridge Trail #1204. There are several, other short access trails out of Ken Wilcox Horse Camp toward the west as well.

Elk

Crystal Ridge #4W319

(To Road 3507)

Distance:	2.6 Miles
Altitude:	4800'-5700'
Map:	GTM 242 Thorp
Difficulty:	Moderate-Challenging
	(Steep & rocky sections)

Directions: Read the directions to Lion Rock in the introduction to this chapter, this trail begins at the end of the pavement before the Lion Rock turn-off. Roadside parking is available where the pavement ends at a 3-way intersection, Crystal Ridge Trail #4W319 leaves toward the west and is signed. This is a shared trailhead with Wilson Creek Trail #1387 (sign for Wilson Trail #1387 reads Wilson Stock Driveway).

Horse Camping: Primitive camping only at the Crystal Ridge Trail #4W319 Trailhead along the roadside. Or camp nearby at Lion Rock Area. See the introduction to this chapter for more information.

Connecting Trails: 1387, 1374

Trail Description: This segment of Crystal Ridge Trail #4W319 is directly across the road from Wilson Creek Trail #1387. Crystal Ridge Trail #4W319 travels west, down across open hillsides, and through forest, with several steep rocky sections. View Mount Rainier and Mount Adams from the top of this trail at 5,700'. Ford a creek and meet with the first of 2 signs for First Creek Trail #1374. The first one goes downhill to the left, a few yards more, you will see the other one to the right going to the uphill side of the road. Continue riding on fairly level terrain with a few ups and downs. There was a water crossing that took up the whole road when I was there. Ford a small creek by a meadow with lots of feed. Crystal Ridge Trail #4W319 has several rugged spots, one rocky section that is above a rock slide and a couple of steep climbs to reach a ledge where you'll find views of the town of Cle Elum. (Before the view you will notice a path going around the hill instead of the rougher route straight down the mogul, rutted and root laden hillside that goes down from the view area, I suggest backtracking after getting your photo shots and go around rather than straight down.) The last ½ mile descends 400' and is quite steep, no switchbacks on this 4-wheel drive road! This section of Crystal Ridge

Trail #4W319 ends at the bottom of the hill on one lane paved Forest Service Road 3507. To make a loop, ride 1 mile down the usually quiet road to ride up a portion of First Creek Trail #1374 back to Crystal Ridge Trail #4W319 and your rig. There are a couple of roads that meet with this 4-wheel road; the signs will guide you on the right path.

*HINT-When using a solar shower leave some room in the shower bag, in case it gets too hot in the sun. Add some cold water and clean up your act.

Sandy and Chris breathe in the view

Josie n' Inky near Tronsen Ridge

Drop Creek #1371.1(A)

Distance:	1.2 Miles
Altitude:	5400'-6100'
Map:	GTM 210 Liberty
Difficulty:	Moderate-Challenging (Steep)

Directions: To reach Drop Creek Trailhead, turn the opposite direction from Lion Rock off Forest Service Road 35, go about ¼ mile and turn right, onto a gravel road; the trail leaves on the right side of the road, and it is signed. I suggest riding to the trailhead from the parking areas described in the introduction to this chapter listed under Lion Rock.

Horse Camping: Primitive camping only, see directions in the introduction to this chapter under Lion Rock Camping.

Connecting Trail: 1371

Trail Description: Drop Creek Trail #1371.1(A) use to leave from Forest Service Road 35 (according to the GTM), now it starts on a small logging road to the east and north of there. The trail travels northeast

Howard Creek Trail, Donna and her mare Dotty

to connect with Naneum Wilson Trail #1371. The trail starts in forest and quickly skims a sage and grass hill going down slightly. Drop Creek Trail #1371.1(A) lives up to its name and drops quickly down a ridge and tops out upon a massive gray rock slide. The views of Table Mountain, Naneum Meadow and Mission Ridge are at your fingertips, it's a good time for photos. The trail plummets down, over sharp rocky terrain. Entering into the forest again, the path glides easily down to an old clear-cut area and finds its way along a stream. Drop Creek Trail #1371.1(A) meets Naneum Wilson Trail #1371 at its end. This trail descends about 700' total, and the mileage has been modified from what the GTM shows due to the change in trailhead location.

*NOTE: The GTM shows Drop Creek Trail #1371.1(A) starting from Forest Service Road 35, its trailhead is now around the corner to the northeast off a logging road, it is signed.

Naneum Meadows Trail, Judy and Dory

Elk Trap Springs #1319

Distance:	1.2 Miles
Altitude:	5300'-5700'
Map:	GTM 210 Liberty
Difficulty:	Moderate

Directions: Follow the directions to Haney Meadow in the introduction to this chapter. Just before reaching Haney Meadow you'll see a sign on the left side of Forest Service Road 9712 that reads Elk Trap Springs Trail #1319. This puts you in the middle of the trail, some on each side of the road. Off road parking is available, or access it from Haney Meadow and Lion Rock on a number of connecting trails.

Connecting Trails: 1209, 1234

Horse Camping: Nearby camping at Ken Wilcox Horse Camp at Haney Meadow, read the introduction to this chapter under Ken Wilcox Horse Camp.

Trail Description: Elk Trap Springs Trail #1319 is a connecting trail between Table Mountain Trail #1209 and Naneum Rim Trail #1234. From Table Mountain Trail #1209, the trail travels downhill through the trees. Pass a water trough and the trail turns into a two-track road, cross Forest Service Road 9712. On the trail again, follow a draw down through a meadow, the path travels along a ridge paralleling Naneum Rim Trail #1234 below. There is a spot where the trail splits. Either way is okay

Josie and Judy at Snowshoe Trail

to go, as it comes back together again. Elk Trap Springs Trail #1319 intersects with Naneum Rim Trail #1234 on a hill overlooking Naneum Meadow area. The lower section of trail from Forest Service Road 9712 is not marked except with a yellow horseshoe.

*HINT-Use your own horse's hair to make small repairs such as a missing screw for glasses.

Josie and Sandy near Tronsen Meadow Trail

Nealy Creek Trail

Distance:	5.2 Miles
Altitude:	3900'-6200'
Maps:	GTM 242 Thorp
	GTM 210 Liberty
Difficulty:	Moderate

Directions: First Creek Trail #1374 starts to the west of Lion Rock Camp; you'll see the sign for the trail from the road. Read the Lion Rock Directions in the introduction to this chapter for parking ideas.

Horse Camping: Primitive camping only, follow the directions in the introduction to this chapter under Lion Rock Camping.

Connecting Trail: 4W319

Trail Description: First Creek Trail #1374 begins to the west of Lion Rock Camp (people camp only). There is a water trough with a "stock water" sign posted next to it. After getting your horses a drink, you'll descend into the forest; be aware of old wire here. The trail starts on an old creek bed and is a bit rocky. This 2-mile section of trail to Crystal Ridge Trail #4W319 is mostly in the trees, and sage hills, and heads downward pretty gently. The path runs in and out of meadows and open forest. Pass a wet area where you can offer water to your animals. There are quick views of Mount Rainier and Mount Adams to the south. Travel down an open hillside where it is rather rocky. A pleasant stroll in the timberland brings you to Crystal Ridge Trail #4W319, turn left (east) to find the trail again on the down side of the road. There are nice signs here indicating where you are. From Crystal Ridge Trail #4W319, First Creek Trail #1374 horseshoes around and down alongside of First Creek, now headed west. Here you'll find a big meadow and the creek is so flat it looks like a murky irrigation ditch. The rock formations along this narrow canyon are awesome, with big blocky gray stone in pillars towering on the far side of the creek. Travel down a connecting draw to a steep spot and ford a small stream, this would be a bit of a scramble if ridden the other direction. The path has a few ups and downs, mostly downs and travels along an open hillside (I saw evidence of recent work done to widen the trail in this area). The trail stays somewhat level as the creek drops beside you. Finally the trail comes to the same level as the creek again. Leaving the creek, the trail flattens out in deep forest to reach the one lane paved Forest Service Road 3507. Cross the road to continue the downhill journey on First Creek Trail #1374, ride above a rock slide on an open hill, the path circles around to the bottom of the rocks and in to the trees. This section seems to be less traveled; you may find trees down over the trail. Down is the order of the day as the trail weaves in and out of trees, and lands in a meadow where you'll see a sign in a tree signifying the usage of this trail is open to: horse, hiker and motor bikes. From here the trail becomes a vague 4-wheel trail, follow the bent grass from the wheels across the meadow and forest. The trail comes out onto a gravel road. First Creek Trail #1374 is signed here, although it is no longer a trail, but a 4-wheel drive trail. It continues down with some steep spots and eventually is a single strand in a web of 4-wheel roads. Loops using 4-wheel roads.

*NOTE: The GTM 210 Liberty, lists First Creek Trail #1374 as Cold Springs Trail #1374 (only 1.9 miles). The sign at Lion Rock Camp and trailhead reads First Creek Trail #1374. The GTM 242 Thorp, lists it correctly as First Creek Trail #1374 (5.2 miles).

Ali gets fitted with and elk antler Josie found

Grass Camp #1219

Distance:	3.8 Miles (see note)
Altitude:	5100'-5775'
Map:	GTM 210 Liberty
Difficulty:	Moderate

Directions: No trailhead. Access from Naneum Creek Trail #1381 or Grass Camp Tie Trail #1219.1(A) near Haney Meadow and Ken Wilcox Horse Camp. Read the introduction to this chapter for more information.

Connecting Trails: 1381, 1234, 1219.1(A), 1372

Trail Description: Grass Camp Trail #1219 starts off of Naneum Creek Trail #1381. Begin at a 4-way intersection with Naneum Creek Trail #1381 and Naneum Rim Trail #1234, go east on Grass camp Trail #1219. Cross an old fence line and a stream, then ride next to a rock slide and gently ascend over open slopes and through an old burn area. Grass Camp Tie Trail #1219.1(A) leaves going north at his point. This is the high-point of the trail at 5,775'. Travel under the pines and take a break on the exposed benches to gain views of Glacier Peak and the North Cascade Mountains to the northwest. Bending to the south, follow a canyon rim, which in the fall displays lemon and golden deciduous tamarack trees on the surrounding hillsides. Traverse across meadows and woodlands ending on Howard Creek Trail #1372. Loops everywhere!

*NOTE: The GTM 210 Liberty, lists the mileage for Grass Camp Trail #1219 as 4.3 miles, the Forest Service says it is 3.8 miles in length.

*HINT-Duct tape is a handy item to include in your saddle, it can be used in many ways to fix broken things, or even to wrap your hands with for a make shift pair of gloves. I've seen it used when a horse looses a shoe and no easy boot would fit, wrap the hoof for protection until a real shoe can be nailed on.

Grass Camp Tie #1219.1(A)

Distance: .	8 Mile
Altitude:	5600'-5775'
Map:	GTM 210 Liberty
Difficulty:	Moderate

Directions: Read the directions to Haney Meadow and Ken Wilcox Horse Camp in the introduction to this chapter. Grass Camp Tie Trail #1219.1(A) exits the Ken Wilcox Horse Camp and Haney Meadow toward the south down by the creek.

Connecting Trail: 1219

Horse Camping: Ken Wilcox Horse Camp is nearby. See directions in the Introduction to this chapter.

Trail Description: Grass Camp Tie Trail #1219.1(A) begins on the south end of Haney Meadow, here you'll see a wooden fence, one side has a trail down to stock water and the other side is Grass Camp Tie Trail #1219.1(A). Cross a stream and head up through the forest, as the trail levels out you'll intersect with Grass Camp Trail #1219. Wonderful soft footing for your animals. Loops are possible from here.

Madeleine and her horse on Grouse Springs Trail

Distance:	3.5 Miles
Altitude:	5300'-5800'
Maps:	Wenatchee National Forest
	GTM 210 Liberty
Difficulty:	Moderate

Directions: Read the introduction to this chapter for more information to get to Haney Meadow. Grouse Springs Trail #1373.1(A) starts off Forest Service Road 9712, several miles past Haney Meadow, but the road is not recommended for trailers.

Connecting Trails: 1373.2(B), 1373

Horse Camping: Nearby camping at Ken Wilcox Horse Camp at Haney Meadow. Read the directions to the camp in the introduction to this chapter.

Trail Description: Grouse Springs Trail #1373.1(A) can be accessed from either end. It will be described from the north end going to the south end. On Forest Service Road 9712 (just up, past where No Name Trail #1373.2(B) meets Forest Service Road 9712) Grouse Springs Trail #1373.1(A) leaves on a hairpin turn. There is a sign and a map box indicating the trail. Multitudes of views await you, so bring your camera! Ride with rocky ledges and rims above you on the ridge, which you'll soon be riding on. The trail begins as an old jeep road on a ridge; it is steep in spots. Odd rock formations entice you to ride further. Grouse Springs Trail #1373.1(A) will take you over the top of rocks and bring you to a rim, which is to the left of an old jeep road. There you'll see some painted signs in the shape of horseshoes, one yellow and one blue. Follow the horseshoes, now on trail around a knoll down through meadows. The town of Wenatchee is to the far left, way below. On the hillsides, the trail levels out to follow more horseshoe markers (they are facing the opposite way you are) to another small old jeep road at Grouse Spring where Old Ellensburg Trail #1373 connects. This is a new trail and was not found on the maps listed above as of 2001. Loops abound!

Wilson Trail- Indian paintbrush flowers

High Creek #1354.1(A) (see note)

Distance:	2.4 Miles
Altitude:	5400'-5600'
Map:	GTM 242 Thorp
Difficulty:	Moderate-Challenging
	(Vague tread)

Directions: No Trailhead. Access from Ragan Trail #1354 or from Wilson Creek Trail #1387. Use the directions to Lion Rock at the introduction to this chapter, except when the road becomes gravel at a 3-way intersection, turn right and drive approximately 3 miles on Forest Service Road 3521 (keep right, the lower road at a split in the road). Parking is on the roadside or there is a campsite with parking, to the left of Ragan Trailhead.

Connecting Trails: 1354, 1387

Trail Description: High Creek Trail #1354.1(A) starts a stone's throw down Ragan Trail #1354 off Forest Service Road 3521. Leaving Ragan Trail #1354, High Creek Trail #1354.1(A) heads up towards the west, in the shadow of old growth trees, on the edge of an aged logging area. The trail becomes wide, almost a two-track, then practically vanishes completely as it skims a sage hillside. Follow rock cairns as you go cross-country down the east side of High Creek's drainage; the trail is now traveling south. In a tree there is a diamond shape marker, gray-silver in color, marking the way. The path works its way into green forest down by High Creek with one small switchback. Pass a sign in a tree, which reads High Creek Trail #1354.1(A) with arrows guiding you. There were several paths here due to range cattle creating new trails. Pass a wet area and continue to descend in the cool shade of the trees. The trail crosses High Creek. HALT! The trail becomes lost in an old clear-cut area. Look west (right) to a ridge and spot the trail at the top. Ride over and pick your path up the hill, the "slow elk (cows)" have had there way with this area and have left lots of paths. On top more rock cairns will lead you up and over the sagebrush covered hillside. High Creek Trail #1354.1(A) heads into an old growth area again, ford a small stream (at one time it had a bridge), then back in to sage again, this time find a post with the number 210 vertically written on it. Turn left here (south). Do not follow the "slow elk" prints onto the wrong path. Go over the knoll and down, passing a grove of dead trees to meet Wilson Creek Trail #1387. High Creek Trail #1354.1(A) is hard to follow in many areas with rocky spots and may not be for everyone. Loops possible.

*NOTE: This trail is listed on the GTM as #1354.

Josie rides Naneum Creek Trail, odd rocks in background

Howard Creek #1372

Distance:	5.2 Miles
Altitude:	5100'-5500'
Map:	GTM 210 Liberty
Difficulty:	Moderate

Directions: Use the directions listed in the introduction to this chapter, listed under Haney Meadow. You'll find a small turnout for parking a few miles past Haney Meadow at the trailhead on the right side of the road. Howard Creek Trail #1372 can be accessed from the trails listed below as well.

Connecting Trails: 1601, 1373, 1373.2(B), 1219, 1381

Horse Camping: Nearby camping at Ken Wilcox Horse Camp at Haney Meadow, see the introduction for this chapter for more details.

Trail Description: Howard Creek Trail #1372 travels south from Forest Service Road 9712. Head down into deep green forest, with nice footing for the animals. There are a few rutty spots as the trail descends, but is short lived. You'll cross several creeks, with roots here and there. Old Ellensburg Trail #1373 intersects from the west (right). Continue on, the other end of Old Ellensburg Trail #1373 departs going east (left). A new trail, I'll call No Name #1373.2(B) also leaves from this area, and goes east. Howard Creek Trail #1372 heads up and over grassy hillsides. The views from this vantage are of the Naneum drainage and Mission Ridge. Ride through a decaying clear-cut area and cross a road. The trail bends toward the west. Grass Camp Trail #1219 exits uphill to the north. The trail ends at Naneum Creek Trail #1381. Loops galore!

*H1NT- Is it going to be fair weather? Ask your "Pringles" potato chip can, unopened, the top will concave slightly when stable, high pressure (fair weather) is present and when low pressure (unstable weather coming in) it will pooch up. Or ask your campfire, the smoke will rise straight up-good weather, if the smoke is erratic and low to the ground-better pack the rain gear.

Magnet Creek #1206·

Distance:	3 Miles
Altitude:	2700'-4285'
Map:	GTM 210 Liberty
Difficulty:	Challenging

Directions: Magnet Creek Trail #1206 can be accessed from Highway 97. From Blewett, Swauk Pass drive about 5 miles down towards the north, the trail begins between mile post 171 and 172 where we found a mere ribbon in the tree marking the path. The traffic is swift; Highway 97 access is not recommended, although there is roadside parking about ¼ mile down the road by the end of the guardrail. Donna and I accessed this trail from the other end at Tronsen Ridge Trail #1209. Use the Haney Meadow directions described at the beginning of this chapter, and refer to the Tronsen Ridge Trail for more information.

Connecting Trail: 1204

Trail Description: Magnet Creek Trail #1206 will be described from top to bottom starting with the intersection of Tronsen Ridge Trail #1204. Magnet Creek Trail #1206 heads west for ¾ mile on an old logging road, it is overgrown and rather brushy. The trail climbs and then levels periodically as it travels over knolls with terrific views of the surrounding valleys and mountains. You can hear the traffic below on Highway 97. The tread is narrow, slouchy with pea size gravel and is on a slant as it travels down and up across an open ridge with cliffs, there is lots of drop off areas here. Magnet Creek Trail #1206 is relentless as it launches downhill to the valley floor; in the green brush, it becomes flat for the last couple of feet.

*NOTE: *Warning-***Only the most experienced rider and livestock teams should attempt this trail, and then extreme caution should be taken! This trail is categorized as "other trails" on the GTM.**

"A RIVER OF FEAR"

I went alone to Haney Meadow to pout, as my faithful old buckskin gelding had a pulled stifle bone and was not able to be ridden. So I went camping without him. I was angry he was hurt and fed up with myself for having so much trouble kicking the cigarette habit, I decided to go for a week and leave the smokes behind. Yup, this was an opportunity not to be missed. I arrived and had the place to myself (after Labor Day and before hunting season), I made camp just beyond what is now known as the Ken Wilcox Horse Camp. The first night out, I fell asleep under the stars; there was no moon. I had taken my sleeping bag on top of my camper shell to make my nest; I woke with a start, but dared not move for my heightened senses petrified my muscles. I heard the crunching, the accelerated breathing and the thud of its hurried feet, wait…no, something is wrong, what could it be? How *many* are there? The noise is louder, like a river of breath and an army of stampeding feet, parting around me, as if my truck were an island. Thank God I'm on my truck, if I'd been in a tent I would have been trampled, or perhaps even worse, eaten alive! I gritted my teeth, and with sheer will power; I pried my eye lids open. Total blackness, even the stars were hiding under a safety blanket of clouds. I ordered my arm to move, silently it slinked over to the flashlight. I had to know what was going to kill me, surely my life would be flashing before my eyes any second now, and I, at least had the right to know what it was! My heart was beating so rapidly and my blood rushed to my temples as my fingers toyed with the "on" button, I aimed the headlight down, I could feel the breeze of chaos below. I'll be brave; I'll click the button. Forcing the pent-up adrenaline into my fingers, I was able push the button and the scene unfolded as the light cut through the unknown. The light beamed through the thick darkness, as I was on the verge of passing out, I saw *them* they were big and hairy and smelly and made me laugh and cry at the same time. Slow elk! A whole herd of cattle, running for their lives, it was a virtual sea of rusty, black, and tan hides, crammed so tightly together, I could have walked on them to the edge of the meadow. The odd thing was they made no cattle sounds, not a moo was murmured, I would have paid handsomely for a *moo,* before the light had been shown. The rest of the night was spent waiting for whatever had spooked them to come and eat me. You'll be glad to hear that when my week was done, I returned home a non-smoker.

Mount Lillian #1601

Distance:	1.7 Miles
Altitude:	5500'-6100'
Map:	GTM 210 Liberty
Difficulty:	Moderate

Directions: Use the directions for Haney Meadow in the introduction to this chapter. Go past Ken Wilcox Camp a few miles. You'll find a small turnout for parking just beyond the Mount Lillian Trailhead at Howard Creek Trailhead, which is on the right hand side of the road. Mount Lillian Trail #1601 can also be accessed ½ mile up the Tronsen Ridge Trail #1204, which is about 1 mile past Haney Meadow. Parking at Tronsen Ridge Trailhead is too tight and can be muddy. I found it most convenient to ride from camp and use this trail in a loop.

Connecting Trails: 1204, 1372

Horse Camping: Nearby camping at Ken Wilcox Horse Camp at Haney Meadow. Use the directions listed in the introduction of this chapter.

Trail Description: Mount Lillian Trail #1601 will be described from Tronsen Ridge Trail #1204, it heads to the southeast. Mount Lillian Trail #1206 begins in forest and climbs to a bluff to attain awesome picture opportunities of the Devil's Gulch area, which is straight down, you can feel the updraft that the birds soar on. The town of Wenatchee and its lake are way below in the distance to the north. Continue onward over a rocky knoll and down the well placed switchbacks that travel over rugged, stony trail. There are unusual shaped rocks here and worth some more pictures. After entering the timber again the trail continues on its descent to Forest Service Road 9712. Loops can be made using Howard Creek Trail #1372, which is just around the corner on the right hand side of the road.

Naneum Creek #1381

Distance:	5.1 Miles
Altitude:	5200'-5500'
Maps:	GTM 210 Liberty
	Wenatchee National Forest
Difficulty:	Moderate

Directions: Use the directions to Haney Meadow listed in the introduction of this chapter. Park at Ken Wilcox Horse Camp at Haney Meadow and ride an access trail to reach Naneum Creek Trail #1381.

Connecting Trails: 1234, 1219, 1389, 1372

Horse Camping: Ken Wilcox Horse Camp is listed in the introduction of this chapter.

Trail Description: Naneum Creek Trail #1381 travels from the north towards the southeast. To begin this trail from Forest Service Road 9712, head downhill through the grassy meadows, under the tall timber to Naneum Meadow and Naneum Creek. You'll find a 4-way intersection of trails. Naneum Rim Trail #1234 takes off headed uphill to the right (west) across the creek, Grass Camp Trail #1219 leaves to the left (east) also headed uphill. Continue on level trail to clip-clop across a very long bridge that goes over wet lands, ride by a rock slide and meet with Naneum Meadows Trail #1389, which departs toward the west. Ride up a hillside to an open steppe to view the Naneum Canyon to the east. Next, Howard Creek Trail #1372 exits going straight as Naneum Creek Trail #1381 veers toward the right (south). The last 2 miles heads downhill and then levels out in a lovely grass dell. On the left (north) side you'll see a lot of odd rock that forms a wall. Travel along side of the West Fork Naneum Creek with old growth timber and small groves of aspen trees keeping you company. Ride across Forest Service Road 3530 (see the note below). Naneum Creek Trail #1381 quickly ends and becomes an old two-track road. This trail is an easy stroll for most any trail horse and rider team. Lots of options for making loops. If you wish to continue riding to make a loop read on, some of the area described is off the GTM map and be advised the trail-road becomes difficult as it goes by a lake. You will cross a rock slide (best done by riding in the creek, rather than risking getting hurt by sharp edges of the rocks and holes in between them). The two-track goes uphill, continue straight to reach another road at the far end of the lake, the trail requires you to go slow and careful as you clamor across another rock slide above the unnamed lake. This time there is no other option but to ride over the treacherous rocks. Turn left (north) on the road. Ride up the road for about 3 miles more to make a loop, keeping in mind to stay on the main road, and towards the left. Ride up to yet another rock slide area, where the road winds its way around and to the top. You will finally arrive at a meadow with sagebrush; this is Grouse Springs where Old Ellensburg Trail #1373 and Grouse Springs Trail #1373.1(A) meet to make a loop. Have fun and stay safe.

*NOTE: A note from the Forest Service-The short stretch of trail below Forest Service Road 3530 is no longer maintained by the Forest Service since it quickly leads onto private and state lands.

*H1NT-Keep a small bag with one full set of dry clothes in your trailer, it can make a delightful difference to a wet, cold and tired rider returning from a ride.

Near Lion Rock

Naneum Meadows #1389

Distance:	3.2 Miles
Altitude:	5100'-6000'
Map:	GTM 210 Liberty
Difficulty:	Moderate

Directions: Use either the Lion Rock or the Haney Meadows directions, listed in the introduction to this chapter. See the map to decide where you want to access it. Naneum Meadows Trail #1389 does have a trailhead, although due to low clearance on Forest Service Road 35, it is better to ride one of the trails listed below to attain access.

Connecting Trails: 1381, 1371

Horse Camping: Nearby camping at Ken Wilcox Horse Camp at Haney Meadow, or Lion Rock Area, see details in the introduction to this chapter.

Trail Description: Naneum Meadows Trail #1389 runs east and west, it will be described from the east-end going to the west-end. Starting from Naneum Creek Trail #1381 Naneum Meadows Trail #1389 heads west through forest skimming the edge of Naneum Meadow on its south end. Cross Forest Service Road 3530 (not a good road to access this trail due to no turnaround) and begin climbing through the forest After about 1 mile Naneum Wilson Trail #1371 leaves headed south (left). The remaining couple of miles are steadily ascending with some steep sections, to reach Forest Service Road 35, where it ends. You'll ford Owl Creek, where your steeds can quench their thirsts. This is a nice medium type trail for those of you who are getting bored with the easy trails. To get to Lion Rock, turn left (south) on Forest Service Road 35. Enjoy the views from the ledge of the town of Cle Elum down below and all the neighboring mountains including the Stuart Mountain Range, it's great time to take some snapshots. Loops possible from the Lion Rock Area.

Naneum Rim #1234

Distance:	1 Mile
Altitude:	5100'-5600'
Map:	GTM 210 Liberty
Difficulty:	Moderate

Directions: Naneum Rim Trail #1234 starts off Forest Service Road 9712 before Haney Meadow, there are a couple of small turnouts to park in, before the trail leaves Forest Service Road 9712. Or, you can ride the connecting trails listed below from Ken Wilcox Horse Camp and Haney Meadow. For directions to Haney Meadow and the camp, see the introduction to this chapter.

Connecting Trails: 1209, 1319, 1381, 1219

Horse Camping: Ken Wilcox Horse Camp is nearby or roadside primitive camp. See details on how to get to Haney Meadow and the horse camp. It is listed in the introduction to this chapter.

Trail Description: Naneum Rim Trail #1234 has a shared trailhead off Forest Service Road 9712 with Table Mountain Trail #1209, which goes uphill, Naneum Rim Trail goes downhill. Naneum Rim Trail #1234 runs west and east. From Forest Service Road 9712 the trail heads down to a treed area where you'll find a water trough in a small meadow. The trail travels atop an open rim made of gray lava. The views to the south are of the head of Naneum Canyon and Naneum Meadow. Straight down is a small valley with Forest Service Road 3530 paralleling the rim you are on. Heading down a hillside toward Naneum Meadow you'll pass Elk Trap Springs Trail #1319, which is marked by a wooden sign in the shape of a yellow horseshoe. Naneum Rim Trail #1234 ends at a 4-way intersection with Naneum Creek Trail #1381 and across the creek is Grass Camp Trail #1219. There are loads of loops to discover in this area.

Naneum Wilson #1371

Distance:	6.5 Miles
Altitude:	5000'-6000'
Maps:	GTM 210 Liberty
	GTM 242 Thorp
Difficulty:	Moderate-Challenging
	(Steep rocky sections)

Directions: No trailhead, access from the north end at Naneum Meadows Trail #1389 or from the south end at Wilson Creek Trail #1387. This trail is used to connect Lion Rock and Haney Meadow. See the map to decide which area you'll park at.

Connecting Trails: 1389, 1371.2(B), 1371.1(A), 1370 (4W315), Ragan (4W316), 1387

Horse Camping: Near the north end of Naneum Wilson Trail #1371, you can camp at Ken Wilcox Horse Camp / Haney Meadow. Near the south end of the trail, primitive camping is available at the Lion Rock area. See the introduction to this chapter for more information.

Trail Description: Naneum Wilson Trail #1371 can be ridden from the north end near Naneum Meadow or from the south, near the Lion Rock Area. The trail will be described from the south end heading north towards Naneum Meadow. Starting from the intersection with Wilson Trail #1387, Naneum Wilson Trail #1371 goes uphill, the path travels across a meadow and a seasonal stream. Follow rock cairns as they take you through another meadow, you'll have views behind you of Mount Rainier, and the far off snow topped Goat Rocks Mountains, and all the ridges in between. The flowers are in bloom in late July here, the reds, purples and white colors are spectacular. Travel into yet another meadow, then cross a road. Head uphill and enter old growth trees with some roots on the trail. Cross another road, more meadows and rock cairns, you may spot the 2 mile-marker in a tree. Meet with Ragan Trail (4W316) the trail levels a bit and dips down. Ford a small creek and go up to intersect with Nealy Creek #1370 (4W315). You're at the 3.2 mile-point on Naneum Wilson Trail #1371. Heading north, ride in the forest slightly downhill. Cross a creek and the trail gets steeper by a huge rock slide area. Go around to the bottom with switchbacks on rocky trail. Ford a creek, then ride next to more of the rock slide area and meet another creek. Here you will find Drop Creek Trail #1371.1(A) coming in from the west. There are several signs to guide you onward. Cross a logging road near an old clear-cut area. Ride on flatter terrain into a meadow, then under more cool trees to another dilapidated logging area, and a stream. The big emerald leaves of the plants are beautiful here. Ride a rocky, steep section of trail down to a creek that is divided into 3 parts to cross. Owl Creek Trail #1371.2(B) leaves toward the west. Now get ready to climb a long steep hill to a ridge. The climb brings you to lush grass filled meadows. (Here is an interesting spot beside the main trail, I haven't decided yet whether this path is a shortcut or the old trail that departs to the west

Madeleine and her mare

marked by post and rock cairns. It takes you across a beautiful meadow and up through trees to intersect with Naneum Meadows Trail #1389, here you'll find a sign indicating so. If you were riding Naneum Meadows Trail #1389 you would not know where this old trail goes, as it is not signed Naneum Wilson Trail #1371 on either end.) Continuing on the well-beaten trail, it travels out and around a rocky rim overlooking both the Naneum and Wilson drainage. Clop across a small new bridge and an open area with more meadows, and old trees. The trail ends as it "T" intersects with Naneum Meadows Trail #1389. Lots of loops to explore here using small amounts of road to connect the trails.

*HINT- Want to be snug in the lawn chair around the campfire? Barrow your horse's clean wool pad to line the lawn chair before sitting down.

Ali, Josie and dog, Tess, ride Wilson Trail

Nealy Creek #1370 (4W315) (see note)

Distance:	2.3 Miles
Altitude:	5200'-6000'
Map:	GTM 242 Thorp
Difficulty:	Moderate

Directions: See the directions to Lion Rock in the introduction to this chapter. The trail leaves Forest Service Road 35 before reaching the turn-off to Lion Rock, it is on the east (right) side, there is no good parking here. Continue on to the next main dirt road and turn left (follow the signs toward Lion Rock). Before Lion Rock there is a road to the left that leads out on a knoll, this is a grand place to park, especially if you're planning to camp. Ride cross-country or follow the road back to the trailhead, about ½ mile.

Connecting Trails: 4W316, 1371

Horse Camping: Read the description of the camping at Lion Rock in the introduction to this chapter.

Trail Description: Nealy Creek Trail #1370 (4W315) can be accessed from either end. It will be described from Forest Service Road 35 going toward the east. The trail starts by going uphill in forest, then levels with a few rocks and roots. Mountain Masters Jeep Club maintains this trail, according to a sign tacked to a tree. Unsigned, Ragan Trail 4W316 meets coming in from the south. Nealy Creek Trail #1370 (4W315) rolls along passing aspen trees, sage and meadows. Naneum Wilson Trail #1371 crosses at the 1 mile-point. Continue on with about 4 steep drops to maneuver down. Pass a rock slide area and a meadow to level out a bit in a meadow with water for your animals. This trail ends at Forest Service Road 3521; there is no good parking at this end either! Loops possible, if you don't mind 1 mile of road that has great views of the Naneum drainage and Mission Ridge (see Ragan Trail #4W316).

*NOTE: Nealy Creek Trail #1370 is listed as 4W315 on GTM.

"YOUR FREE & I FEEL BETTER, THANKS!"

Sometimes you just need to go for a drive, alone. I found myself at Haney Meadow one fine spring afternoon, on a Sunday, I think. I came for quiet and solitude to just "be". There was still lingering snow on the roads; it was a challenge to get my old 69' Chevy truck up to this point because it was only a 2-WD, although it does have a stick shift and a hell of a granny gear. I turned off the engine to hear the silence, which I did for a few seconds. A loud cry of relief echoed off the mountains as a man emerged from beyond Haney Meadow on the slippery road. He was half running as he shuffled in his big boots laden with mud, part of me wanted to leave, and the other part said stay and see what he wants. You can rely on your inner self, it will always tell you when there is danger, this time I felt none. He had sweat on his brow and a worried look on his mouth. He told me he was stuck in the mud and had been there since early morning, hoping to hear someone come up the mountain to help him. Well that must be me, I thought since no one else was there! I had a big roll of yellow nylon rope in the back of the truck, however it was narrow gage. After breaking several ropes, we finally quadrupled it and were able to free him from the grip of the sucky mud; it took about 45 minutes or so. I felt great, helping him totally made my day and he was very grateful!

Josie

276

Mount Lillian Trail

Distance:	1.6 Miles
Altitude:	5600'-5900'
Map:	GTM 210 Liberty
Difficulty:	Moderate

Directions: Read the directions to Haney Meadow in the introduction to this chapter. No Name Road 224 starts past Haney Meadow on Forest Service Road 9712 and heads uphill; the other end is also off Forest Service Road 9712 near Tronsen Ridge Trail #1204.

Connecting Trails: Access Trail, 1205, 1204, 1601, hiker only trail

Horse Camping: Ken Wilcox Camp is nearby at Haney Meadow. See the introduction to this chapter for more information.

Trail Description: Road 224 makes a loop off of Forest Service Road 9712. This is a "must see" for the view of the Stuart Mountain Range, Mount Rainier and far off snow capped mountains in the North Cascade Mountain Range. The road goes uphill and crosses Access Trail, and then at the top of the ridge it meets with Tronsen Meadow Trail #1205. There are a few rough spots in the tread as it climbs then rolls up toward a rock outcropping area. Take out the camera. A hiker only trail leaves to the north, which connects to Tronsen Ridge Trail #1204. Going away from the ridge and in to the trees the road levels somewhat to reach Tronsen Ridge Trail #1204. Road 224 and Tronsen Ridge Trail #1204 become one for a short distance across a meadow. Ride down to where Mount Lillian Trail #1601 hooks in, this is where Road 224 splits with Tronsen Ridge Trail #1204. The Tronsen Ridge Trail #1204 and Road 224 run parallel with each other, a small creek divides them. Road 224 ends at Forest Service Road 9712. Used for making loops and great snap shots!

*NOTE: The GTM shows part of this road as #4W312, and part of the road is not shown at all. It is not listed at all on the back of the GTM.

No Name #1373.2(B)

Distance:	1.5 Miles
Altitude:	5200'-5700'
Maps:	GTM 210 Liberty
	Wenatchee National Forest
Difficulty:	Moderate

Directions: There is no trailhead for No Name Trail #1373.2(B). Access is attained from Howard Creek Trail #1372 or Grouse Springs Trail #1373.1(A). Read the directions to Haney Meadow at the beginning of this chapter.

Connecting Trails: 1372, 1373.1

Horse Camping: Nearby camping at Ken Wilcox Horse Camp at Haney Meadow. Read the directions to the camp at the introduction to this chapter.

Trail Description: No Name Trail #1373.2(B) is a connecting trail for making loops. It joins Howard Creek Trail #1372 to Grouse Springs Trail #1373.1(A). This is a newer trail and was not found on the maps listed above as of 2001. From Howard Creek Trail #1372, No Name Trail #1373.2(B) exits and travels west. Cross a creek and switchback up through trees with good footing. Travel up and over a knoll passing many grassy hillsides. The trail rolls along, you'll see Forest Service Road 9712, which parallels the trail and in a few turns ends on it. For a loop, ride the road up to the right towards a wooden sign on the side of the road by an old two-track. This is the beginning of Grouse Springs Trail #1373.1(A), at one time the trail number was listed on the sign and another time it was missing from the sign.

Old Ellensburg #1373

Distance:	3.6 Miles
Altitude:	5100'-5300'
Maps:	GTM 210 Liberty
	Wenatchee National Forest
Difficulty:	Moderate

Directions: Use the directions listed in the introduction to this chapter to reach Haney Meadow. Old Ellensburg Trail #1373 starts about ½ mile past Haney Meadow on the east (right) side of Forest Service Road 9712. Park at Haney Meadow and Ken Wilcox Horse Camp.

Connecting Trails: 1372, 1373.1(A)

Horse Camping: Ken Wilcox Horse Camp is listed in the introduction to this chapter for more information.

Trail Description: Old Ellensburg Trail #1373 begins off Forest Service Road 9712 and heads southeast. Ride downhill slightly to cross a creek, level out and curve around Haney Meadow's north end, which you can barely see thorough the trees. Climb a knoll and start a gradual descent. Crossing open hills sprinkled with tall old growth timber, you'll ride down a dell for about 1-mile to intersect with Howard Creek Trail #1372. Here you need to turn right (south) on Howard Creek Trail #1372 for about ¼ mile or less. Now catch Old Ellensburg Trail #1373 again, headed southeast (left). Ford Howard Creek, the path rolls along down toward Grouse Springs mostly in timber with some meadow and sage hillsides. When reaching the springs you can decide which way to go to make a loop. A newer trail, Grouse Springs Trail #1373.1(A) is marked by wooden horseshoe signs, and it takes off toward the northeast, or you can ride a road for 3 miles and connect with Naneum Creek Trail #1381 (see Naneum Creek #1381 for details). The last part of this trail is off the GTM and the connecting GTM has yet to be released, use the Wenatchee National Forest Map for a general idea of the area.

*NOTE: The Forest Service has informed me that these horseshoe markers and the trail mentioned above are not part of the Forest Service trail system, and is not authorized or maintained by them. The actual Grouse Springs Trail follows the old jeep trail (now closed to jeep travel) and goes from Forest Service Road 9712 to Grouse Springs.

"EVER HEARD A COW BARK?"

One beautiful summer day Judy, Sandy and I were trail riding along Old Ellensburg Trail near Haney Meadow. The forest was thick with undergrowth and logs in this area. We startled some huge cow elk, and we noticed they were somewhat reluctant to budge from the path, so we yielded to the wildlife, we sat and waited, and waited, one big ol' brazen female was very stubborn. We looked for a way around her, although the forest was too jam-packed to get around, so we waited some more, a good lesson in practicing patience, I figured. We inched our way forward slowly, then she started to move toward us, 'taint natural we thought, and we backed off, this could take a while. She was clearly upset with us invading her nursery, we figured she must have a little one close at hoof. Once she came straight at us, head craned up, and her "U" shaped neck stretched out and let out a series of baritone barks, the horses were transfixed, but calm. After about 30 minutes, she ultimately moved enough for us to very cautiously walk on by.

Josie

Donna and Josie delight in their trail ride

Owl Creek #1371.2(B)

Distance:	1.7 Miles
Altitude:	5000'-6100'
Map:	GTM 210 Liberty
Difficulty:	Moderate

Directions: Read the directions to Lion Rock in the introduction to this chapter, I like to park on the knoll and ride to the trailhead. Backtrack to the intersection that has the Lion Rock sign, this time go straight. This section of Road 35 going towards the trailhead is rough and parking is limited and tight. Ride the rough road and pass through the gate beside a cattle guard, Owl Creek Trailhead is on the right (east) side of the road, and is signed; it is a shared trailhead with Snowshoe Ridge Trail. This trail is accessed from Haney Meadow by using the trails listed below.

Connecting Trails: 1368, 1371

Horse Camping: Read the Lion Rock information listed in the introduction to this chapter.

Trail Description: Owl Creek Trail #1371.2(B) can be ridden from either end. The top end is from Forest Service Road 35 (shared trailhead with Snowshoe Ridge Trail #1368) and the bottom end is from Naneum Wilson Trail #1371. This trail has an elevation change of 900' in 1.7 miles. Owl Creek Trail is mostly in forest with some meadows and some steep spots. It crosses roads 4 times. When riding up the trail, you'll find the trail continues to the south (left) when crossing the roads, and when traveling down the trail, the trail continues to the north (left). Towards the top of the trail you may spot an old sign in the tree that reads Owl Creek Spur Trail #1371.1(A). The sign off of Forest Service Road reads Owl Creek Trail #1371.2(B) and they're only a few feet apart! There are a lot of rocky spots on this trail; it seems to follow an old creek bottom. The only water we found was a puddle near one of the road crossings. There is a seasonal creek bed toward the middle of the trail. Loops possible if you don't mind a little road riding.

Ragan #1354 (see note)

Distance:	1.4 Miles
Altitude:	5300'-5600'
Maps:	GTM 242 Thorp
	GTM 243 Colockum Pass
Difficulty:	Moderate

Directions: Use the directions to Lion Rock at the introduction to this chapter, except when the road becomes gravel at a 3-way intersection, turn right and drive approximately 3 miles on Forest Service Road 3521 (keep right, the lower road at a split in the road). Parking is on the roadside or there is a campsite with parking, to the left of the trailhead.

Connecting Trail: 1354.1(A), 4W316

Horse Camping: Use the directions to Lion Rock listed in the introduction to this chapter for the closest camping or primitive camp alongside the Forest Service Roads.

Trail Description: Ragan Trail #1354 starts at a former logging area and travels southeast. It looks like a two-track at first glance, but soon you realize it is a real trail. The path enters old growth timber and intersects with High Creek Trail #1354.1(A), which leaves toward the right (west). You'll travel across meadows, sage hills and rocky spots. The trail contours a ridge. The path is almost lost in the deep grass. There is a milepost "4" in a tree (must have been an old sign, when the whole trail was trail, now part of the original trail is Ragan 4W316 Road). Travel along a hillside and the trail becomes less noticeable. Follow a vague two-track across sage fields marked with rock cairns, which are hard to see due to the growth of the sage. On the other side of the sage field, enter an old growth area again, the trail disappears at the National Forest Boundary and a newer logged area. I found this to be a delightful little trail to add on to a day ride in the area.

*Note: The sign at Ragan Trailhead reads #1354, and the High Creek sign as #1354.1(A). The GTM reads Ragan 4W316 and High Creek as #1354.

Distance:	2.9 Miles
Altitude:	5600'-6187'
Map:	GTM 242 Thorp
Difficulty:	Moderate

Directions: No Trailhead. Access from Nealy Creek Trail #1370 (4W315). Follow the directions for Lion Rock for the closest camp and trailhead information.

Connecting Trails: 1370 (4W315), 1371, 1354

Trail Description: Ragan Trail #4W316 will be described from Nealy Creek Trail #1370 (4W315). This trail travels northwest to southeast. It is a beautiful stroll for any level of horseman and mount it goes gently down under a canopy of trees and through old logged areas. Naneum Wilson Trail #1371 crosses at about the 1 mile-point. You'll ride pass a dead end gravel road (not on the GTM). Ride across an open rim to view Mission Ridge and the Naneum drainage. The trail ends at Forest Service Road 3521. A Loop is possible with Nealy Creek #1370 (4W315) by taking Forest Service Road 3521 to the left for about 1 mile, keep in mind that Ragan Trail 4W316 is much gentler than Nealy Creek #1370 (4W315).

*NOTE: The GTM shows this trail continuing across Forest Service Road 3521, and it does. The trails are labeled differently, one as a 4-wheel drive, and the section across the road as Ragan Trail #1354, so they are listed separately.

"HARE DINNER INTERUPTED"

My friend Donna and I decided on a late autumn ride at Haney Meadow, as we made our way down the Naneum Creek Trail we came upon a snow-white mound of velveteen fur at the base of a mammoth tree. My horse usually doesn't spook much, however, she sidestepped this area where the fur ball lay. We reined up for a second for a closer look and were able to identify the remains of the animal, a snowshoe hare, but even dental records wouldn't help, because the head was missing, a clean decapitation I might add, no blood except the tiny ring around the spinal cord. My horse blew and snorted a bit. It felt eerie and the forest was deadly silent. Donna and I think that we interrupted someone's dinner and the smell of that someone was still in the air, alerting the horses to danger. The predator may have been in the nearby scrub watching us pass by.

Josie

Naneum Meadows Trail, Madeleine, Josie and Sandy on a pleasure ride

Snowshoe Ridge #1368

Distance:	2.5 Miles
Altitude:	5400'-6100'
Map:	GTM 210 Liberty
Difficulty:	Moderate-Challenging
	(Steep rocky sections)

Directions: Read the directions to Lion Rock in the introduction to this chapter, I like to park on the knoll and ride to the trailhead. Backtrack to the intersection that has the Lion Rock sign, this time go straight. This section of Road 35 going towards the trailhead is rough and parking is limited and tight. Ride the rough road and pass through the gate beside a cattle guard, the Snowshoe Ridge Trailhead is on the left (west) side of the road, and is signed; it is a shared trailhead with Owl Creek Trail.

Horse Camping: See the camping for Lion Rock listed at the beginning of this chapter.

Connecting Trail: 1371.2(B)

Trail   Description: Snowshoe Ridge Trail #1368 departs Forest Service Road 35 directly across from Owl Creek Trail #1371.2(B) and goes west down the ridge. Slink down the open sage hillside on rocky terrain and switchback underneath the cover of the trees. Now you're on a somewhat level area next to a huge rock slide. Ride on to find a wet green mossy spot next to what must be a spring. Travel down a mini ridge where the trail is intermittently mixed with a 4-wheel road. Remember to look for blazes, rock cairns and metal triangles in the trees. When you reach a knoll, ride down the hogback of the ridge, ignoring the tempting 4-wheel roads that cross here, (although the one to the south has a creek at the bottom, if your steed is in need of a drink). The trail is a 4-wheel drive road at this point, go beside a shale rock mound on the north (right) side of the road. Continue on and you'll see where this road ends at 4W119. Ride 4W119 to the left (downhill) a few yards to where Snowshoe Ridge Trail #1368 ends at Forest Service Road 3507.

*HINT- Carry your gun with an empty chamber at the 12 o'clock position. This way if the gun gets banged around the gun won't go off, although if the trigger is pulled it advances and the next round if will go off.

Table Mountain #1209

Distance:	2.5 Miles
Altitude:	5500'-5900'
Map:	GTM 210 Liberty
Difficulty:	Moderate

Directions: Use the directions at the beginning of this chapter for Haney Meadow. Table Mountain Trail #1209 starts about ½ mile past Haney Meadow on the west (left) side of Forest Service Road 9712 directly across from Old Ellensburg Trail #1373. Table Mountain Trail's other end can be accessed from Forest Service Road 9712, directly across from Naneum Rim Trail #1234, about 1.5 miles before reaching Haney Meadow. Parking also available at Haney Meadow and Ken Wilcox Horse Camp.

Connecting Trails: 1234, 1319, 1205, 1373

Horse Camping: Nearby camping at Ken Wilcox Horse Camp at Haney Meadow. Read directions at the introduction of this chapter.

Trail Description: Table Mountain Trail #1209 can be used to make loops in the Haney Meadow Area. The trail rolls along mostly in forest, the middle section is on a flat rocky area with a ledge overlooking Tronson Meadow area. Looking off this ridge, you'll see the Teanaway Area with the Stuart Mountain Range and Red Top Mountain. Either end of this trail starts on Forest Service Road 9712, Elk Trap Springs Trail #1319 departs to the south, the southern end of Table Mountain Trail #1209 connects with Naneum Rim Trail #1234. Table Mountain's eastern end intersects Tronsen Meadow Trail #1205, which leaves to the north, and Old Ellensburg Trail #1373 goes toward the east on the other side of Forest Service Road 9712. The trail has a split near the Haney Meadow end, which leads to Ken Wilcox Horse Camp.

*HINT-For those of you that like to trot, but your gun feels lopsided and uncomfortable. Try sliding the holster in the center of your back so the gun is balanced better, you can trot all day like this! Or consider getting a shoulder holster.

Tronsen Meadow #1205

Distance:	2 Miles
Altitude:	4400'-5600'
Map:	GTM 210 Liberty
Difficulty:	Moderate-Challenging (Steep)

Directions: Read the directions to Haney Meadow at the beginning of this chapter. Tronsen Meadow Trail #1205 starts about ½ mile past Haney Meadow on the west (left) side of Forest Service Road 9712, a few yards past the trailheads for Table Mountain #1209 and Old Ellensburg #1373.

Connecting Trails: Access Trail, X-country ski

Horse Camping: Nearby camping at Ken Wilcox Horse Camp at Haney Meadow.

Trail Description: Tronsen Meadow Trail #1205 starts off Forest Service Road 9712 just past Haney Meadow, or can be ridden to from Ken Wilcox Horse Camp via the Access Trail going north out of camp. This trail begins as an old road, then turns into a trail. Climb slightly to the top of a ridge, here you'll see a wonderful view to the west of the Stuart Mountain Range and other surrounding mountains; pass another old road headed north. Ride down over a bald area with a rock out-cropping. This path intermittently goes through forest and open spots. Tronsen Meadow Trail #1205 is very steep in spots; the top part has the steepest pitch, and was obviously made before switchbacks were visualized, although there are several tiny switchbacks near the bottom. There are 2 small springs, one big enough to get a drink for your horses. You'll intersect with a ski trail marked with a blue diamond and an arrow, leaving to the right (north). Tronsen Meadow Trail #1205 ends on Forest Service Road 7240. To appreciate this trail to the fullest, visit in the fall when the deciduous tamarack trees are turning a lemon drop yellow. By the way, Tronsen Meadow is no where to be seen. This trail is open to motorcycles.

*HINT-Sap on your hands got you stuck? Rub oil on your hands, and then wash em' off. I like chunky peanut butter best, it has some grit to loosen the sap, but you can use butter, vegetable oil, even motor oil works, but peanut butter smells better!

Tronsen Ridge #1204

Distance:	9 Miles
Altitude:	4400'-5800'
Map:	GTM 210 Liberty
Difficulty:	Moderate

Directions: Read the directions to Haney Meadow at the beginning of this chapter. Tronsen Ridge Trail #1204 starts about 1 mile past Haney Meadow on the north (left) side of Forest Service Road 9712. The Access Trail that leaves out of Ken Wilcox Horse Camp can be ridden to avoid riding Forest Service Road 9712 from camp. Parking is tight and I recommend riding from Haney Meadow and the horse camp.

Connecting Trails: Access Trail, 1601, Road 224 (4W312), hiker only trail, 1223, 1206

Horse Camping: Nearby camping at Ken Wilcox Horse Camp at Haney Meadow.

Trail Description: Tronsen Ridge Trail #1204 begins off Forest Service Road 9712. You can ride there via Access Trail from Ken Wilcox Horse Camp to avoid road riding. Begin in forest and quickly intersect with Road 224 (4W312) and then Mount Lillian Trail #1601, exits to the east. Turn left as Tronsen Ridge Trail #1204 and Road 224 (4W312) merge to become one for a short distance. Follow the road up through

Table Mountain Trail, Josie and Inky

a meadow, the road and trail split, it is very clear that the Tronsen Ridge Trail #1204 becomes a trail again. Head down on the north side of the hill, on somewhat rutty tread. Hiker only trail (unmarked) merges, coming in from the left, up a ridge. Continue on the ridge to the first of various views of the Stuart Mountains, Mount Rainier and the valleys below with Highway 97 way down in the distance. At the 4.5-mile mark, Red Hill Trail #1223 joins from the northeast. The path stays on top of Tronsen Ridge dipping only slightly to one side or the other. There is an open switchback that has some pea-size gravel on it, overall this ridge trail is in pretty good shape. There is no water for stock and the ground is soft in some spots and rocky in others. The path is still relentless in its trek downward. Reach a Forest Service Road, where there is a sign indicating the trail's name and number. Tronsen Ridge Trail #1204 climbs several steep knolls and finally makes its way to the end where there are 2 choices; either one drops you off a ridge onto a road, this is the end of the trail. For a point-to-point ride, continue west on an old brushy logging road for about ¾ mile to find Magnet Creek Trail #1206.

Where do the buffalo roam?

"WE PUSHED IT TO THE LIMIT"

The last camp out of the season is usually the coldest, I seem to have a pattern of pushing it to the limit with the weather. I talked Sandy into taking one last trip after hunting season was over. We chose to go to Ken Wilcox Horse Camp. The forecast was for possible drizzle, oh well, lets go for it, if we end up not riding, we can always hunker down in my camper with the heater on, lots of food, and drink and a deck of cards. When we pulled in we remarked, "We have the place to ourselves, cool". We rode a full day, and were pleased with ourselves for coming so late in the year and having full run of the camp. We had well-laid plans for the next day's trail ride. We turned in early, and the rain started, camp was a massive puddle by morning when Sandy knocked on my door, ready for coffee. We had a leisurely breakfast, no use in saddling in the rain; it *will* quit by the time the dishes are done. **NOT!** Well one more cup of coffee, maybe two, by the third or fourth cup we had the caffeine jitters and were ready to ride, unconditionally. Then it happened, the rain quit and we were elated, grabbed our coats and opened the door…a whiteout! The rain had turned to snow and it was like looking through a lace curtain, so thick we could not see Sandy's rig, and it was only a matter of yards from mine. Oh well, the horses were cozy in their blankets, but their haunches were turned into the torrent of snow with heads slumped down to their ankles, which were submersed in icy water. I've never packed up so quickly in my life, our bodies were white, head to toe. If you've ever been to Haney Meadow, you can imagine what we were up against getting down the mountain on those steep roads with a full load, it looked like a blizzard!! It was a slow moving train of sad hearts coming off the mountain, as we realized this was the last camp out of the year. Always optimistic, we thought, next year will be just as fun, and maybe it will be an open winter.

Josie

Distance:	3.9 Miles
Altitude:	5400'-5700'
Map:	GTM 242 Thorp
Difficulty:	Moderate

Directions: Use the directions to Lion Rock listed at the beginning of this chapter. Before reaching Lion Rock, parking is available where the pavement ends at a 3-way intersection. Wilson Creek Trail #1387 leaves toward the east in a meadow and is signed Wilson Stock Driveway #1387. This is a shared trailhead with Crystal Ridge #4W319, which exits to the west.

Connecting Trails: 4W319, 1371, 1354

Horse Camping: Primitive camping along side roads. Or read the introduction of this chapter for Lion Rock.

Trail Description: Wilson Creek Trail #1387 starts at an intersection of roads and heads east through a meadow. Directly across the road Crystal Ridge Trail #4W319 departs going west. In the meadow is where Madeleine and I spotted a bull elk with a huge rack. Cross a small stream and ride through old growth timber and head up slightly on nice footing and travel across open sage and rocky terrain. Cross an old clear-cut area and ride down to ford Wilson Creek. Ascend a steep section and travel around a rock slide. Views of Mount Rainier can be seen. A sign in a tree lets you know where Stock Driveway Boundary is. You pass lots of meadows and old logging areas. Rolling trail is the name of the game here. Cross 3 more creeks, some may be dry, depending on what time of year you visit. Ride up 1 switchback around a rock slide and small rocky section of trail to the 2.8 mile-mark. Intersect with Naneum Wilson Trail #1371 where you'll find a sign post in a small meadow. Rock cairns will guide you along as the trail goes from forest to meadow and sagebrush. The purple daisy plants are gorgeous in July as well as the paintbrush flowers. You can see Ellensburg in the distance to the south. Wilson Creek Trail #1387 crosses a creek and rolls along. You may notice to the left (north) a series of rock cairns going across a sage hill; this is the unmarked High Creek Trail #1354. A sign under the shady limbs of an evergreen, mark the trail with the words, Wilson Creek Trail #1387, although there is no mention of the less traveled High Creek Trail #1354.1(A). You may see "cow-patties" made by "slow elk" (cattle). I guess the bovine couldn't read the "Stock Boundary" sign. Wilson Creek Trail #1387 ends as it "T" intersects with an old two-track road. Loops possible from this trail using a verity of trails mixed with some road.

"SPOTTED BY THE CHICKEN COOP"

On a cold winter day a small female bobcat, lay in wait by the chicken coop for a chance to eat one of my fluffy fat laying hens. She was caught in the act, and never got her meal, later we discovered that she was dying, for she had a huge tapeworm in her belly. We have named her "Peaches" because of her coloring.

Josie

Peaches, the bobcat

ANCIENT LAKES AREA

The Ancient Lakes Area is located along the east bank of the Columbia River in Central Washington, between the towns of George and Quincy. It is a desert type area with loads of canyon-land riding laced with lakes. My friends and I frequent the canyons in the winter and early spring. It can be snow-free when the mountains are getting dumped on, and it is quiet during elk and deer season, although it is open to bird hunters, and fishermen after April. There are trails on the upper shelf of the canyons at the 1,200' level and sandy trails on the lower shelf going into the canyons to captivate you. You can ride to the Columbia River from the canyon lands to the 800' level, although the shoreline is rocky. The access roads by the upper lakes and trails may be closed from October to April. You can drive in and camp in this area when the gate is open in April. When the gate is shut you'll need to have your mount step over a very low metal gate to access the area. Ancient Lakes Area has many more rides than are listed. Some people even ride to a winery that is nearby for kicks. There are two fascinating hiker trails to explore on foot. One is the signed Ancient Lake Trail. A gate blocks it, so horses can't get in from the main road, (a portion of it that is suitable for riding will be described coming in from H Lake). Another hiker trail is Dusty Lake Trail, which is across the way from Burke Lake. It has a metal guardrail and narrow path on a cliff with low hanging rock outcroppings that make it unsafe for horses to wander down. There are rattlesnakes in this area, usually from the middle of April through October. There are port-a-pots by Quincy and Burke Lakes. You'll find a large parking area near Burke Lake. From April to October you may drive in to the lake areas, however, H Lake Road is a bit narrow to get your rig turned around.

Upper parking: From 1-90, take the George/Quincy Exit 149. Drive north for 5 miles. Turn west (left), on NW 5 (White Trail Road). There is a golf course on this corner for a landmark. Go about 3 miles on NW 5 Road and turn south (left) on a gravel road marked with a sign that reads, "Public Fishing and Public Hunting". Drive ¼ mile to the trailhead. This trailhead is large enough for 3-4 rigs, but can have hunter rigs parked here, especially on the weekends.

From Wenatchee, take Highway 28 east toward Quincy, turn south (right) on U NW Road for about 6 miles, the road changes into NW 5 Road on the

"S" curve. Turn south (right), on the gravel road marked with the "Public Fishing and Public Hunting" sign. Drive ¼ mile to the trailhead. This trailhead is large enough for 3-4 rigs, but can have hunter rigs parked here, especially on the weekends.

Lower parking: From I-90, take the George/Quincy Exit 149. Drive north for 5 miles. Turn left on NW 5 (White Trail Road). There is a golf course on this corner. Go about 8 miles on NW 5 Road (after the "S" curves it becomes U NW Road) and turn left on NW 9 Road. Go about 5 miles. The last 3½ miles are gravel. The trailhead is at the end of the road; there is room for about 6 rigs to park. There is a port-a-pot there. The lower trailhead has a permanent cable gate, use the trail around the gate to gain access.

From Wenatchee, take Highway 28 east toward Quincy, turn right on U NW Road for 1-mile, then turn right on NW 9 Road. Go about 5 miles. The last 3½ miles are gravel. The trailhead is at the end of the road; there is room for about 6 rigs to park. There is a port-a-pot there. The lower trailhead has a permanent cable gate, use the trail around the gate to gain access.

Northwest Forest Parking Passes are available at Forest Service offices, they are required at designated trailheads.

Put the hat and gloves on and ride...

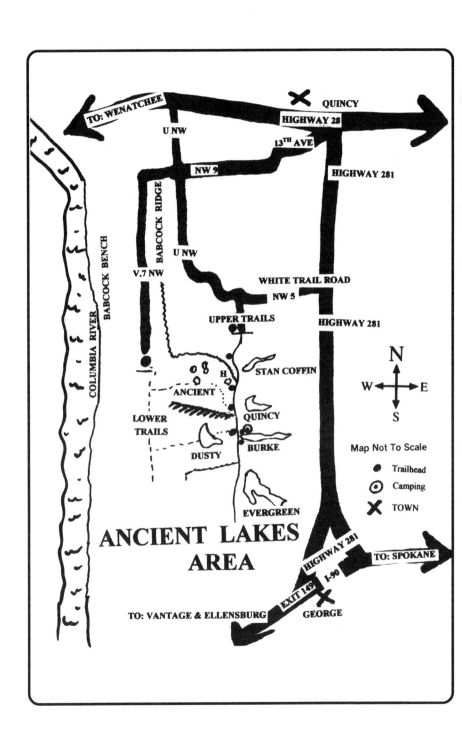

ANCIENT LAKES
AREA

Ancient Lake

(On the canyon rim above near H Lake)

Distance:	¾ Mile
Altitude:	1200'-1200'
Map:	Washington Atlas & Gazetteer
Difficulty:	Moderate

Directions: Follow the Upper parking directions listed in the introduction to Ancient Lakes. Access from H Lake Loop Trail.

Connecting Trail: H Lake Loop

Trail Description: To begin riding the portion of the signed Ancient Lake Trail that is horse accessible, start at H Lake, after crossing the cement inlet to the lake, keep right and follow the power line road north. The power line goes slightly uphill around a corner, then down to join Ancient Lake Trail in a small meadow area. (You're meeting the Ancient Lake Trail in its mid-section because the beginning of it is fenced so horses can't get through.) Head west toward the Columbia River on the Ancient Lake Trail. Follow the path as it heads across an open steppe and skirts a hillside on somewhat narrow tread. Ride the trail as it takes you to a view, high on a bluff overlooking Ancient Lake, with a waterfall and several other lakes below (it may have been one giant lake long ago). This is the spot you'll need to do an "about face" on your horse. There is a fence line a short way after this and boggy areas that are not suitable for horses.

If you want to hike, you can access the canyon by scrambling down beside the waterfall and then follow the rock slide around the lake. For a loop see "Ancient Lakes (From Quincy Lake to canyon floor unsigned trail)".

*HINT-Do your knees hurt after a long ride? Try the newer type of stirrups that cushion your feet and absorb shock when you put your weight in them. Endurance riders use them all the time. "Sportack" carries a whole line of them (www.sportack.com).

"RUN-A-MUCK CANYON"

One February day at dawn, my friend, her husband and I went for a 40-mile ride in the Quilomene-Whisky Dick area, east of Ellensburg, WA., riding down to the Columbia River. It was cold and gray with some snowflakes drifting through the air, periodically. We stopped for lunch after riding about 5 hours. Then, after re-mounting and riding about 10 minutes or so, it happened! The six-foot tall, bone-dry reeds, and grasses were rustling against one another in the swampland beside the trail, as a slight breeze grazed them, it was an eerie sound. All three horses spooked at once, jumping sideways ten feet, and all hell broke loose. My friend's young horse promptly dismounted her, and took off, rider-less at a dead run. I looked down, under my horse's nose, to find my friend staring up at me, my horse, Ali, leapt over her body, arching to the right. My friend's horse was a runaway, and was getting away! The split second jar of the jump caught me off guard, and I was now hanging on my horse's neck, with my right leg over the horn-less saddle and no reins in my fingers. I thought about bailing off, but the longer that I thought about it, the faster we went, until jumping was not an option any longer. I clutched Ali's mane for dear life, knowing I needed to align myself with her spine to center myself. Inch by painstaking inch, I worked my way back on, thanking myself for going to Jazzercise as often as I do. I used every ounce of muscle I had to regain composure, I knew I had to perform at the top range of my abilities or beyond. One hand at a time I got the reins, I never did get my feet to reclaim the stirrups. Going about 40 mph down the canyon as trees rocketed past me on either side, along the narrow, twisting path, the icy wind whipping my eyes into wet pools of blur. Ali and I caught up with the runaway horse. After about a half-mile, still running all out, I was praying that no bucking would accompany this adventure, I used this brief time to rest for a moment, I was exhausted. I could see the horse in front of me, metal shoes flashing with every stride, an occasional spark from the few rocks in the trail, his taunting hoof beats echoed back to me, the reins bouncing aimlessly around his neck and his mane flying in the wind. At one point, I completely relaxed and felt the awesome power of Ali, and was totally amazed at how calm I had become in the midst of all this chaos. I stayed steadfast and the chase was stunning to watch. I thought Ali was ready to give to my commands, not pushing or pulling, but simply asking for a give to the bit, after all, I didn't want any sharp turns or sudden stops, as I still had no stirrups. I murmured softly to her in our secret language, and I saw her ear rotate slightly toward me, and I knew she was responding. She gave, and I was able to coax her to a halt, my companion's horse still at a dead run ahead of us, down what we now call, "Run-A-Muck Canyon". We were able to complete our journey and reached the almighty Columbia River. My friend was very sore and my muscles talked to me for the next several days. We beat the end of the daylight back, as we finished our ride at a good clip, with no mercy to our runaway mounts. We have told ourselves that the horses must have caught wind of a predator to spur such a wild reaction, the truth is, we will never know and they aren't telling!

Josie

Ancient Lakes Canyon

Distance:	2 Miles
Altitude:	1000'-1000'
Map:	Washington Atlas & Gazetteer
Difficulty:	Moderate

Directions: Use the Lower parking directions listed in the introduction to Ancient Lakes.

Connecting Trails*:* Two-track, Ancient Lake (From Quincy Lake to canyon floor)

Trail Description: Follow Two-track Trail until you can see the first canyon with its many soft grassland and sage hills. You need to turn east (left) and follow the small road, or choose any path to go see the Ancient Lakes and waterfalls. The Ancient Lakes is a glorious spot to ride, especially in the spring to condition for the summer rides, or late fall to wind down for the long winter months. The jointed columns of rock standing up on end shoulder to shoulder look like "Tootsie Rolls". The lakes are huddled together at the end of the canyon. Notice the chalky bathtub ring left behind on the north canyon wall, marking telltale long ago water levels. Envision how the valley floor you're riding on may have been the bottom of an ancient lake! To intersect

with the Ancient Lakes Trail (Quincy Lake to canyon floor) look on the south (right) side of the canyon for beige colored rocks near a lake. Keep in mind the trail going up toward Quincy Lake is a bit more challenging. I am sure anyone will enjoy this easy sandy-footed ride in to see Ancient Lakes down in the canyon. You may add on hours of riding in this area using the trails listed in this chapter.

*HINT-Do yourself a favor, brightly paint your "Easy Boot" so you can spot it easier if it falls off. Some people even attach small bells to them, so they can hear them when they are on. The "Easy Boots" are now sold in a red color also

Ridge Between the Canyons Trail

Madeleine and Josie ride the canyons

Ancient Lakes

(From Quincy Lake to canyon floor, unsigned trail)

Distance:	¾ Mile
Altitude:	1000'-1200'
Map:	Washington Atlas & Gazetteer
Difficulty:	Moderate

Directions*:* Follow the Upper parking directions listed in the introduction to Ancient Lakes. Lots of roadside parking near Quincy Lake.

Connecting Trail: Ancient Lakes Canyon

Horse Camping: Primitive camping along the gravel road, leading in toward the upper Ancient & Burke Lake Area after April and before October.

Trail Description*:* Ancient Lakes Trail (From Quincy Lake to canyon floor) begins across the road from Quincy Lake. Look for a path just beyond the lake on the west (right) side of the road. It is marked with 2 boulders, one on each side of the path. The trail begins flat and weaves across the rock-strewn desert dropping to the first of several shelves. There are views of the canyon floor below. It looks pretty awesome from here with the lakes shimmering below; the terrain has a riot of shapes and colors to tantalize you with. The trail dips and then contours the shoulder of a bluff on a rock slide to reach the next step. This is a place

Beaver dam

to get some great aerial shots of the Ancient Lakes. The trail wanders across a bench. The last effort to the ground level is somewhat steep with unforgiving sharp rocks. From here you can explore this magnificent area at your leisure on the Ancient Lakes Canyon Trail. The Ancient Lakes area is ideal to picnic in.

Sandy rides Ancient Lakes Trail

Cliff, Josie's husband hikes while she rides in the Ancient Lakes Area

Burke Lake Loop

Distance:	3 Miles
Altitude:	1200'-1200'
Map:	Washington Atlas & Gazetteer
Difficulty:	Moderate

Directions: Follow the Upper parking directions listed in the introduction to Ancient Lakes. You'll find a large parking area near Burke Lake.

Connecting Trail: Dusty Lake Trail (Hiker only).

Horse Camping: Primitive camping along the gravel road leading in toward Burke Lake, April to October.

Trail   Description: Burke Lake Trail is a conglomerate of trails and roads encompassing Burke Lake. You can begin the trail from either side of the lake, both ends start as roads, as they go through the parking areas they become paths. The route takes you around the lake on a rolling trail, and dirt roads; watch for fishermen and hikers. At the far end you'll cross a boat launching area and a wet grassy spot with a small steep hill. Lots of views of the mountains to the west from here. It takes about an hour to travel the long blue lake's shore.

Josie and Ali above the canyons

303

*HINT-Add a "Leatherman" type of tool to your belt, along with your gun. It is a good idea to be wearing the essentials on your person. You'll be glad you did if you and your mount get separated.

Josie and Inky on a bright fall day

Dusty Lake Canyon

Distance: 2 Miles	
Altitude: 1000'-1000'	
Map: Washington Atlas & Gazetteer	
Difficulty: Moderate	

Directions: Access from Two-track Trail. Use the Lower parking directions listed in the introduction to Ancient Lakes.

Connecting Trails: Two-track, Ancient Lakes Canyon

Trail Description: From the Two-track road going south. Dusty Lake will be found in the 2nd canyon. Pass Ancient Lakes Canyon Trail, which is in the 1st canyon. Leave the main Two-track that goes north and south, and take any of the overgrown roads or small paths into the canyon to the east (left) and ride from the maze of trails that crisscross the lava sprinkled valley. The rocks look like the giants have been playing a game of "Chinga" with the stones. Yell to hear your voice ricochet off the canyon wall. In the late afternoon, shadows play with the sides and

Sandy by Ancient Lake

305

rock pillar formations of the canyon. They are layered and stacked in odd and wonderful ways. At times you may see mirages, the walls appear to be different from a distance than they are when you ride closer. The shore of the lake appears distorted. To my delight, I am not the only one that noticed this! Dusty Lake is set at the end of the canyon, with waterfalls all around, one-waterfall cascades down the rock face and disappears into rock, never to reach the ground. This is a sandy area that is nice to ride on. I highly suggest you come and play here!

It is possible to hike from Dusty Lake Trail down to the Dusty Canyon by way of trail and rock slides, for a loop you would need to go around the end of the canyon to reach Ancient Lake Canyon.

Three hoots

Burke Lake

H Lake Loop

Distance:	1 Mile
Altitude:	1200'-1200'
Map:	Washington Atlas & Gazetteer
Difficulty:	Moderate

Directions: Follow the Upper parking directions listed in the introduction to Ancient Lakes. There is roadside parking by Quincy and Burke Lakes, don't try to drive in to H Lake parking area.

Connecting Trails: H Lake, Ancient Lake (via a pole-line road)

Horse Camping: Primitive camping along the gravel road leading in toward the upper Ancient Lakes Area is allowed April through October.

Trail Description: H Lake ride begins off of the main gravel road that heads in toward Quincy and Burke Lakes. The small road that leads to H Lake is marked with a metal sign with the letters burned out of it spelling "H LAKE". Follow the road in and see H Lake. Ride across the inlet on a cement pad that may have water flowing over it. Ride up a hill and go left on a dirt pole-line road, (right is your return route). This is a good place to view the quaint lake with its island. Keep going around the knoll and the road becomes trail and drops onto a small road, keep right, going back toward H Lake. By-pass the cement pad by the inlet and ride the small overgrown 2-track road, back out to the main gravel road. You'll ride next to swampland that connects Stan Coffin Lake to H Lake.

*HINT-Rain hood got you down? Wear a visor or a baseball cap underneath the hood, to keep the brim from collapsing down on your nose.

Pheasant

Trail Between the Canyons

Distance:	¾ Mile
Altitude:	1200'-1200'
Map:	Washington Atlas & Gazetteer
Difficulty:	Moderate

Directions: Follow the Upper parking directions listed in the introduction to Ancient Lakes. Park at Burke Lake.

Connecting Trails: Ancient Lakes (From Quincy Lake to the canyon floor), Dusty Lake (hiker only).

Trail Description: Directly across from Burke Lake you'll find a small parking area. An unmarked hiker only trail goes from Dusty Lake Trail to the rim of the canyons I call "Trail Between the Canyons". Take the rather vague path that leads directly up a small hill. The tread goes out on open and somewhat rocky terrain to a breathtaking view of the razor sharp wall that divides the two magnificent canyons. You can see both canyons and part of the lakes below from this viewpoint. If you feel like cross-country riding go north (right), when the trail gives

Bald Eagle

out and you can connect with the trail that goes from Quincy Lake to the canyon floor, turn right on it to follow it back to the road and your rig, or go explore the canyon below.

*HINT- If caught out on the trail at night, tape your glow stick onto the breast collar. Or illuminate a flashlight by draping a transparent rain poncho over the top of the light. You'll be surprised how much light this puts out. The horse only needs to see a shadow to enhance his vision.

Dusty Lake Trail

Two-track

Distance:	9 Miles
Altitude:	1000'-1000'
Map:	Washington Atlas & Gazetteer
Difficulty:	Moderate

Directions: Use the Lower parking directions listed in the introduction to Ancient Lakes.

Connecting Trails: Ancient Lakes Canyon, Dusty Lake Canyon

Trail Description: Two-track Trail starts by going up and around a gate next to a fence line in the sagebrush, just beyond the parking area. The beginning of the trail has a few rocks. They melt away as you ride to the 1st of three canyons. Near a thicket you'll see Ancient Lakes Canyon, and its trails and old roads. The footing is sandy and wonderful here. Continue on and ride uphill slightly, around a rocky ridge descending to the second canyon, this is Dusty Lake Canyon. The Two-track Trail will take you to the far south side of this canyon, which has many small roads and paths to entice you to ride up to see the lake, and waterfalls. Continue on the Two-track, riding towards the south with a few hills and some rocky spots, then ride to a large hill. Ride up and over it, then cross a sometimes-rapid rushing creek that may have some mud on the edges. When the irrigation is running on the farmland above, the stream flows quite fast. "The Gorge" is above you where summer concerts are held. It is a bit brushy here, however, the path will be quickly found again. The next couple miles are on rolling terrain with some small ponds and maybe a little mud in the spring. Get out your camera for there are beautiful scenes of the deep blue Columbia River here. Follow the Two-track up to a parking area, cross a paved road and regain tread again. The footing is very sandy here, ride about 2-3 miles to gain access to a final canyon and some more waterfalls, this area is popular for rock climbers, Two-track Trail ends at this canyon and a paved road.

*HINT- For cuts consider this, fishermen have used Super Glue to close small cuts and wounds in the skin for years. Liquid Band-Aid is available now and reduces pain as well as protecting cuts.

TAYLOR MOUNTAIN AREA
Maple Valley

Taylor Mountain is a part of the Seattle watershed, not far from I-90 and Highway 18, near the town of Maple Valley. It is a nice area to ride because the roads are all gated. Only a few locals and workers have keys to get in. You can ride around the gate, through the woods on a path to gain access. It is in a jungle type setting, thick undergrowth, sea foam green moss hangs like tattered rags on the trees. The air is heavy and humid, the ferns and vines are huge. You'll find riding of all types here. Road riding for the novice horsemen, a challenging mud laden trail (Hobart Trail) for the adventurous, and nice moderate trails with few obstacles for the pleasure rider (I'll call these "Little Loop Trail & Valley Trail" because their were no titles or numbers assigned to these trails). Wildlife includes black bear, deer, and slugs. Blackberries are prolific, however after we ate a bunch, we saw a sign discouraging picking of the wild black treats. Taylor Mountain is not in National Forest or Wilderness. I know that it will be helpful for those of you that need a suggestion for a place to ride and have perhaps newly moved to Washington State. The area is small, it's only 3 or 4 square miles or so, and houses are near. A half a day of riding can be had here. We rode several trails, but only 2 are written about. Sandy and I decided to yield to the "**3 bears**" on the Hobert Trail, and another unmarked trail was too overgrown to get through.

Directions to Taylor Mountain: Drive on Highway 18, south of I-90 and take the Hobart Exit. Turn left Go under the overpass and turn right on the next road and drive up a hill. When you see a fire station turn left, it is a dead end road. Drive 2.2 miles to reach a gated road on the left, there is a pull-off on the right side of the road. There is room for a couple of rigs to park.

Northwest Forest Parking Passes are available at Forest Service offices, they are required at designated trailheads.

Make noise so the bears can hear you...

Trail	Page

UMMMM Blackberries

Little Loop

Distance:	¾ Mile
Altitude:	500'-500' (about)
Map:	Washington Atlas
Difficulty:	Moderate

Directions: Read the introduction to this chapter to find the paved road to the area. The "Little Loop Trail" begins by riding around the gate, through the woods, and up the gravel road from the parking area. Then ride left on the next main gravel road. The trailhead is on the left side of the road.

Connecting Trail: Valley Trail

Trail Description: The trail I'm calling "Little Loop" is only about ¾ mile long. It begins on the left side of the road. It has nice gravel patch with wooden barriers on the side replacing what use to be a muddy area. It is all in deep forest and gently makes its way downhill and then curves to the right and comes out onto an old road. This is where the trail I'm calling "Valley Trail", which intersects from the left. Turn right on this old road to reach the end of the trail and the same road the trailhead came off. If you are going to make a loop to the trailhead turn right. The other loop that can be made uses "Valley Trail".

Brushy trail

Valley Trail

Distance:	2 Miles
Altitude:	500'-500' (about)
Map:	Washington Atlas
Difficulty:	Moderate

Directions: Read the introduction to this chapter to find the paved road to the area. The "Valley Trail" begins by riding around the gate, through the woods, and up the gated gravel road from the parking area. Then ride left on the next main gravel road. The trailhead is on the left side of the road (1-mile or so down this road) it is past "Little Loop Trail" and is across from Hobart Trail, which is on the right hand side of the road.

Connecting Trails: Hobart, Little Loop

Taylor Mountain Area

Trail Description: The path that I'm calling "Valley Trail" begins from a gravel road on the left side. It travels down a valley on good tread, it has great footing and is glorious as it makes its way through dark, old growth timber and coastal flora. Ride along the side of a creek. A section of trail has wooden bars bracing the ground on the side of you, some workers in the area said it is an old railroad grade. The trail meets an intersection of unmarked trails. Sandy and I kept to the far left and were rewarded as the trail continued to go on. (We had heard that there was one trail that was closed do to a wash out area.) The path switchbacks down and you'll need to ford the wide stream. Head up on good trail (may be challenging if it is wet) and come out onto an old grassy road. Here we turned left and found we were on the same old road that "Little Loop Trail" hooks onto. Ride this old road to connect back onto the original road that the trailhead is on. Loops possible with some road riding and use of "Little Loop Trail".

A small swamp

Coastal forest

Sandy and Chris

So long, and may you never stop chomping at the bit!

MORE TRAILS I HAVE RIDDEN

M=Moderate **C**-Challenging   **GTM**=Green Trails Map
TH=Trailhead

AREAS:

SALMON LA SAC (Near Cle Elum)-WA

Diff.	Trail Name	Trail #	Mile	Description	Map
M	**Cooper River**	1311	3.9	Wide wooded trail that follows the river, with some drop-off areas.	GTM 208 Kachess Lake
M	**Deep Lake**	1396.1	5	Flat trail into alpine lake.	GTM 176 Stevens Pass
M	**Escondido**	1320	1.8	A steep wooded trail to lake.	GTM 208 Kachess Lake
M-C	**Jolly Mountain**	1307	6.2	Valley trail, climbs to ridge, gaining 4,000'.	GTM 208 Kachess Lake
C	**Kachess Ridge**	1315	14.5	Climbs steeply to a ridge with narrow drop-offs sections, and meadows.	GTM 208 Kachess Lake
M	**Lake Michael**	1336	6	Forested trail with rocky spots goes to lake.	GTM 208 Kachess Lake
M-C	**Paris Creek**	1393.1	8	Steep forest trail with narrow spots.	GTM 208 Kachess Lake
M	**Pete Lake**	1323	7.5	Forested trail to lake small climbs.	GTMs 208 Kachess Lake & 207 Snoqualmie Pass

Diff.	Trail Name	Trail #	Mile	Description	Map
C	**Pollalie Ridge**	1309	8.8	Forested trail that's extremely steep on the south end, goes to an old lookout and lakes. Better if started at north end!	GTM 208 Kachess Lake
C	**Sasse Mountain**	1340	9	Open ridge trail with narrow spots & drop-offs after the first 3 miles.	GTM 208 Kachess Lake
M	**Spinola Creek**	1310.1	9	Forest trail along creek, connects to PCT.	GTM 176 Stevens Pass
M	**Trail Creek**	1322	5.5	Ford Waptus River, forested trail with stair step climbs, and a waterfall.	GTMs 208 Kachess Lake & 176 Stevens Pass
M	**Waptus Pass**	1329	6	Forty-five switchbacks up and Forty-five down, mostly in forest. Meadows, flat trail and muddy on top.	GTM 208 Kachess Lake
M	**Waptus River**	1310	11.2	Forested trail, small elevation changes, ford a wide river and it connects to the PCT.	GTM 208 Kachess Lake and 176 Stevens Pass

TANEUM (Near Ellensburg & Cle Elum)-WA

Diff.	Trail Name	Trail #	Mile	Description	Map
M	**Blazed Ridge**	1333	4.6	Ridge trail climbing up on open terrain with drop-offs.	GTM 240 Easton
M	**Cle Elum Ridge**	1326	15.1	Ridge Trail mostly forest lots of elevation changes with a few switchbacks.	GTMs 240 Easton and 241 Cle Elum
M	**Fishhook Flat**	1378	4.2	River bottom to ridge, forested with meadows and creeks.	GTM 240 Easton
M	**Gooseberry Flat**	1227	1.1	River bottom up the hillside to a road, with steep tread in the forest.	GTM 241 Cle Elum
C	**Granite Creek**	1326.1	2.5	Extremely steep, rutty forest trail.	GTM 240 Easton
M	**Greek Creek**	1321.2	3.2	Steep trail connecting 2 ridges, cross creek, it is not on the map.	GTM 240 Easton
M-C	**Lightning Point**	1377.1	2.4	Steep lower section, forested trail connects valley to ridge.	GTM 240 Easton
M	**Little Creek Basin**	1334	4.8	Forested trail, connects 2 ridges, climbs.	GTM 240 Easton
C	**Mount Cliffty**	1321.1	1.7	Ridge trail, narrow with long drop-offs in open terrain.	GTM 240 Easton
M	**North Fork Taneum**	1377	15.7	Valley trail in the forest to a ridge at the end, some climbs with lots of creek crossings.	GTMs 240 Easton and 241 Cle Elum
M	**North Ridge**	1321	9.5	Valley floor, then climbs on an open ridge with switchbacks.	GTM 240 Easton
M	**South Fork Taneum**	1367	6.4	Forest valley trail, follows a river to a clear-cut ridge and down to another river valley.	GTMs 240 Easton and 241 Cle Elum
M	**Taneum Ridge**	1363	12.1	Ridge trail with lots of climbs, mostly in forest. Easton &	GTMs 240 241 Cle Elum
M	**"User built trail"**	no #	¾	Steep forest trail, not on map.	GTM 241 Cle Elum

MANASTASH (Near Ellensburg & Cle Elum)-WA

Diff.	Trail Name	Trail #	Mile	Description	Map
M	**Hereford Meadows**	1207	3.8	Follows creek along a valley with sagebrush hillsides and meadows.	GTM 240 Easton
M	**Hoyt Mining**	1347	8	Part trail and part 4WD Road in forest with some steep spots and goes over several ridges.	GTM 241 Cle Elum
M	**Keenan Meadow**	1386	3.1	Forested trail with meadows, creek and has small climbs.	GTM 241 Cle Elum
M	**Lost Lake**	1350.1	1	Starts at lake and goes through forest to ridge, part on 4WD Road.	GTM 241 Cle Elum
M	**Manastash Lake**	1350	4.4	Forested trail goes to 2 lakes, switchbacks.	GTMs 240 Easton, 241 Cle Elum & 273 Manastash Lake
M	**Manashtash Ridge** (To Mt. Cliffty)	1388	6	Ridge trail in forest, some narrow tread.	GTM 240 Easton
M	**No Name**	30	4	Small climb in new-growth forest.	GTM 241 Cle Elum
M	**Plantaion**	1350.2	1	Travels through new-growth part trail and part road, flat.	GTM 241 Cle Elum
M	**Shoestring Lake**	1385	3.8	Climbs to lake in forest, creek crossings, with some mud.	GTMs 241 Cle Elum and 240 Easton
M	**South Fork Manastash**	1385.1	3	Starts in a river bottom and climbs to a ridge, then back down again, it has meadows, creek and bridge.	GTM 241 Cle Elum
M	**Tripod Flat**	4W307	4	Rough jeep road, big meadow and mostly forest.	GTMs 241 Cle Elum & 240 Easton

Diff.	Trail Name	Trail #	Mile	Description	Map
M-C	**Bean Creek**	1391.1	3.5	Valley to a ridge on narrow switchbacks with drop-offs, then vague trail on open hillsides down on other side.	GTM 209 Mt. Stuart
M-C	**Beverly-Turnpike**	1391	6	Forested trail switchbacks up to a ridge to another valley with rocks and mud at the river.	GTM 209 Mt. Stuart
M	**Boulder DeRoux** (To Gallagher Head Lake)	1392	4.1	Forest trail up steep & narrow in spots goes to a lake.	GTM 209 Mt. Stuart
M	**County Line** (Miller Peak to Rd. 113)	1226	5.4	Open bowl, switchbacks, brushy and climbs with some forest. Good views.	GTM 210 Liberty
M-C	**DeRoux Spur**	1392.1	2	Climbs in forest from the valley to a ridge, some brushy switchbacks and narrow tread. Nice views.	GTM 209 Mt. Stuart
M	**Esmerelda Basin**	1394	5.1	Valley to ridge ride, with some forest, switchbacks and open hillsides. Bring the camera.	GTM 209 Mt. Stuart
M	**Iron-Bear**	1351	5.3	Valley to ridge. Iron-side open bowls drop-off. Bear-side forested along creek.	GTMs 209 Mt. Stuart and 210 Liberty
M	**Iron Peak**	1399	3.5	Climbs from valley to ridge and down again. Open hillsides and forest some loose footing on other side of ridge. Take a picture.	GTM 209 Mt. Stuart
M-C	**Johnson-Medra**	1383	6	Medra-side not recommended for stock, extremely steep with treacherous footing, rocks and drop-offs some forest, mostly open to ridge. Johnson-side forested valley and climbs to ridge on switchbacks. Awesome view on ridge!	GTM 209 Mt. Stuart

Diff.	Trail Name	Trail #	Mile	Description	Map
M-C	**Jolly Creek**	1355	3.5	Forested valley to rugged steep open ridge.	GTMs 209 Mt. Stuart 208 Kachess Lake
M	**Jungle Creek**	1383.1	4.5	Forest valley up to ridge on switchbacks with some narrow spots.	GTM 209 Mt. Stuart
M	**Middle Fork Teanaway**	1393	10.5	Forested valley some climbs lots of creek crossings.	GTM 209 Mt. Stuart
M	**Miller Peak**	1379	3.6	Valley to ridge in forest most of the way, switchbacks to open ridge with lots of views.	GTMs 209 Mt. Stuart and 210 Liberty
M	**Stafford Creek**	1359	6	Valley to open ridge with some narrow tread, rocks and steep drops.	GTM 209 Mt. Stuart
M-C	**Standup Creek**	1369	5.9	Steep switchbacks to open ridge. Bring the camera!	GTMs 209 Mt. Stuart
M	**Teanaway Ridge**	1364	4	Ridge trail in forest with brushy areas lots of views.	GTM 210 Liberty
M	**Way Creek**	1235	5	Valley to ridge narrow and steep in spots with drop-offs near top, all forested.	GTM 209 Mt. Stuart
M-C	**West Fork Teanaway**	1353	9.6	Follows creek up narrow canyon to ridge on narrow trail with drop-offs, switchbacks and rocky spots.	GTM 208 Kachess Lake
C	**Yellow Hill**	1222	9.2	Open razor ridge, loose footing most of the way, with drop-offs. South end has some trees and climbing, lots of views.	GTMs 208 Kachess Lake and 209 Mt. Stuart

ICICLE & INGALLS CREEKS
(Near Leavenworth)-WA

Diff.	Trail Name	Trail #	Mile	Description	Map
C	**Blackjack Ridge**	1565	6	Steep switchbacks in trees, meadows and vague in spots.	GTM 177 Chiwaukum Mts
M-C	**Cascade Creek**	1217	2.7	Valley floor to ridge in forest. Vague in spots, narrow places and ford the river, views.	GTM 209 Mt. Stuart
M	**Forth Creek**	1219	4.2	Forest valley up and over a ridge, river crossing, mud and climbs.	GTM 209 Mt. Stuart
M	**French Creek** (To French Ridge)	1595	3.5	Valley trail in forest.	GTMs 177 Chiwaukum Mts and 176 Stevens Pas
M-C	**French Ridge**	1564	7.2	Forested valley to ridge with views and back down. South end steep brushy narrow switchbacks, the other end has a waterfall with some steep sections.	GTMs 177 Chiwaukum Mts and 176 Stevens Pas
M	**Icicle**	1551	12.1	River bottom trail with long high bridges, may encounter old bridges and mud, it switchbacks near the end.	GTMs 177 Chiwaukum Mts and 176 Stevens Pas
M	**Ingalls Creek**	1215	15.5	River bottom, some narrow open areas in first 3 miles, then deep brushy spots with rocks.	GTMs 209 Mt. Stuart 210 Liberty
M	**Jack Creek** (To Jack Ridge Trail)	1558	3	Forested valley follows the creek, some mud.	GTM 177 Chiwaukum Mts

INDIAN HEAVEN WILDERNESS
(Near Trout Lake)-WA

Diff.	Trail Name	Trail #	Mile	Description	Map
M	**Filloon**	102	1	Wide flat trail in trees.	Indian Heaven GTM 366 & Mt. Adams West
M	**Indian Heaven**	33	3.3	Valley to ridge, meadows and lake. View of Mount Adams.	Indian Heaven & GTM 365 Lone Butte
M	**Lemei**	34	5.3	Climb to an open area and above crater rim by a lake basin, views of Mt. Adams and Mt. Rainier.	Indian Heaven GTMs 366 Mt. Adams West and 365 Lone Butte
M	**Lemei Lake**	179	1.9	Fairly level with a small climb to lake, meadows mud.	Indian Heaven & GTM 365 Lone Butte
M	**Middle Trail**	26	6	Trees and rolling trail with bridges, some mud and lakes.	Indian Heaven GTMs 366 Mt. Adams West and 365 Lone Butte
M	**Placid Lake**	29	3.5	Forest trail with short climb to a lake, rocky spots & wide trail.	Indian Heaven & GTM 365 Lone Butte
M	**Race Track**	171	2.3	Rocky spots in trail in forest with a pond and big meadows.	Indian Heaven & GTM 397 Wind River
M	**Shortcut**	171A	½	Flat trail through meadow and timberland.	Indian Heaven & GTM 397 Wind River
M	**Thomas Lake**	111	3.5	Climbs to a ridge in forest with views of Mt. St. Helens, lakes and lots of meadows.	GTMs 397 Wind River and 365 Lone Butte

Diff.	Trail Name	Trail #	Mile	Description	Map
M	**Bear Creek**	943	7	Forested valley along a creek to an open ridge.	GTMs 239 Lester and 240 Easton
M	**Dust Dodger**	963B	3.4	Valley, then up and over a ridge with meadows & timber with short steep sections with the trees very close together.	GTM 240 Easton
M-C	**Louisiana Saddle**	945A	3.6	Narrow loose trail in timber goes from valley to a ridge.	GTM 239 Lester
M	**Lower Sand Creek**	963A	1.5	Valley to a ridge and down other side in timber.	GTM 240 Easton
M	**Middle Fork Naches**	945	7.5	Forest valley trail, follows creek, old bridges, then up a ridge with a steep pitch, and switchbacks. Views of Mount Rainier.	GTM 239 Lester
M	**Naches Historical and Wagon Road**	1913-684	6.5	(To PCT) Narrow old wagon road in the forest, it goes from a valley to a ridge, where it meets the PCT at Government Meadow shelter.	GTM 239 Lester
M	**Pyramid Peak** (Kaner Flat to Rd. 1903)	941	15.1	Parallels Little Naches Road on a hillside in the forest with streams and bridges some narrow spots.	GTMs 239 Lester and 240 Easton
C	**Quartz Creek**	949	7	Climbs from valley to ridge with steep open hillsides with rock and some forest.	GTM 240 Easton
M-C	**Quartz Mountain**	948	7	Climbs in forest from valley to ridge with rock, meadows and some rutty spots. View of Mount Rainier.	GTM 240 Easton
M	**Raven Roost**	951	4.5	Open hill down to forest on old road, then becomes trail, it has rocky spots, meadows, and some rutty areas. View of Mount Rainier.	GTM 239 Lester
M	**Sand Creek**	963	9	Climbs from the valley floor to ridge, crosses a creek with open spots to a ridge on good trail.	GTMs 239 Lester & 240 Easton
M	**South Fork Naches**	946	5.3	Forested trail with short steep sections and bridges in the middle, runs beside a creek and goes to a ridge.	GTMs 239 Lester and 240 Easton
M	**West Quartz Creek Loop**	952	11.6	Goes from a valley to a ridge and down again with bridges and some rock, view of American Ridge.	GTMs 272 Old Scab Mt. & 240 Easton

OLYMPIC MOUNTAINS (Near Pacific Beach)-WA

Diff.	Trail Name	Trail #	Mile	Description	Map
M	East Fork Quinault River		10	Mostly flat trail in the rainforest, goes to a river.	GTMs 166 Mt. Christy & 167 Mt. Steel
M	North Fork Quinault River (To 16 mile camp)		12.1	Valley to ridge trail in rainforest, log bridge and a shelter.	GTM 166 Mt. Christy

MISCELLANEOUS TRAILS-WA

Diff.	Trail Name	Trail #	Mile	Description	Map
M	Chiwaukum Creek (To Timothy Meadows) (Near Leavenworth & Stevens Pass)	1571	7.5	Climbs in the forest along a creek through alpine meadows. Chiwaukum Mts.	177
M	Dewey Lake (Near Chinook Pass)	968	8	Valley to ridge and lake in forest with climbs and a river to ford.	271 Bumping Lake
M	Greenwater	1176	10.4	Valley trail in coastal woods, bridges, and lots of river crossings with some mud. I only got to the 4-mile point, although I understand the remainder has mud and roots and ends at a lake.	GTM 239 Lester.
M	John Wayne (Iron Horse State Park)		50	Old railroad grade, (Snoqualmie Pass to Columbia River) it is wide with some high bridges and a few tunnels.	207 Snoqualmie Pass 208 Kachess Lake 240 Easton 241 Cle Elum 242 Thorp no GTM from E-Burg on to river
M-C	Skyline		18	Climb an open slope to ridge, then ride narrow drop-off along ridge and down to a grassy valley and up other side to a second ridge.	USGS Badger Pocket, Selah and Ellensburg

327

WILLIAM O' DOUGLAS WILDERNESS & AREA
(Naches & Yakima)-WA

Diff.	Trail Name	Trail #	Mile	Description	Map
M	**Bumping Lake**	971	10.1	Valley trail along lake, some rock and creek crossings it goes to the PCT.	GTM 271 Bumping Lake
M	**Fish Lake**	971.1 (A)	1.8	Forest trail with some rock, goes by a rock slide to a river.	GTM 271 Bumping Lake
M	**Swamp Lake**	970	4.6	In timber, travels by rock slide and meadows to a lake with a shelter.	271 Bumping Lake GTM

OLALLIE LAKE BASIN
(Near Estacada & Detroit)-OR

Diff.	Trail Name	Trail #	Mile	Description	Map
M	**Fish Lake**	717	2.8	Valley to ridge trail, then back down again to a lake, in forest. Narrow trail above the lake.	GTM 525 Breitenbush
M	Horseshoe Saddle	712	7	Valley to ridge trail, go past a lake, all in forest. Meets the PCT.	GTM 525 Breitenbush
M	**Lodgepole**	706	5.2	In pines, with rocky spots and a meadow, view of Mount Jefferson, it meets the PCT.	GTM 525 Breitenbush
M-C	**Olallie Butte**	720	3.8	A must see. Rocky climb to the top of the butte, views of Mt. Jefferson, Mt. Hood and lake.	GTM 525 Breitenbush
M	**Olallie Lake**	731	1.7	Flat with nice footing. Great view of Mt. Jefferson, all in forest and goes around a lake.	GTM 525 Breitenbush
M	**Red Lake**	719	5.8	Very rocky, rolling trail, all in forest with gentle slopes and passes lakes. Meets with the PCT.	GTM 525 Breitenbush
M	**Russ Lake**	716	.9	Connects to PCT. Boulder sprinkled hills and goes up between 2 lakes.	GTM 525 Breitenbush

THREE SISTERS WILDERNESS
(Near Sisters & Bend)-OR

Diff.	Trail Name	Trail #	Mile	Description	Map
M	**Cultus Butte**	2		Road no number Old road spirals around butte to the top, views of Mt. Shasta, 3 Sisters Mts. and Crane Prairie.	3 Sisters Wilderness
M	**Fall Creek**	17	4.4	A must see. Use Green Lakes TH. Valley to ridge trail, with lakes and waterfalls, lots of climbing on nice trail, mostly in trees to the timberline view the Three Sisters Mountains.	3 Sisters Wilderness
M	**Foley Ridge** (Near Racetrack Meadow & PCT)	3511	1	Terraced trail in alpine meadow connects to the PCT.	3 Sisters Wilderness
M	**Green Lakes**	4070	14.6	Timberland to open alpine ridge and lakes, narrow around Green Lakes View of 3 Sisters Mountains, some switchbacks.	3 Sisters Wilderness
M	**Many Lakes**	15	4.5	Timberland trail goes by many lakes connects to Little Cultus Lake to un-maintained forest road, not always cleared!	3 Sisters Wilderness
M	**McBee** (From Mink Lake N. to its end)	3523	6.5	Use Six Lakes TH. Forest trail, some climbs, follow signs toward Spy Lake and Platt Lake.	3 Sisters Wilderness
M	**Metolius Windigo** (By Sisters Cow Camp)	99	7	Easy trail in forest, dusty, ford a creek. View of North Sister Mountain.	3 Sisters Wilderness
M	**Millican Crater**	4066	4.5	Near Whispering Pine Camp. Easy trail in forest, goes to Lava Lake. View of North Sister Mountain.	3 Sisters Wilderness
M	**Mink Lake**	3526	4	Easy timberland trail to lake.	3 Sisters Wilderness
M	**Mirror Lake**	20	3.1	Use Mirror Lake TH. Must see. Easy trail in forest, lava and meadows it goes from Road 46 to Mirror Lake, view of the Sisters.	3 Sisters Wilderness

Diff.	Trail Name	Trail #	Mile	Description	Map
M	**No Name**	3542	1	Connects two trails in forest, goes by a lake.	3 Sisters Wilderness
M	**No Name**	3515	1.6	Use Elk Lake TH. Forest trail used to make loops, high use area.	3 Sisters Wilderness
M	**No Name**	3547 (3546)	3	Goes by James Creek Shelter near the PCT to Foley Ridge Trail, all in forest.	3 Sisters Wilderness
M	**No Name**	12	4.6	Connects Devils Lake Trailhead to Elk Lake Trailhead, Flat and sandy trail that parallels road.	3 Sisters Wilderness
M	**Obsidian**	3528	5.7	Use Obsidian TH. Must see, high use area, day pass required. Valley to ridge ride, to the foot of Sisters Mountains, creek, lava flow and waterfall.	3 Sisters Wilderness
M	**Scott Pass**	4068	5.9	Use Scott Pass TH. Valley to ridge ride, mostly in forest, sandy and open toward pass, connects to the PCT.	3 Sisters Wilderness
M	**Scott Spur**	3531.	1.1	Use Obsidian TH. Connects 2 trails in area, flat and all forested.	3 Sisters Wilderness
M	**Scott Trail**	3531	5	Use Obsidian TH. Valley to ridge ride, connects to PCT. There are some seep spots in the trail toward the valley, views of Sisters Mountains and alpine meadows.	3 Sisters Wilderness
M	**Six Lakes**	21	2.5	Use Six Lakes TH. Valley trail up and over a ridge to meet PCT, will pass a lake.	3 Sisters Wilderness
M	**Snowshoe Lake**	33	2	Lakes and more lakes, connects Winopee Lake Trail to the PCT, all in timber on nice trail.	3 Sisters Wilderness
M	Tam Mc Arthur Rim	4078	2.6	Must see! High elevation 6,800'-7,600', climbs from Three Creek Camp area to Broken Hand. Views of the Three Sisters Mountains and Bachelor Butte, very busy!	3 Sisters Wilderness
M	**Trout Creek Tie**	4067	1	Forest trail connects 2 trails and crosses 2 creeks, located near McMillican Trailhead.	3 Sisters Wilderness
M	**Wickiup Plain**	12.1 (A)	1.3	Easy trail that connects 2 trails near Wickiup Plain by South Sister Mountain.	3 Sisters Wilderness
M	**Winopee Lake**	16	9.6	Easy trail that connects Cultus Lake area to the PCT on forested trail, goes by Muskrat Lake, shelter, and meadows.	3 Sisters Wilderness

MOUNT JEFFERSON WILDERNESS
(Near Sisters & Santiam Pass)-OR

Diff.	Trail Name	Trail #	Mile	Description	Map
M	**Big Meadows**	3456	2.4	Travels from Big Meadows Camp to lake basin in forest.	GTM 557 Mt. Jefferson Wilderness
M	**Blue Lake**	3422	7.6	Use Big Meadows TH. Goes across a lake basin in forest to Marion Lake, views of Three Sisters Mountains nice footing.	GTM 557 Mt. Jefferson Wilderness
M	**Booth Lake** (Jack to Square Lake)	4014	5.6	Use Jack Lake TH. Rolling trail in forest connects Jack Lake Camp to Booth Lake.	Mount Jefferson Wilderness
M	**Bowerman Lake**	3492	3.3	Use Big Meadows or Jack Lake TH. Fairly flat tread goes to 8 Lakes Basin, bushy and has lakes.	GTM 557 Mt. Jefferson Wilderness
M	**Dixie Lakes**	3494	1.5	Use Big Meadows TH. Flat trail runs by Dixie Lakes in forest.	GTM 557 Mt. Jefferson Wilderness
M	**Duffy Lake**	3427	3.5	Use Big Meadows TH. Goes to Duffy Lake in forest with some climbing.	Mount Jefferson Wilderness
M	**Marion Lake** (Portion of total trail)	3436	.8	Use Jack Lake TH. All in forest along lake to outlet of lake.	GTM 557 Mt. Jefferson Wilderness
M	**Marion Lake Outlet**	3495	.8	Use Jack Lake TH. Thick forest connects to Blue Lake Trail.	GTM 557 Mt. Jefferson Wilderness
M	**Minto Pass**	3437	4.7	Use Jack Lake TH. Connects Marion Lake area to PCT. Travels climbing from lake to ridge in timberland with waterfalls and long bridges.	GTM 557 Mt. Jefferson Wilderness
M	**Minto Tie**	4006	4.2	Use Jack Lake TH. Switchbacks in timber and meadows, connects 2 ridges.	GTM 557 Mt. Jefferson Wilderness

Diff.	Trail Name	Trail #	Mile	Description	Map
M-C	**Pacific Crest Tie**	4015 (GTM65A)	¼	Use Jack Lake TH. Climbs steeply through a rock slide area from Wasco Lake to the PCT.	GTM 557 Mt. Jefferson Wilderness
M	**Pine Ridge**	3443	4.4	Use Big Meadows TH. Connects Blue Lake Trail to Camp Pioneer on a ridge with good footing in the forest.	GTM 557 Mt. Jefferson Wilderness
M	**Wasco Lake** (Jack Lake to Minto Pass)	4014 (GTM 65)	3.4	Use Jack Lake TH. Connects Jack lake to Minto Pass and the PCT, goes by lakes in forest.	GTM 557 Mt. Jefferson Wilderness

TIMOTHY LAKE AREA (South of Mount Hood)-OR

Diff.	Trail Name	Trail #	Mile	Description	Map
M	**Headwaters**	522	1	Near Joe Graham Horse Camp. Newer forested trail with views of Clackamas Lake, meadows and clear-cuts. Connects to the PCT, not on the map.	GTM 494 Mt. Wilson
M	**Joe Graham**	524	½	Spur trail from Joe Graham Horse Camp to PCT, all in forest, not on the map.	GTM 494 Mt. Wilson
M	**Miller**	534	2.5	Connects PCT to Timothy Lake. Goes by Clackamas Lake and a seed orchard.	GTMs 494 Mt. Wilson 493 High Rock
M	**Timothy By-Pass**	529	1	Starts as a road and turns into a trail all in forest on Timothy Lake's south shoreline area, not on the map.	GTM 493 High Rock
M	**Timothy Lake**	528	7.8	Treed loop off of the PCT, circles lake goes over a high bridge and a dam.	GTM 493 High Rock

MOUNT HOOD AREA (East of Portland)-OR

Diff.	Trail Name	Trail #	Mile	Description	Map
M	Twin Lakes	495	2.9	Climbs and switchbacks, makes a loop to 2 lakes, all in trees, connects to PCT.	GTMs 462 Mt. Hood and 494 Mt. Wilson
M	Upper Twin Lake	533	4	Goes around lake with a view of Mount Hood.	GTM 494 Mt. Wilson

BULL OF THE WOODS AREA (Between Corvallis & Santiam Pass)-OR

Diff.	Trail Name	Trail #	Mile	Description	Map
M	Bagby (To hot springs)	544	10	Starts at Elk Lake up and over ridge to valley and hot springs, clothes optional. Some narrow trail in deep woods, small bridges, call ahead for trail conditions.	GTM 524 Battle Ax
M	Elk Lake Creek (To Mother Lode Trail)	559	4.1	Starts at Elk Lake, valley trail all in forest, mud and narrow sections, call ahead to see if it is clear.	GTM 524 Battle Ax

NORTH FORK UMATILLA (East of Pendelton)-OR

Diff.	Trail Name	Trail #	Mile	Description	Map
M	Beaver Swamp		¼	Flat trail goes by a swamp in deep forest.	North Fork Umatilla Wilderness
M	Lick Creek	3070	4.5	Valley to ridge mostly in forest open at top, travels by a spring view on top of hills and valleys	North Fork Umatilla Wilderness

INDEX – Trail, State and Page

INDEX – Trail, State and Page

INDEX – Trail, State and Page

INDEX – Trail, State and Page

INDEX – Trail, State and Page

INDEX – Number, Name, State & Page

INDEX – Number, Name, State and Page

INDEX – Number, Name, State and Page

NOTES

NOTES

NOTES

NOTES